EXPERTS ADVISE PARENTS

EXPERTS ADVISE PARENTS

*A Guide to Raising Loving,
Responsible Children*

LOUISE BATES AMES, PH.D.

DOROTHY CORKILLE BRIGGS, M.S.

MYRA CATES, M.ED.

DON DINKMEYER, PH.D.

FITZHUGH DODSON, PH.D.

RICHARD FERBER, M.D.

SOL GORDON, PH.D.

MARTIN GREENBERG, M.D.

EARL GROLLMAN, D.D.

MICHAEL MEYERHOFF, ED.D., and
BURTON WHITE, PH.D.

EILEEN SHIFF, M.S.

BENJAMIN SPOCK, M.D., and
MARY MORGAN

Edited by Eileen Shiff

*Illustrated with photographs by
Betty David and Suzanne Arms*

DELACORTE PRESS/NEW YORK

Published by
Delacorte Press
1 Dag Hammarskjold Plaza
New York, N.Y. 10017

Manufactured in the United States of America

First printing

Library of Congress Cataloging in Publication Data
Experts advise parents.
    Includes index.
    1. Parenting—United States.   2. Parent and child—United States.   3. Child
psychology.   I. Ames, Louise Bates.   II. Shiff, Eileen.
HQ769.E96   1987   649'.1
ISBN 0-385-29522-7
ISBN 0-385-29526-X (pbk.)
Library of Congress Catalog Card Number: 86-24024

Dedicated to
—our parents
—and children
who have taught us firsthand the joys
and challenges of parenting.
And to our loved ones who have shared the adventure.

Every book has a silent partner at the publishing company—the book editor. Ours, Emily Reichert, deserves special recognition. She has nurtured our project with care, providing boundless confidence, creative freedom, and wisdom—and has been a pleasure to work with.

CONTENTS

WELCOME TO A
UNIQUE EXPERIENCE

As a parent education teacher, I've shared the concerns, frustrations, and joys of mothers and fathers who have made effective parenting a high priority. Together we explore the latest parenting research on subjects from self-esteem to sexuality, learning skills to anticipate and deal with issues as they occur rather than wait until they become unmanageable. Ever since my first class, in the early 1970's, I've fantasized about inviting the leading authority on each subject to be our guest speaker for the specific topic, so the students could hear directly from the experts rather than depend on interpretation from a textbook or from me.

Experts Advise Parents is the fulfillment of that dream—a parenting course in print, offering firsthand exposure to a select group of the most respected child-rearing authorities of our times. Our course is a team approach to parenting, written for mothers and fathers who are not content to parent by instinct, the latest trend, or trial and error alone. It is for those who see parenting as a creative adventure and are willing to invest time and energy to prepare themselves to meet each challenge.

Working with this illustrious faculty has been an incredibly gratifying experience, both personally and professionally. Parents have benefited from their individual contributions to the field of parent education for years. Now, for the first time, these nationally acclaimed authors join forces creating a comprehensive course designed to help you strengthen your child and enrich your relationship with him. Welcome to *Experts Advise Parents!*

—Eileen

A NOTE
TO PARENTS

The miracle of the birth of a firstborn is, in essence, the birth of three: the birth of a child, a mother, and a father. Parents are filled with a rush of powerful emotions as they experience the wonder of new life and the anticipation of endless responsibilities! It isn't until the baby of your dreams becomes a reality in your home that you realize how exhilarating—and exhausting— parenting can be.

Most prospective parents have theories about "babies" in the generic sense and have strong feelings about how they will raise their own. But from the moment of birth, it's evident that your infant is no silent partner in this production. Each child is a unique individual, with his specific combination of genes and his own family dynamics. Just as you influence him, he influences you. It's natural to respond warmly and enthusiastically to an attractive, bright, friendly baby. The unattractive, slow-to-learn, cranky baby who keeps a parent up all night is not quite so easy to enjoy.

When you care about your child, you can't help being affected by his behavior, but it's important not to let it be the measure of your success or failure as a parent. That makes you dependent on his moods and achievements for your sense of self-worth. For example, if your child responds to new experiences with tears rather than enthusiasm, understand that his attitude is in part shaped by his nature. His nature is not his fault any more than it is yours. Recognizing its impact on his approach to life can diminish your frustration and anger with him and your disappointment in yourself. Instead of blaming him for his fearfulness, difficulty adapting to new situations, and oversensitivity to stimuli, help him learn to deal constructively with his stress so he can learn to enjoy life more fully.

Parents quickly discover that taking care of a new baby compromises resources: sleep, energy, money, and time (the more difficult the child, the greater the demands); but total self-denial drains the parent and the parent-child relationship. In demonstrating healthy self-respect you gain the respect of your children. Learn to balance the needs of all family members, including your own. In addition to reducing your stress, you're teaching your child the art of cooperation, compromise, and sensitivity to others' needs as well as his own. Those skills will be valuable to him in future relationships.

To avoid burnout, recharge your parent battery by seeking out personally satisfying activities for yourself: reading, painting, playing tennis, jogging, practicing a musical instrument, or even taking a bubble bath. The activity doesn't have to be noteworthy, just pleasurable. In discovering creative ways to renew yourself, you'll have more energy and enthusiasm to share with your child.

Single parents have even greater need for renewal. With their increased responsibilities and diminished adult support, they often report that they feel as though they are "running on empty." Single-parent groups can help you develop new friendships and gain emotional support. Children benefit from your enhanced self-esteem and from the sense of extended family that other single-parent families can provide. Some parents try to fill the space of the missing parent by trying to be both mother and father to their child. It is not practical for the parent, or in the best interest of the child, to try to assume both roles. Instead, provide opportunities for him to interact with consistent role models of the opposite sex. Above all, when you think you can't possibly do it all, don't! Set priorities.

It's important for those in two-parent families to keep the marriage a high priority. Too often parents begin to see each other as "Mom" and "Dad" and lose their connection as friends and lovers. They find their energy consumed by child care, housework, and jobs outside the home, leaving their spousal relationship with the leftovers. At the end of the day, especially when the children are young, there usually aren't any leftovers. Parents who schedule a few minutes alone together each day and a date with each other at least once a week find it easier to maintain the romantic quality of their relationship.

It's easiest when both parents share the same parenting goals and techniques. (It's helpful to take parenting classes together, if possible, so you'll work as equal partners.) But while it is valuable to come to terms with a general philosophy, parents need not provide a united front on all issues. Children learn early to adapt to differences in the way they're treated by parents, grandparents, teachers, and club leaders. For example, a five-year-old recently explained to her three-year-old brother, "At Grandma's we have to make the bed before breakfast, but Mommy lets us wait till we get home from school." Her brother responded, "Yeah, but Grandma lets us have soda. Mommy says we hafta drink milk." Children recognize that just because they get away with something with one authority figure doesn't mean there will be a carryover to another.

What *is* important is recognizing that you and your spouse are two different people with different perspectives, not "he's wrong, I'm right." In that way, you demonstrate respect for one another and tolerance for your spouse's viewpoint. Each parent needs the freedom to discipline the children without the other's interfering or undermining, unless a parent is abusive.

Keep expectations of yourself and your youngsters realistic. When expectations are too high, you're programming yourself and your interaction with your children for disappointment and failure. Often parents become overwhelmed with guilt over their children's mistakes and their own. If guilt helped, most of us would be superparents by now. Unfortunately, guilt is counterproductive. It creates stress and drains one of our most valuable resources—energy. As parents, we are fallible humans with fallible children. All we can ask of ourselves is to make the best judgments we can at the time. There are no easy answers. Those come only with hindsight. Rather than allow negative emotions to immobilize you, turn your mistakes into learning experiences. Most of us have had quite a few.

Good parenting doesn't eliminate problems and conflicts. Conflict is part of any healthy relationship, part of being separate individuals with different needs and interests. Instead, work to reduce conflict in numbers and intensity, with the goal of resolving issues rather than hurting each other. When you begin to use a technique that's new to you and your child, expect conflict to become worse before it gets better. Your child is used to your responding to him in a predictable way. It takes time for him to realize that you are committed to doing things differently.

It helps to remember that when your child tests you in a new area, it is the first time you've had to cope with that child facing that particular situation. As your child moves on to new stages of development, the challenge continues as you learn and grow together.

While it will be tempting to deal with several issues at once, it's more productive to focus on only one behavior at a time to increase the likelihood of success. If you want to make a significant change in your child's behavior, work on a problem that happens repeatedly. Resolving an issue that happens daily eliminates 365 conflicts a year.

Parents often don't recognize the importance of learning effective parenting skills until after a child develops behavior problems. But it's far more difficult to undo complicated negative behavior patterns after the fact than to help shape positive ones from birth. As one father tearfully explained after facing a crisis with his teen-ager:

> *I wish I'd known what to do years ago. I would have handled things very differently and then we wouldn't be in this mess today. I didn't know you could study how to become a parent. I thought that just came naturally—all you had to do was love your kid.*

While loving is crucial to effective parenting, love alone doesn't make one a competent parent, any more than love of fine music makes one an accomplished musician. Both require education and practice.

Children don't come with "Care and Handling" manuals. Without formal training, most of us simply respond instinctively to our child's misbehavior the same way our parents responded to ours when we were children. It's incredible that this, one of the most critical jobs in shaping society, doesn't require minimal standards of education. Preparation for parenthood is basically learned in childhood from observing our own parents in action—and early programming leaves indelible impressions! Many of us remember thinking, "When I have children I'll NEVER make my kids feel guilty, compare them with other children, or pressure them the way my parents did to me." Yet we often hear the echo of our parents' words escaping from our own mouths. That's how parenting behavior gets passed on from generation to generation.

Even those of us who were fortunate enough to have had warm, loving, competent parenting find that our parents' methods aren't always adequate to meet the pressures of our complex, changing society, with its conflicting values and overwhelming choices. Changes are occurring at such a fast pace, we find ourselves preparing our children for a world about which we can only speculate.

Change doesn't always signify progress. In elementary school my parents warned me about the long-term effects of smoking and drinking. Who had even heard about "designer drugs" like crack? I wonder what dangerous substances my children will be discussing with their youngsters.

Many look for easy answers to solve our evermore complex parenting challenges: "We just have to get tougher!" That's the old "If some is good, more is better" philosophy. It doesn't work in parenting. Just as too much fertilizer, water, or sunlight can damage a plant, parenting extremes are damaging to children. Children need motivation, not pressure; loving, not hovering; consequences, not punishment; and consistency, not rigidity—all tempered with flexibility and love.

Permissiveness and authoritarianism both tend to produce children with similar problems—low self-esteem, fearfulness, inability to think for themselves, limited resources to cope with stress, and irresponsibility. Yet there are major differences between the two.

In permissive homes, parents communicate weakness as they hand over their power to the children. They are afraid to discipline because they are trying too hard to be their youngsters' friends. Parents need to be more than friends, willing to stand firm when a loving "no" is in their children's best interest. As their children get older and become more demanding and manipulative, parents often belatedly recognize the need to establish their parental authority. Children don't give up power easily. As they get older, they expect more freedom, not less.

Authoritarian parents communicate lack of confidence in their children through their need to control them. They act as family policemen, setting rigid rules and demanding blind obedience. They assume that intimidation teaches "respect." On the contrary, intimidation teaches fear. Victims of authoritarian parenting learn to sneak and lie to avoid being caught, rather than develop self-discipline. These children avoid the company of their parents for obvious reasons, and often rebel against parental values as well. As the children mature, the fear and anger they've stockpiled often block their ability to form meaningful, trusting relationships with others. And when they become parents, they usually become authoritarian themselves, taking out their revenge on the wrong generation.

Overprotective parents make their children's decisions for them and save them from the consequences of their behavior. Since the children don't have the opportunity to tap their inner strengths, they see themselves as weak. As a result, they are dependent on others to make decisions and solve problems for them, becoming overly vulnerable to negative peer influence.

Today indifference and indulgence exist in many homes simultaneously. When parents are too preoccupied to demonstrate caring to children, they often indulge them with "things." Children need warmth, respect, and interaction to feel valued. Material goods are no substitute for involvement.

"Hurrying," a recent trend described by Dr. David Elkind, is the result of parents' encouraging or pressuring children to dress, act, and achieve skills that are developmentally advanced for them. Children are not just tiny adults. Pushing them into adulthood before they have had a chance to be children is like picking fruit before it's had a chance to ripen. Quality is compromised.

Children need nurturing parents who build self-esteem and communicate caring while assuming their rightful role as loving, supportive leaders. Since parents have more life experience and have far more responsibilities within the family, it is appropriate that *they* be the family guides—not the children. Discipline is a special kind of love; it says, "I care about you enough to remain firm about issues that are important to your well-being." Just as executives in the corporate world establish basic guidelines for their employees but give them latitude in carrying them out, you can learn to be an effective manager in your home. It's important for children to have the guidance of competent, confident parents to give them a sense of security in their complicated world rather than parents who simply react to their behavior.

Experts Advise Parents is an eclectic approach to parenting—it is not a "system." Systems limit options, locking you into one method of parenting as though there is only one right way to approach a particular issue. Instead, this course increases your parenting options by offering a number of constructive routes to specific parenting goals. After you define your goal and explore which pathway works best for you and your child in any given situation, you'll develop skill in applying the strategies to him.

While each of the authors offers her or his own unique perspective on parenting, they all agree on the importance of:

- Valuing your child enough to spend quality time with him, helping him to feel your love and appreciation.

- Helping him to know and appreciate himself so he can better appreciate and relate to others.

- Respecting the developmental tasks that are a child's "business" at each important life stage.

- Nurturing the development of the whole child, seeing him as more than just a "brain," an "athlete," a "socialite," or a "beauty," but as a balanced, well-integrated individual.

- Teaching your child independence by giving him greater freedom and more privileges as he takes on more responsibility.

- Helping him learn to act according to his own principles, not to gain acceptance from others.

- Teaching values by setting your own priorities and living by them, being clear on which issues you'll stand your ground and which are open for negotiation.

- Limiting your child's choices when the decision affects his or another's well-being, even if your firmness arouses his fury from time to time.

- Giving your child increasing opportunities to learn to make responsible decisions as he matures, so that by the time he reaches adulthood you lose your role as "needed parent" and become, instead, his trusted friend.

The contributing authors are all renowned in their respective fields. React to their theories, process them, integrate those ideas that fit you and each of your children, and incorporate them into your own style of parenting. But remember that the professionals can only provide suggestions. In reality, *you* are the final expert. The challenge is yours to make the decisions on a day-to-day basis about how to best motivate, teach, and reinforce each of your children in specific situations.

With any complicated new job, you develop confidence in your personal resources and a sense of fulfillment as you gain more knowledge and experience. When you've finished reading *Experts Advise Parents,* you will have greater faith in your own judgment because you'll have more insight into your child, and a larger, more versatile repertoire of effective parenting strategies from which to choose. Your confidence will be reinforced as you experience the more positive interaction that comes as a result. Just don't take your responsibility so seriously that you stifle the spontaneity that comes from simply *enjoying* your child. Appreciate the miracle of growth as you did the miracle of life!

(Because of our concerns about sexism, we tried to come up with a narrative format which would include both male and female pronouns. However, using "he or she" throughout the book detracted from its readability, and so we opted to refer to the child with the universal pronoun "he." We have included a greater number of examples of girls in each chapter, to correct this imbalance.)

EXPERTS
ADVISE PARENTS

DOROTHY CORKILLE
BRIGGS

Meet the Author

Mrs. Dorothy Corkille Briggs has received worldwide acclaim for her pioneering and continuing work on self-esteem. Her book, Your Child's Self-Esteem, *which has sold over 400,000 copies, remains the definitive child-rearing book to focus on self-esteem.*

After graduating Phi Beta Kappa and magna cum laude with an A.B. in psychology from Whitman College, Mrs. Briggs received a B.Ed. and M.S. from Washington State University. Her postgraduate work included studying with Carl Rogers, Virginia Satir, William Glasser, Fritz Perls, Muriel James, and S. I. Hayakawa.

In 1957, following ten years as a teacher, counselor, school psychologist, and dean of girls, Mrs. Briggs became a parent/teacher educator in adult education departments at UCLA Education Extension and Long Beach Memorial Hospital. Her central focus has been on building high self-esteem in adults and children through her classes and her private practice as a marriage, family, and child therapist. Her skill as a presenter for national conventions and major universities across the United States and Canada has brought accolades. She not only educates and inspires, she also "feeds the soul."

Elected to the Board of Directors of the California Association of Marriage and Family Counselors, she has been a parent–education consultant for public television and film projects, and a sought-after television guest on numerous national programs. Her best-selling books have been translated into all the major foreign languages. She is listed in Who's Who in California, Who's Who in Contemporary Authors, *and* The World's Who's Who of Women.

Mrs. Briggs makes her home in Southern California and is the mother of two married daughters.

YOUR CHILD'S SELF-ESTEEM

THE KEY TO LIFE
DOROTHY CORKILLE BRIGGS, M.S.

Space Age

Do you believe Sputnik launched the space age? Not so. Human beings have always been in the space age. For it is what goes on in the person-to-person space around the child that creates "personhood" as we know it.

Children use the ingredients found in their person-to-person space to build their self-image, self-concept, sense of self. And the kind of self-image built determines how they live their lives. In short, the quality of the interpersonal space between children and the important others around them directly affects whether they become winners or losers in life.

The discovery of the rare child reared by a mother wolf gave evidence that "selfhood" is learned. The wolf-person was a human being. But such individuals could not later be taught language. Nor did they develop the human characteristics we associate with people.

When a baby is born, he comes into the world with his total uniqueness, unlike any other. But he has no sense of identity at all. However, he has the *potential* to build one. Whether that identity becomes positive or negative depends on what happens between that baby and his caretakers, others around him, his own comparisons of himself with others, and the culture he lives in. Even the seriously handicapped have the potential to build self-confidence and a positive self-image.

Parent Goals

Over the years I've routinely asked parents what they want for their youngsters. They have little trouble listing their goals. Universally, it seems we all want children to

- be happy
- be responsible
- be caring, loving
- be creative
- be curious
- be thoughtful of others
- be spontaneous
- be flexible
- be cooperative
- be motivated to learn
- be honest, truthful
- be friendly
- be self-confident
- contribute to society

- have good marriages and happy family lives
- have good physical health
- have initiative, courage
- have a sense of humor
- handle stress constructively
- enjoy life
- have integrity
- have moral values to live by, active faith
- avoid destructiveness to self, others
- do well in school and at work
- develop their potential

The list goes on and on. Ordinarily, the conclusion is, "I just want the best for my child." What about you? Wouldn't you honestly like your youngster to have all the above?

How does it feel to face so many goals? Overwhelming? If you are like most parents, it *is* an overwhelming list to face. Yet, which quality would you eliminate if you wanted to feel less burdened?

Wouldn't it be a relief to head for just one goal? Believe it or not, massive research shows that high self-esteem is our best guarantee that a youngster will not be a problem child. Children with a strong sense of self-worth are physically healthier. They are more motivated to learn. They get along better with others. They are more able to tolerate frustration and ambiguity. They are more likely to tap their creativity and risk expressing it. They tend to be leaders and avoid loser choices. Their energy is freer to scale the challenges of life; they are not easily discouraged. Their inner self-confidence makes them less likely to go for the cop-outs of promiscuity, substance abuse, and neurotic defenses.

To fully nurture, our primary challenge as parents is to build strong self-worth in children. With inner sureness, children are more likely to use their energy positively. They bound out to life and bring their own inner contentment with them. They are more able to give to life. And they are fun to be around. *The goals we want for children are the outcroppings, the harvest, of high self-esteem.*

All the issues involved in parenting can be seen in the light of this question: "Does this particular approach build or shred self-worth?" If you have any doubt, simply ask yourself how you would feel on the receiving end of what you dish out. Ask yourself, "Would I like to be my own child?" You'll quickly get your answer.

Building self-esteem is *not* a side issue in parenting. It is the cornerstone to nurturing that allows children to fulfill their promise, to become the most they can become.

Levels of Self-Esteem

In general there are three levels of self-esteem with variations in between. The high self-esteemer has self-confidence.

The mid self-esteemers live with self-doubt. It is as if they are saying, "I'm not so sure I'm okay so I must prove my value to myself and others." There is a drivenness to the self-doubter. The Type A personality, the over-achiever, the perfectionist, most often live with self-doubt.

Low self-esteemers are convinced of personal inadequacy. They live with self-hate. This painful place can result in the choice to go for "anesthesia." Alcoholism, drug abuse, overeating, gambling, and promiscuity are choices that numb pain and keep the low self-esteemer's loser belief alive.

The need to escape from the pain of self-hate can result in building a Pretend Self, a false mask to present to the world. But no amount of positive feedback helps, because low self-esteemers "know" what lies beneath . . . their own self-discounts, self-doubts.

How the Self-Image Is Built

Primitive peoples built their homes out of materials available in the environment. For some, that meant caves; for others, the house was built from animal skins, adobe mud, or the ice of igloos. Since brick and mortar were not available to them, they obviously could not build brick homes.

This exact same process occurs in building the House of Self—the self-image. The developing child uses the material from the interpersonal space around him to create his self-concept. The building materials used are the words, body language, and treatment of important others. These building materials are intangible, of course. But they make a tangible difference.

From their earliest moments, infants are sensitive to their environment. They know whether they are picked up with tender or tense arms. Long before they know language, infants are tuned into whether tones and looks are friendly and kind or harsh and angry. Each infant is affected by the "vibes" around him. And from those messages he forms generalized impressions as to how safe and trustworthy this new world is. The child soon learns whether his needs will be met with reasonable constancy and friendliness.

Once the child learns his name, he begins to attach certain qualities to himself. If the child receives a barrage of verbal and silent messages that he is an inconvenience, impossible, and "never gets it right," that child builds a picture of himself that fits those messages. If he gets more positive feedback, he builds a positive self-image. None of us would feel good about ourselves if we were continually told we were mean, clumsy, selfish, and naughty. The mix of words, body language, and expectations of important others, then, is the material used by the child to build his self-image.

Of all the many things the developing child learns, none is more important than this collection of messages from others. These messages form his answers to the question, "Who am I?" In short, each child takes the image of himself that others reflect to him and sees himself accordingly. The child gathers the thousands and thousands of inputs he receives. He then puts together a set of beliefs about himself. We call this "belief package" the self-image. The child calls that package "me." Each child borrows the views of others and makes those views his own.

So, we can have a handsome, bright, curious child who learns to see himself as ugly and inadequate because he lives with constant putdowns and expectations he cannot meet. *His self-image matches how he is treated in spite of the reality of his assets.* How can this be?

The younger the child, the more the primary caretakers (parents, relatives, teachers) are seen as godlike. *How* these others see him is how that child believes he is. Their view is infallible. The child simply does not question what is reflected back to him by others. They become the looking glass that reflects who he is. And he can only come to respect himself to the degree that he is respected.

Self-Image Is Flexible

Because the very young child is building his first set of self-impressions, the self-image formed in the early years is of vital importance. However, it is crucial to know that the self-concept is not forged for all time. Since the self-image is learned, a negative one can be improved. How? By changing the messages coming to that child. Just so, a positive self-concept can be eroded by later on-going destructive messages.

The process is really quite simple. It is actually no different from growing plants. You know that if you put a little bush in nonnurturing soil, it would grow quite differently than if you gave it nurturing soil—an environment that met its specific needs.

If we want a child to blossom as he is meant to, we need to attend to the climate—the nurturing soil—around that child.

What Self-Esteem Is

We've all had snapshots of ourselves that we don't like. We may make a value judgment about that picture and say, "Yuk!" Similarly, the child makes a value judgment about his collection of self-pictures and judges the overall picture of himself accordingly.

We often hear people say, "He has lots of self-esteem." They imply *high* self-worth. But the person filled with self-hate has lots of self-esteem. The problem is that it is very negative.

Strong self-worth is simply the child's quiet, inner feeling that adds up to, "I'm glad to be me." High self-esteem has nothing to do with conceit, which is nothing but noisy whitewash for self-doubt or low self-esteem. People don't spend energy hitting you over the head with how terrific they are if they live with inner confidence.

Beliefs of High Self-Esteemers

High self-worth rests on two inner beliefs:

- "I am *unconditionally* lovable."
- "I am competent. I can handle myself and my world. I have something to offer. I count."

Of these two statements lovability is the more important. In the House of Self, competencies are like the walls and the roof. But they rest on the foundation belief, "I am unconditionally lovable."

The child who believes, "I'm okay if . . ." ("I am quiet, achieving, get the lead part, etc.") places his self-confidence on the line. Self-worth tied to performance is forever conditional. And *conditional lovability* does not do the trick where high self-esteem is concerned.

If a child believes he is unlovable or lovable only on condition, he may develop all kinds of competence. However, these skills are hollow victories. No amount of competence ever substitutes for lovability. Indeed, the suicide note of a high-achieving sixteen-year-old who ran into academic difficulties read: "If I fail in what I do, I fail in what I am."

Each child needs to be cherished for his sheer existence. Apart from skills. And even when behavior needs to be limited or stopped. The belief, "I, as a person, count and am valued," gives the child the zest to build competencies. This belief in lovability allows the child to bound out to others in more socially acceptable ways.

A "hole" in the child's lovability can create a *love of power* to prove his importance to himself and others. Such a stance almost always sets up problems in getting along with others.

Conversely, the child who knows he is unconditionally lovable is much more apt to operate from the *power of love*—love and respect for self and others. Such a child gets along much more smoothly. He doesn't have to "use" others or have power over them to feel good inside.

We have far too many extremely competent adults who are unhappy people. They are destructive to themselves and in their relationships because deep within themselves they believe they are unlovable. And they act accordingly.

Thus competence is important to high self-esteem. But, in and of itself, competence does not amount to a hill of beans unless that competence rests on lovability. As nurturers, parents and educators need to give love first billing and competence-building second priority. Both lovability and competence are important for strong self-worth. But as in all structures, the House of Self needs the firm foundation of love for the walls of competence to rest on.

Dr. Abraham Maslow discovered that we humans have a hierarchy of needs. The loudest claim on each person's attention is having physical needs (food, shelter, and clothing) met. As parents, we take care of children's physical needs, of course. We are all largely familiar with the importance of these needs. Once they are met, the next loudest claim is the selfhood need to know that "I count; I have personal value; I am cherished." Only then are human beings free to move up the ladder to constructively meet their needs for positive social interaction, achievement, and creative expression.

This concept is basic and crucial. A "hole" in selfhood needs (self-worth) means that all social interaction, achievement, and creativity rest on deficiency, on a void. When social interaction is less smooth, achievement may come, but at a negative price to self and others, and creativity comes from neurosis and not health.

Behavior Matches the Self-Image

The child with negative beliefs about himself tends to make loser choices. Naturally, these choices lead to negative experiences that support the negative self-belief, "I'm not okay." We call this the self-fulfilling prophecy.

The child with self-confidence lives with a different focus. He makes positive choices that lead to positive experiences. These feed his basic "I'm okay" belief. He finds ways to work around the hurdles of life because of that very self-confidence. The belief, "I count; I can do it or learn how to do it," gives this child the energy for forward thrust in spite of obstacles. Inner sureness means outer uncertainty is less threatening. Such a child knows that, one way or another, he can accomplish.

High self-esteemers have a healthy sense of reality. They are not afraid to take responsibility for their behavior. Inner self-confidence gives them freedom to work with what *is*. It gives "go-power" to try the new because such children do not come from fear and doubt. Self-confidence literally spurs such children to seek challenges. It supplies the energy to try, to stretch, to trailblaze.

Love's Importance

We often hear the statement, "So-and-so has a 'way' with children." If we are around such a person, we notice a particular quality between that person and the child. The "magic" of their way lies in *how* they connect; *how* they relate. Certain ingredients are in the person-to-person space so that the child on the other end of that adult feels valued, cherished, and loved.

Since high self-esteem is founded on the belief that "I am unconditionally lovable," we do not build strong self-worth in children until we put love's ingredients in the space between us and them. The issue is not "Do I love my child?" Rather, it is "Does my child feel and experience my love?"

Later chapters in the book will deal with behavior management skills (environmental control, natural and logical consequences, time-out, contracting, reality therapy, etc.). However, *the success of all such skills rests on the kind of climate existing between adult and child*. The same skills are far more likely to work when the person-to-person space contains love's ingredients. If they are absent, specific skills may not bring the desired results.

Such behavior management techniques become an art when they are used in the context of love's climate. Love alone is not enough. Specific techniques are not enough. *Love and techniques need to be wed one to the other*. It is the marriage of these two that you find existing in the person-to-person space of those who have a "way" with children.

The magic of unconditional love has very definite ingredients that can be looked at one by one. They interweave to form a particular kind of interpersonal climate. No child can *feel* lovable if he does not *experience* love. This basic truth cannot be ignored.

Trust

Each child needs to know first that he can trust the adults around him. This means promises are kept. The child learns that he can trust that adults will help him get his real needs met.

Trust is built only when words and body language match. When we are uptight, we don't smile and say, "Nothing's wrong," as we bang about the room. We may not choose to go into detail, for what we are experiencing may not be appropriate to share. But nothing destroys trust faster than double messages—mismatching ones from mouth and body.

Trust comes when adults are real persons, not role players. Loving adults are not afraid to apologize, to say "no" when a refusal is needed; yet they are able to have fun with children also. As real people we do get tired, frustrated, and have legitimate needs of our own. But, as nurturers, we do not use children as the dumping ground for our inner hangups or other frustrations. We let them know that we're perhaps uptight about a grown-up problem that we don't care to discuss.

Children need to experience us as fair and reasonable. When we fall short in any area, we work on our own case to eliminate what in us is causing us to work against attitudes and actions that build trust. There is no question that trust is the bedrock of loving relationships.

Focused Attention

To feel cherished, a child needs to be *seen,* not looked at. Too often a child is only really seen when he is misbehaving. Then adult attention is totally focused upon him. The child who is only seen when misbehaving has good reason to act out. Negative attention is better than none at all.

To get a feel for this kind of focused attention, think of your own experience. How often have you been in a grocery line and had the clerk look at you as just another body? His "look" makes you feel like just one of many who have passed through. There is no meeting, no connection of one person with another.

You know the difference when that special clerk "sees" you. There is a brief moment of connection, of involvement. You feel your existence as a person actually recognized by another in that brief contact. We have all experienced the qualitative difference between being *looked at* and *seen.*

It takes no more time to see than to look. But seeing takes a definite internal shift in focus. Seeing means you connect with fresh eyes. You connect with the other's "particularness." Even if brief, at that moment you are *involved* one-on-one. Dr. Martin Buber, the Jewish theologian and philosopher, has called this "the meeting." It is the "I–Thou." When we truly see, we literally *touch* the other.

Touching is a necessity for life. Both physical and psychological touching. Visual touching carries the message of bonding—so essential for emotional and physical health. Focused attention literally validates the child's very existence. It carries the potent message, *"You* are important enough for me to want to focus away from me . . . outward to *you."* This kind of focus gives the child the experience that "I am worth connecting with." And remember, it is experience that counts. It is experience that carries the message of love. The child (or adult) who goes for too long a time without being "seen" soon starts feeling unloved. Noninvolvement erases the feeling of being loved.

Preschoolers are walking examples of focused attention. Watch their eyes as they connect with everything in their environment. They are drinking in everything they see; they seem to see uniqueness, specific details. They see afresh. They do not see in terms of categories (dogs-in-general; people-in-general). They see with specificity. They are in the "here and now," moment by moment.

If you observe adults who have a way with people, you'll notice that they

are attention-connectors. On the other end of them you experience being seen afresh. You sense their absorption in the very details of you.

As busy adults, we can become so focused on the task at hand, on schedules, on inner pressures, that we never really see. We only look.

This habit can be broken. But it does require awareness and an internal "gear shift." It requires a willingness to move our focus outward. And a willingness to connect with the freshness of the other in the present moment. Sounds simple. Right? Yet, for most of us to completely let go of our inner world even for short periods is often very hard. The more stress we are under, the more difficult this shift in attention will be.

If you find yourself thinking of excuses, just recall how quickly we drop everything internally when children misbehave or when they are in danger. The challenge here is, Can we attend with focus *in the positive times* as well as in the negative ones?

Taking Time

Children cannot feel loved if the important people around them are so busy they rarely take time to just "be" with them—to visit, to chat, or to share. We do this with our friends. We need to do it with our children as well.

We can be so busy doing things *for* our children, so busy teaching them and monitoring them, that we are never truly *with* them as persons. If you are playing a game, is your attention on the game or on enjoying your youngster? When you bathe Jenny, is your focus on getting her clean, or is there focus on her as she enjoys the bubbles of water dripping from the cloth?

Many parents say they don't know what to "do" with their children, if they are not taking them to the park, the library, or scouts. We are a nation preoccupied with "doing" rather than with "being" together. Recall your courtship days. It really didn't matter what you and your loved one did. What was important was simply being with the other. This is the quality that spells caring. Two people connecting in the moment; and, two people *enjoying* that connection.

How long has it been since you reveled in the miracle of watching your child's face light up as Susan watches the flames in the fireplace make moving patterns? Enjoyed her excitement as you dropped "leaf boats" in a rain-filled gutter? Winked at her as she sat at the dinner table? Ruffled her hair, appreciating its color and texture as you passed in the hall?

Enjoying-the-other time is precious. It is imperative that we commit to this internal gear shift periodically (not every moment). Each time we do, we feed the child's belief, "I am enjoyable. This important adult *makes* time for me. And makes me feel important by what I experience coming from his eyes."

Being seen, being fully attended to, helps your child feel loved. But along with that encounter, the child needs to feel safe. Safety has a number of specific ingredients that give your youngster the experience of being loved.

Nonjudgment of Person

Probably no one quality makes us pull in and feel less adequate than to be on the other end of someone who continually judges our person. "Judge not" is an imperative if our children are to feel loved.

Do not misunderstand. Children definitely need to know when their behavior is out of line. Part of loving is setting limits and being firm, declaring your "ouch" line when their behavior interferes with your needs.

The trick is to be friendly toward the child even when behavior needs changing right away. Imagine hearing these statements tossed your way: "You are so rude"; "You're acting like a baby"; "Class, you are being very bad." Can you feel the judgmental sting?

Dr. Haim Ginott said, "Labeling is disabling." There is no question. Slapping *labels on children blasts self-esteem.* They put boxes around children. They give inputs about *who they are* that may later be acted out!

How can we let children know when behavior needs changing without touching self-esteem? Simply switch from judgments-of-the-person to reactions-toward-behavior. This change of focus removes you immediately from the judge's bench. It puts you into limiting-behavior shoes.

If we use the examples above, notice the difference in how you might feel if, instead of calling you a "rude person," I say, "I don't want any more interruptions." Can you see that with this statement I am not attacking the person of the child? Instead, I am limiting behavior without the child's worth as a person being an issue. Rather than calling the child a "baby," you can say, "Right now I need to finish this, so I can't hold you." You state your needs and set the limit without damaging personal worth. The disruptive class is spared the "bad" judgment when the adult says, "Stop talking, please."

Praise

Many of us would not use negative labels against children. But we may overlook the fact that we are judging when we dish out benign judgments or praise.

The idea of avoiding praise and instead sending positive reactions-toward-behavior cuts across many adults' beliefs. It cuts across old-fashioned teacher training. Avoid praise? It almost sounds sacrilegious.

Yet, if we examine the issue closely, we can see the danger of using praise. As used here, praise is a *positive label of the person.* "Aren't you wonderful for doing that!" "I'm proud of you for those grades." "You are a good girl."

Do you catch the silent yet dangerous message that lies beneath such talk? Implicit in this way of communicating is the good-behavior-equals-good-person formula. Automatically, its opposite is bad-behavior-equals-bad-person.

Praise ties personal worth to behavior. It is the essence of conditional love. The very words "I'm proud of *you* for these grades" literally puts the focus on *self*-being-praised (and therefore better) rather than on *behavior* that is being recognized and appreciated. Such conditionality fosters the self-doubter and low self-esteemer's belief, "I am what I do."

Praise subtly encourages the child to go after "What-is-in-it-for-me?" rather than encouraging the child to focus on cooperative ways to live with others. Praise puts the spotlight on the *person.* Positive reactions-toward-behavior spotlight the *act.*

When children behave in positive ways and we comment on such behavior, we underscore their contributions to harmony and getting along. Our focus on the pluses of positive behavior obviously reinforces it. We all need recognition and appreciation for our efforts and accomplishments. The issue is not *do* we recognize the positives, but rather *how* we recognize them.

To build self-worth, to give children experience in love, we need to focus on *behavior* that is appreciated rather than imply that they have more worth as *persons* if they shine. How do we shift from benign judges and still give those needed reinforcers positive strokes? We send positive reactions-toward-behavior.

"How much I appreciate your remembering the rules!" "Look! You figured how to do that all by yourself. That's a new skill for you." "How enjoyable our day was!" "Thank you for picking that up. It's such a treat to have everyone pitch in here." "Thank you for using your soft voice." In each of these sharings, the adult's positive reaction is directed toward the *behavior* and not the person. Part of feeling loved is knowing that your person is cherished, independent of behavior. And that behavior and attitudes that work together for the common good are given recognition. We all like to feel that our positive contributions are appreciated. And we like to hear that appreciation.

The underlying principle is that as children are judged, so they will judge themselves. Reactions-to-behavior (whether positive or negative) rather than person-judgments take the conditionality out of love. Nonjudgment is proof that allows unconditional love to be felt. Judgment needs to be removed from the person-to-person space.

Respectful Treatment

Ask yourself what you need to feel loved. Surely you have trouble feeling loved when you are treated with disrespect.

Watch those who have a "way" with children. You'll notice a stream of person-to-person respect flowing. Such adults do not talk down to children, even though they may simplify their language where needed. They help children save face by talking to them privately for needed corrections. They avoid dissecting the child's character in front of other adults as the child stands by. They avoid sarcastic, humiliating, or belittling remarks. They model "please," "thank you," and "I'm sorry." They avoid long harangues and shriveling tones. They model the Golden Rule in their contacts with children.

Most adults treat other adults with respect. Yet, at times, unthinkingly, we may forget that even wee human beings are enormously sensitive to how they are treated.

Part of respect for children is not asking them to be adult before their time. Respectful adults avoid asking children for more than they can handle in light of their age or abilities. They avoid trying to redesign the child's basic temperament. Quiet, slender Frank is not a natural athlete. His parents' respect is shown when they don't put expectations on him that work against his inborn nature.

The simple act of stooping down to eye level when talking to the young child is an act of respect. Telling children what to do rather than what not to do, when possible, is further evidence of respect. Slowing our adult pace down is yet another courtesy. Advance notice of a change ("In ten minutes it will be time to leave.") allows children to experience consideration.

Basically, when we as adults are sensitive to others, it is easier for children to be respectful. When we model respect, we teach by what we do. To repeat, our respect becomes the child's self-respect. The child who does not receive respect has trouble respecting self and others. *No child can give back what he has not received.*

Conversely, as parents, we need to ask for respect in return. Children may be treated respectfully, but be allowed to behave toward others disrespectfully. Part of parenting positively is teaching them that certain behaviors are acceptable and other behaviors are not. The socialization process is not taught the first time around. It takes patience and repeated teaching, just as teaching potty rules or reading or math do.

Children often try out behaviors they see other youngsters model. As parents we need to let them know when behavior that has been copied from friends is not acceptable by our standards.

Right Versus Wrong

Love comes through more clearly when we have our major focus on what is right rather than on what is wrong. The more we see children's strengths, the more likely those strengths and new ones are to blossom.

Some adults say nothing when children are behaving, but they really let them know when they are misbehaving. Again, think about yourself. How valued would you feel by your boss if all you heard about were the "fall shorts"? Wouldn't you prefer to have one who made a point to support and recognize your strengths and successes as well as calling your attention to the areas that need changing? Children are no different.

When a child brings home a paper with ten math problems, two of which are checked as wrong, where do your eyes go first? This is not to say that we don't deal with errors that need correction. But what about the eight problems that are done correctly? How many parents will spend eight tenths of the time on that paper getting excited about the ones done right? Probably not many. Why?

Watch adults who have this magic "way" with children. You'll find they are "strength bombarders." They get excited about the smallest improvements. They recognize and comment about the progress, no matter how small. Their general attitude is "for" the child. They reflect joy in the pluses and are not quiet about them. They let children know. If pluses are hard to find, they communicate a positive faith that "soon you will learn this." "Margo, you are having trouble remembering it, but soon you'll have it down pat, I know." And their words match their inner feelings of positive expectation. Perhaps this adult might add, "What could we work out that would help you to remember?" The nonloving comment would be, "When are you ever going to get this through your head?" Remember, our positive faith becomes our children's positive faith in themselves.

Children need adults who are in their "cheering section." They need us to root for them. Children know if our expectations are positive or negative. And they respond accordingly.

Part of being a loving adult, then, is having a mental set that looks for, sees, and shares positives with children. We can tell a child daily that we love him. But if he largely hears about his failures, he cannot *feel* loved. Loving adults are "warm, fuzzy" givers. And children thrive in such a climate.

DOROTHY CORKILLE BRIGGS, M.S.   17

Realistic Expectations

In spite of loving intentions, parents often create enormous pressures for children by expecting too much too soon. Children do not question our expectations, particularly when they are younger. They invariably question their personal adequacy. If they feel they are not measuring up, they assume something is wrong with them. *Parental love and valuing is the child's oxygen line.* Without it, they shrivel. Realistic expectations for this age, this child's temperament, this child's pressures, and his history are part of loving. Finding the balance means keeping eyes open, observing, watching the child's particular uniqueness.

In some communities there seems to be a subtle competition among parents revolving around how soon. And the sooner, the better. The more Brownie points for parental pride. How soon is the baby sleeping through the night? How soon on solids, out of diapers, talking? How soon reading and handling numbers? And how much? How often in the limelight? How often the star?

Dr. Jack Canfield reports in a study tallying the number of negatives versus positives two- and three-year-olds heard on any given day. The tally showed 432 negatives to 32 positives. Very young children need limits, as do we all. But they need an environment that does not overwhelm them with expectations for behavior they are not up to giving.

Did you hear about the kindergarten boy who, when asked his name the first day of school, replied, "Johnny Don't"?

Most parents of several children say they expected far more of their first child than later ones. Natural enough. First time around, we usually have little or no experience. We are unsure of what to expect. First children are often expected to bear the family flag. The family reputation for excellence lies on their shoulders. Remember the psychiatrist who said, "Every parent should be allowed to toss out the first two kids"?

Notice how often you ask the parent of a third baby how things are going and you hear, "Oh, we are really *enjoying this one.*" By the third time round parents tend to be more relaxed in terms of expectations. They have more faith that this too shall pass. They are less into overkill.

Knowing the developmental tasks of each age is extremely important if our expectations are to be in line. We do not get upset with our children when they do their school homework. But we often get upset when they do their developmental homework. Why? Because we often do not know what that homework is.

As nurturing parents, it is essential that we do *our* homework. We do

that by becoming familiar with these developmental tasks, and by working
with them. The work of Dr. Louise Bates Ames of the famous Gesell Institute, Erik Erikson, Piaget, and child study centers of the major universities all
highlight facts we need to know. Their studies show a sequential pattern to
growth and development. Love is more apt to come through when we work
with the nature of the human fabric rather than against it.

Empathic Understanding

If you feel another rarely understands you, it is hard to feel loved by that
person. Empathic understanding is a powerful and needed ingredient if your
child is to feel loved. How each child experiences his own individual world is
that child's personal reality. Your youngster may be quite upset over something that seems quite minor to you. To prove love to children it is necessary
to periodically set our world aside and come into their world, to walk in their
shoes temporarily.

For example, Sarah is upset that you're leaving her with the sitter. She
starts to cry. You can ignore her message or discount her feelings with a
"Don't be a crybaby." If you do, her feelings go unheard. On the other hand,
if you reflect back in an understanding tone, "It's *so* hard to have me leave,"
she gets proof that at that moment you can understand her sorrow. Briefly,
yet with an understanding heart, you have walked in her shoes, even though
you need to leave.

The greatest craving in the human heart, regardless of age, is to be
heard. Even when nothing changes in the situation. No question, hearing is
healing.

Typically, unaware parents handle children's feelings in ways that leave
youngsters alone to handle their feelings by themselves. Most frequently,
again unknowingly, parents tell youngsters their feelings are unreasonable or
off-base—from the adult point of view. They may try to set the child's feeling
aside with cheery advice, forbidding the feeling or judging the child for the
feeling. It is enough to say at this point that it is hard to feel loved when you
do not periodically feel *understood from your point of view*. That is what
empathy is all about.

Most of us are quite unaware that we place great pressure on our children to feel as we do. This is the "Match Me" syndrome. It is as if we say at
times to youngsters by our responses, "If I think something is good, you
should too." (Naps, for instance. Do you remember how you felt as a child
about naps?) If I think something is logical, you should too. (Were you
overjoyed about practicing the piano even though you didn't want to flub the

dub at the recital?) If I tell you you'll feel better about it tomorrow, your "right now" feeling of disappointment is not heard.

If children buy into the "Match Me" blueprint, they may learn to build a disowned self. This is the part of them that houses all the feelings they've learned are not acceptable to have. Low self-esteem is folded around "The Bad Feeling Me." As Father John Powell has said, "You never bury a feeling dead; you only bury it alive." Repressed, suppressed feelings require energy to hold them down. That energy is not free for constructive use. And those repressed feelings bubble underneath to crop out in lowered scholastic ability, psychosomatic symptoms, heightened jealousy, and other undesirable behavior toward self and others.

The crucial point to understand here is that feelings exist. Children's feelings may be different from ours at times. We honor their integrity as little human beings by accepting that their particular feelings are real for them at that time. But we hold the line on how, when, where, and to whom those feelings are expressed, acted out, and dealt with.

Even we adults have trouble dealing constructively with our own negative feelings. Part of loving children is giving them constructive outlets for the expression of their feelings; outlets that do no harm to self, others, or property. Such outlets can be working feelings out with clay, drawings, pounding materials, puppets, talking, or writing about them. When feelings are given a safe outlet, the energy in them is dissipated and they do not remain as an old slush fund to be added to as the years go by.

Feelings simply do not disappear on command. So while we limit *behavior* that is antisocial, we find an outlet where such feelings can be safely "dumped."

It is harder to allow children to do this if we repress our own feelings. Part of giving ourselves the ticket of admission to the human race is to acknowledge that we all have all kinds of feelings.

Part of growing up whole is learning how to handle negative feelings in constructive ways. And denying or repressing feelings is simply not constructive, no matter how we look at it. Countless hours of adult therapy involve going back to the old awful feelings of the past—to that frozen pain buried years ago—and getting safe discharge. Part of therapy is learning that such feelings do not wipe out lovability. Part of growing free is knowing that feelings are one thing, actions are another.

Countless adults today live life on "automatic pilot" because they disconnect from their feelings in childhood. They are literally out of touch with their inner experiential world. But, as we've mentioned, repressed feelings push for some kind of outlet. Repression works only up to a point without a price being paid. And so often those old pains are worked out destructively later in relationships with others.

Feelings are a package deal; to the extent that negative ones are held in, so will the positive ones be repressed. If we want children to be warm, whole, loving adults, it is imperative that we be empathic to their feelings and give them ways for safe expression. Just as there is sunshine and rain, so there is anger and love. Love is communicated when we make children feel no less lovable because sometimes they feel "rainy" inside.

Parental Self-Worth

When a child hears English spoken, he learns to speak that language, of course. Just so, the parents' degree of self-worth is contagious. Children pick up the "psychological language" they hear.

We each connect with children from our own sense of OKness or Not-OKness. When we feel confident and inwardly sure, we relate much more smoothly to all others, particularly our children. We are the child's primary models. So our degree of self-worth affects them as they watch and imitate us. Each step we take as adults to enhance our own self-esteem is an indirect gift to our child.

It is important to remember that whatever goes on within parents and between them is part of the climate the child lives with. Does the child watch a master–slave relationship being acted out by parents? Or does the child hear the language of cooperation and mutual respect spoken between parents?

Pain in the parental relationship can be acted out in the parent–child relationship. Mother may be upset with Dad but take it out on the child. Working on our own self-worth and working to build positive adult relationships indirectly but tangibly makes a positive mark on the self-worth of children.

It is important to note that part of getting our love across to children, part of helping them to strong self-esteem, is to understand and work with the guilt and personal recriminations that are triggered off when the family unit is broken. As an increasing number of families go through such crises, it is helpful to keep this guideline in mind: "How would I feel under these circumstances?" Usually this question gives an immediate clue as to what is needed to lessen the pain. The powerful feelings of loss, grief, fear, depression, rage, and abandonment need to be heard. And, above all, children need to be spared the role of pawn when divorce is involved. They need to be spared being placed in the role of the absent parent, the role of therapist, the role of go-between.

Parenting has never been an easy or uncomplicated job. It is even more difficult when separation, divorce, remarriage, or death occurs in families. Children can make good adjustments if they feel supported emotionally, heard empathically, and are eased through family crisis. When family crisis hits, it is important to have as much of an emotional support network for family members as possible and at times to get a professional assist.

Children are remarkably resilient; yet they are children with dependent needs. Our role as parents is so important because we are operating on the growing edge of the upcoming generation. However, we each know adults today who are stable, loving, and functioning well in spite of childhood crises in their lives. How we adults handle family crisis is a model for our children.

Nevertheless, parents do not need to be perfect. Indeed, we couldn't be if we tried. Parenting is a challenging job. All any of us can do is our best and to learn along the way. We can seek help if situations call for that.

The greatest strength-giver, however, for both children and adults, will be high self-esteem. Through both peaceful and stressful times children need to be connected with in a particular way—the way of loving and caring, no matter what.

Guilt

It is easy to read this kind of book and brew up guilt when you learn of constructive methods you have not used. Most parents have enough guilt. They need more as much as they need a hole in the head. New ideas for parenting can be used as ideas to beat yourself with or as areas for growth.

Be aware that at all times you are probably doing the best you can, given the modeling you had, the pressures you are under, and the amount of awareness you have. If you are trying parenting approaches different from those you were raised with, remember you are trailblazing. And it is not easy to go across virgin territory.

It is often helpful to search for positive models and watch them. We humans are born imitators and we need positive examples to follow. Parenting classes, books, lectures, and professional help are all available.

Remember, if you try to be a "perfect parent," you are a prime candidate for burnout. There truly is no such thing. When you fall short of what you would wish, go to your child and say, "I am sorry I handled that this way. I want to erase that and handle it this way." Just as you would appreciate an employer who came back to you in his humanity and "re-did" the scene, so children appreciate human parents who model humanity rather than ones who hold themselves out as perfect.

As you are gentle and compassionate with yourself, so you are more likely to be with your child. "Fall-shorts" are part of the parenting trip.

If things are going amiss with your child, the first place to start is with a general physical checkup. Recent research has pointed up the effect of food allergies and neurological imbalances on behavior. Next, look to the climate

—the psychological climate—around your child just as you would with a plant. What kind of emotional soil is he living in? How would you feel living in a similar climate? Behavior is caused. Look for the cause, for that will determine the solution.

It is important to remember that books can only give general guidelines. You are living with a unique individual. It is therefore most important that you watch for your particular child's way and work with that child's unique temperament.

It is hard not to compare one child with another. Yet comparisons are rarely productive. Even with the same parents, children are often as different as day and night. Part of constructive parenting is being aware of uniqueness and finding creative ways to work with it.

Regardless of individual differences, however, every child needs experience in trust, focused attention, nonjudgment, firm-not-harsh limits, respectful treatment, empathic understanding, realistic expectations, and appreciation expressed for strengths. The need for love's climate is universal. It is *feeling loved* that allows the child to go out to others constructively, to be eager to learn, and to develop his gifts. It is that lack of feeling loved and valued that often leads the child to seek out inappropriate and, often, self-damaging ways to temporarily feel a sense of belonging.

Final Note

You are not the only influence in your child's life. Other family members, peers, teachers, and physical, social, and cultural pressures, along with the media, *all* play a part in forming your child's personality.

Laugh with, play with, take pleasure in, your child. All too soon he will be grown and gone. Children are truly only on loan to us. The more we can live the Golden Rule with them, the more they will be able to know they are lovable. And that they count. Remember, you are the parent; the child is the child. It is important not to get the roles confused.

Your positive faith that they will make it becomes their faith in themselves. That inner self-confidence gives youngsters the stuff with which to meet life's challenges. They will live out to a large degree what they believe to be true about themselves.

Long after they forget the words to the stories we read to them, they'll remember the song in their hearts because we made them feel valued by how we lived with them. By what was in the space between us and them . . . the Love space.

By the Author

for parents about their children

Your Child's Self-Esteem: The Key to His Life. New York: Doubleday, 1970 (hardback); Dolphin Books, 1975 (paperback).

for adults about themselves

Celebrate Yourself: Increase Your Own Self-Esteem. New York: Doubleday, 1977.

Enhance Your Self-Esteem: Teaching Manual (self-published). 1982.

Embracing Life: Growing Through Love and Loss. New York: Doubleday, 1985.

cassette for adults

Who You Truly Are. Creative Communications, Inc.

MARTIN GREENBERG

Meet the Author

Dr. Martin Greenberg's innovative research on father–infant bonding has been called classic. His studies have been published in psychiatry, medical, and child development journals and have been translated into several languages as well.

Dr. Greenberg received his M.D. and completed his internship in Pediatrics in San Francisco at the University of California School of Medicine, and did his psychiatric training at the Langley Porter Neuropsychiatric Institute at the University of California School of Medicine.

In 1965 he was awarded a National Institute of Health Award to study in Sweden for one year. There he worked with the renowned pediatrician John Lind at the Department of Pediatrics of the Karolinska Hospital, Stockholm, Sweden, completing studies on mothers rooming-in with their babies as well as on behavior and cry patterns of newborns. Dr. Edith Jackson, a pioneer in the development of rooming-in, was a particularly important influence at this time both through her writings and personal contacts.

In Zurich, Switzerland, he carried out research on sandplay with Frau Dora Kalff, a pioneer in the use of sandplay therapy with children and adults, and studied at the C. G. Jung Institute of Analytical Psychology.

Though Dr. Margaret Mead expressed skepticism early on of the father's importance, nevertheless she provided valuable assistance to Dr. Greenberg in his work. Years later, when she saw his completed research on Engrossment (a term he coined to refer to the father's absorption, preoccupation, and interest in his newborn baby), she noted the importance of his work in demonstrating the intense bond that fathers can potentially have with their infant children.

Dr. Greenberg is in private practice of psychiatry in San Diego, working with adults and families. He is particularly interested in the bonding process for parents, especially fathers, and in understanding and helping families when untoward events interfere with that process.

He and his wife, Claudia, are the proud parents of two boys, Jonathan and Jacob.

2

FATHERS: FALLING IN LOVE WITH YOUR NEWBORN

FATHER–INFANT BONDING
MARTIN GREENBERG, M.D.

In generations past, the father had no direct personal role with his baby. Everyone seemed to treat the birth as an event between the mother, doctor, and the infant. The father was seen as an outsider. So, although excited about the birth of his child, he seemed to be experiencing this momentous event from a distance.

He noted the close relationship between his wife and child, and assumed that this was the way it was supposed to be—no space for him. While a mother's role was to nurture her infant, a father's was to work, to provide for his family. That was his responsibility, what was expected of him. Even experts in child development emphasized the importance of the father's supporting his wife rather than mutual support and cooperative parenting. New fathers were told that men didn't have much of a relationship with their children, at least during the first two years.

My father's experience as a new parent seems to be fairly typical of his generation. During my mother's labor with me, he was out pacing the street in front of the hospital. When my grandfather finally came bearing the news that I was born, the two of them went out to celebrate, getting drunk together at a local bar.

Until fairly recently, fathers were denied early contact with their children, a practice that discouraged their involvement as fathers. They waited for news at the workplace, in the hospital waiting room, or, like my father, as they paced outside the hospital. Their presence was forbidden at one of the most thrilling events of their lives, their children's births. And they were permitted only infrequent visits to their wives once a day in the hospital, rarely being permitted to see their babies except through a dividing wall of glass.

The gradual movement of fathers into hospital delivery rooms was a recent development in Western society, producing significant change in father-child relationships. The opportunity for fathers to see their children being born resulted in a tremendous outpouring of feelings. Whereas previously it was thought that fathers were by nature emotionally uninvolved with young children, fathers who participated in the birth process felt swept off their feet—carried away with their feelings. They described themselves as "falling in love with their newborns."

The second significant development that strengthened the bond between fathers and their children was the movement of women into the workplace. Fathers began to spend more time with their children out of necessity because, with mothers working, children needed more attention and care from fathers. And as fathers assumed more responsibility, they developed close relationships with their children.

Perhaps no single event made me more aware of the power of the newborn infant than the birth of my own child on Tuesday, June 11, 1974. My wife, Claudia, had already been in labor for fourteen hours. After spending twenty minutes of pushing in the delivery room, Claudia made one last effort and it was enough. My son was born!

I was stunned by the size of the baby before me. He looked absolutely gigantic; he seemed to take up the entire room. He had a full head of hair and looked very alert from the beginning, gazing about the room. When I saw him, I began to laugh; it was a laugh that released all the weeks and months of waiting, a laugh of joy and happiness. I hugged my wife as I kept repeating, "Look, Claudia, look at the baby. Look, we have a baby. We have a baby boy!"

I was absolutely swept off my feet and carried away by the power of the moment, unable to resist giving in to all the excitement. I felt like shouting, singing, and dancing; but instead, I laughed so hard that I cried. I was completely flooded with emotion. This was the most incredible experience I'd ever had, seeing him born, seeing him for the first time. It was as though I was drunk and reeling from the power of the birth.

My experience with my own newborn mirrored what so many other fathers had already described to me. In 1971, in London, I studied first fathers' feelings toward their newborn babies. Those fathers vividly talked about their sense of a connection, their link with their infants. It was from this study that my concept of father bonding developed.

Engrossment

I coined the word "engrossment" to describe the father's absorption, preoccupation, and interest in his baby. It refers to the bond or linkup of the father to his newborn from the father's point of reference. The father wants to look at, hold, and cuddle his baby. His attraction to his baby is so powerful that it appears to be something over which he has little control; it is like an irresistible force, a magnet. All of his attention is focused on his baby. "Engrossment" means more than involvement. The derivation of the word engross means to make large. When the father is engrossed in his infant, that baby assumes gigantic proportions for him, larger than life.

The concept of engrossment is an important and revolutionary idea. First of all, it smashes the myth that fathers are emotionally detached from their newborns. Furthermore, the fact that the baby has such tremendous power over the father suggests that this is an innate potential for all fathers. It is the opportunity for early involvement with the newborn that triggers the release of engrossment. And there is exquisite pleasure in this experience!

Engrossment has tremendous ramifications for the entire family. Fathers who connect early with their children have a significant impact on their children's development. Children whose fathers know how to really "play" with them tend to be more sociable, get along better with their peers, and are more popular. Children feel better about themselves and are more open to others when they know their fathers care about them. And women who see their husbands relating to their children with warmth and affection feel closer toward their husbands, enhancing the quality of the marriage.

The major benefits, of course, go to the fathers themselves. When a father falls in love with his baby, he gets tremendous enjoyment from looking at, holding, and touching his infant. The pleasure in contact results in his feeling drawn to the baby and wanting to spend time with him, and in an increase in the father's self-esteem.

These positive feelings have dramatic consequences for the new family. They will help the father weather the trials of the first year and more easily cope with his jealousy over his wife's preoccupation with their new baby. And increasing the level of caring and loving of fathers for their newborns will inevitably shape the kind of society we live in.

At this point you may ask why we are focusing on engrossment for fathers. Don't mothers also develop a bond with their children? Certainly they do, but society has always recognized the mother's instinctive bond to her children. It is the fathering connection that is newsworthy. Furthermore, the experience of the father is different from that of his wife.

A woman begins to develop both an intense emotional as well as physical bond with the baby well before the baby's birth—it begins during the pregnancy. As she feels her baby move, kick, and shift positions, she has the unique ability to experience him within her own body.

A man's relationship to the fetus is obviously different. While his wife is experiencing the relationship from the inside—this baby is part of her, connected with her—he is experiencing the relationship from the outside and can't feel the depth of emotion and commitment that she does. She spends the pregnancy as the go-between, describing the sensation of their child moving within her, inviting him to touch her belly to share the excitement. She has to mediate his experience.

A husband whose wife was in the last trimester of pregnancy vividly described his sense of awe at his wife's ability to experience the baby from within:

> *I wonder what it would feel like to actually feel the kid inside of you, to feel an elbow inside of your stomach. I ask her all the time, "What does it feel like from the inside?" A man can only feel things from the outside. When someone walks up to you and touches you, you feel it on the outside of your flesh. What does it feel like on the inside of your flesh? What would it feel like to have something besides your stomach growling, your heart beating? What would it feel like to have somebody in there, to have a hand hitting you or a foot kicking you from the inside instead of being external? It would be internal and you'd be feeling it. That would blow me away.*

At the birth, the new mother may experience a feeling of loss as the biological connection with the infant is severed. They are no longer one. This is why it is so important for the new mother to be able to hold the baby as soon as possible after the birth, thus replacing the severed pregnancy with the new baby.

The father-to-be, on the other hand, is coming from much further back in terms of his relationship to his child. Suddenly at the birth, after nine months of waiting, of wishing he could feel more toward his child, of feeling unconnected and uncertain and wondering what will happen and what he will experience when his baby is born, he finally gets to meet the baby for the first time on his own—and he feels like a father.

When he assumes that it is his wife's role to continue as mediator, he continues to be an outsider. When he is welcomed to love and care for his new child, and he does, he can become fully and completely engrossed.

One of the most dramatic aspects of engrossment consists of the "swept away" experience. The baby explodes upon the father's consciousness despite his preconceived notions, his plans for the future. The explosive power that newborn babies have over fathers leads us to believe that this experience is out of the father's voluntary control.

In my own case, I desperately wanted to feel involved, to feel hooked up with my baby during the pregnancy, but I wasn't able to experience the intensity of emotion that Claudia did. I was convinced that having completed research on the concept of engrossment, I was going to be the one unengrossed father. I thought I knew too much. I couldn't seem to get emotionally involved in my wife's pregnancy despite the fact that I had read many books on pregnancy and birth and spent time practicing the childbirth exercises with her. Massaging her belly, talking and singing to our baby in utero, going to her doctor's appointments, listening to the heartbeat with her, and seeing the sonogram of our child helped make the baby more real, but it was still Claudia's pregnancy. I was experiencing mixed feelings of excitement and insecurity, disruption, and chaos. I was concerned about losing my freedom; no, terrified would be a better word.

So I was surprised and pleased that I, too, became overwhelmed with excitement when my son was born. It proved to me that engrossment occurs on a deep emotional level, not a rational one.

Now we can reassure new fathers, "You don't have to do anything to fall in love with your baby. All you have to do is be present early on—to allow your senses to be open and aware."

Fathers in the past have not given sufficient recognition to their loving and nurturing feelings. By learning more about engrossment a father will better appreciate the magic of the birth experience for himself as well as for his wife and baby. By being more aware of her husband's experience, the wife can also be a source of support for him during this incredibly exciting period. As a result, in addition to increasing the father's opportunity to bond with his child, the parents will be able to use this as an opportunity to bond with each other.

Engrossment actually consists of seven different aspects. To help you capture the true flavor of each, I'll describe them in the words of the fathers themselves:

Visual appeal of the baby. The father sees his baby as attractive. He enjoys looking at his own baby, as opposed to babies in general. For example, one English father said:

> *I couldn't get over it. I walked up and down and looked at all those babies in that room up there, and they all looked a bit ugly, a bit rubbery, and then when she came out, she looked so beautiful, really a little gem, so beautiful!*

Pleasure in touching the baby. Fathers enjoy holding, touching, cuddling, and playing with their babies. Another father said:

I feel great, just great; can't stop picking her up—really a strong feeling of pleasure. She wriggles in your hands; she wriggles when she's against your chest and in your arms.

Fathers are impressed by the softness and smoothness of the baby's skin. A father who was asked how it felt to touch his newborn replied:

One hears the expression "soft as a baby's backside," I suppose, but when I touched it, it did seem incredibly soft, like velvet.

Awareness of the newborn's distinct characteristics. Some fathers can describe the unique features of their infant in quite elaborate detail and even think they can distinguish their own baby from others.

One first-time father whose baby was three days old stated that he felt very good about his baby as it looked like him. "He looks like you?" I asked in surprise. "Oh, you didn't get a good look at him," the father responded matter-of-factly. He then described in detail how his child resembled him.

He's got a longish body already, although he's very light in weight. He's got large hands like me; he's got long feet; he's got large ears; he's got a broad nose like me; he's got a little chin with a cleft, I think. He's got my wife's hair, long black silky hair, and her eyes. I definitely would be able to recognize him by his face, and if I wasn't sure about the face, I could definitely go by the hands and feet. I think I could pick him out of a crowd.

Perception of the baby as perfect. Though the father may admit that the baby is awkward or not completely coordinated, he sees his infant, nevertheless, as the epitome of perfection. One father said:

The little nervous system seems to be in its first stages. It's not completely coordinated yet. The legs are shaking about as if they're a bit uncoordinated. But it all seems just right. It's as though all these little systems are going into action, the eyes, the ears, the neck, the nervous system. And everything is just right, just right.

Another exclaimed:

I had the feeling—this is miraculous that he could come out and be perfect. I remember looking at his hands and seeing the fingers and the fingernails. Everything was so perfectly formed. What an incredible miracle that nature works this way.

Strong attraction to the baby. Many fathers describe this feeling of being drawn to the baby as beyond their control. One English father told me:

When I come up to see my wife I say, "Hi! How's things, everything all right? You need anything?" And then I go look at the kid and then I pick her up and then I put her down and then I say, "Hi! Is everything all right?" And then I go back to the kid. I keep going back to the kid. It's like a magnet. That's what I can't get over, the fact that I feel like that.

Focusing on the baby can even make her appear larger. The same father also commented:

Hey, she looked a bit bigger that night than she does tonight. I suppose, the birth, things are perhaps exaggerated or magnified a bit.

A feeling of elation. Often fathers describe themselves as feeling high. This is expressed in many ways; as feeling stunned, stoned, dazed, drunk, ten feet tall, different, taken out of themselves. For example, a father who was present at his child's birth marveled:

I took a look at it and I took a look at the face and I left the ground—just left the ground! I thought, "Oh! This is marvelous."

Many fathers are surprised at the impact of their infants upon them and the intensity of their emotions, especially when they felt uninvolved during their wife's pregnancy. For example, one father explained:

Well, up to now, I wasn't really all that involved, I suppose. I didn't have much strong feeling one way or another. It was just my wife was pregnant and I was happy for her and that's about as far as it went. But the little something was born and—I did a complete switch, just a complete switch! Just felt tremendous about it. And I was surprised because I thought I wouldn't take too much interest in it until it was old enough to be a small human being. But it already is a human being.

Increased sense of self-esteem. After seeing his baby for the first time, a new father will often describe himself as feeling prouder, bigger, stronger, more mature. A twenty-three-year-old first father commented:

> *It's a lovely little thing. I don't really want to leave . . . I just feel a bit older now. I'm a father, a father at last. I've got something of my own. I look at it and I say, "I did that—I did that; it's mine." I think it's just realizing that I'm a father and the baby's there and letting that sink in.*

When fathers are engrossed in their children, they experience a bond, a connection, a link. They describe feeling that the child is a part of them. And they emphasize over and over, when asked about the importance of the birth, "When you see your child born, you know he's yours, something that the two of you produced." It's truly the beginning of a powerful relationship—father and child.

As a father discovers his child, he finds a whole world of new sensations opening to him: the path to the child is also the road to discovering a more open, feeling side of himself. As a father interacts with his child, he finds the child within himself. It is as if the birth of the child leads to his own birth as a father as well as his maturation into a more complete human being.

Absence of Engrossment: The Emotional Impact

Although engrossment is a potential phenomenon for all fathers, it is not always experienced at the birth. For some fathers, emotional bonding evolves more slowly. So don't be alarmed if you don't become engrossed immediately.

Physical Absence

The crucial ingredient necessary for bonding is contact. This is why the father's presence at the birth can be so valuable, for it is a unique and powerful kind of contact. Its importance in the development of engrossment is demonstrated by the words of a twenty-four-year-old first-time father who did not see his child born:

> *After the birth, the nurse came up to me and said, "Here's your baby." The nurse just sort of plopped him in my hands. I didn't feel*

much of anything. I didn't feel like a father. I didn't feel like he belonged to me.

But in the next several days the father came to the hospital and had an opportunity to visit his son, to hold and cuddle him. He described the turnabout in his feelings, saying:

I began to feel more and more like a father. I began to feel that he was really mine!

If you have to be absent due to ill health, military, educational, or occupational demands, you may have a harder time establishing that special connection on your return. Don't wait for the stirrings of love to envelop you before approaching your child. When you play with him, the baby himself can trigger closeness, breaking down your feelings of isolation.

Society's Influence

If there is a generally accepted norm in your community or your cultural group that fathers just don't get too involved with their children, this can be a significant block to your emotions. Taking childbirth education classes will force you to be aware that the birth is coming; it's inevitable. You are going to become a father! Seeing other men helping and coaching their pregnant wives will help you get yourself psychologically ready to assume your role as an involved, loving father.

Lack of Preparation

Childbirth classes also significantly reduce anxiety. If your wife has had no preparation for childbirth, she might be overly frightened during labor and birth. Watching her, you may feel helpless, unable to alleviate her pain and fears despite your caring. Through education, mothers and fathers gain an understanding of what to expect and they learn specific exercises to help facilitate labor and delivery. Parents develop a sense of control as they work as a team to get ready for the impending birth.

In your preparation, keep in mind that while engrossment is valuable in helping you link up with your baby immediately, the first priority is the welfare of your wife and baby. Many times parents have in mind a specific script—natural childbirth, no medication, no forceps, and so forth. But when the unexpected, such as a necessary caesarian section, intrudes on that ideal, parents often think that they have failed their child and themselves. The guilt over not doing things the "right way" can interfere with their joy over their newborn. Instead, recognize that planning can only go so far and then, in the interest of a healthy baby, your childbirth attendants might have to use methods that were not in the original plan.

Emotional Absence

It's important for you to realize that basically anything that causes you to be preoccupied (thoughts about your career, your job, your schooling, money, and housing, or the responsibilities ahead of you as a new parent) can distance you from your baby at the birth. Youth and emotional immaturity can also be contributing factors.

If you are worried about an illness in your family, if you are overwhelmed by the loss of a loved one, or if you are severely depressed, you might have even more difficulty becoming engrossed in your child. Don't compound your difficulty by heaping guilt on yourself for your seeming disinterest in him. Understand that the problem is that all your energy is currently being taken up by your feelings of loss or concern. It's as if your system were burned out and you just had no more energy to feel. As you recover and have the opportunity to interact with your baby, you'll develop your connection to him.

If your wife is in poor health, or if she has been ill during the pregnancy or the birth, you may focus all of your energy on your concerns for your wife's welfare. You might need to find out that she is well before you can allow yourself to enjoy your child. Some fathers even blame the baby for their wife's problems, as though the child consciously hurt her. At the other extreme, if you are going through struggles with your wife, it may be difficult for you to enthusiastically welcome your newborn's arrival. You and your wife need to talk out some of your concerns during this time. In either case, if feelings are intense, get some help from a therapist so you don't direct your anger to your baby.

The Birth Process

The doctor's attitude and hospital procedures can enhance or interfere with your engrossment in your baby. If you have a lack of communication with your wife's doctor or nursing staff, or if your presence is excluded by what you see as arbitrary hospital rules or procedures, you might feel uninvolved in the birth process. In this age of increasing options, it's important to choose a doctor who not only is a skilled clinician, but is also supportive of family bonding. And choose a hospital with staff that treats fathers with respect and dignity.

Something Wrong with the Baby

If your child is born prematurely, you may not be ready for the birth. You may need eight or ten more weeks to fully emotionally accept the reality of your baby. In addition, watching your newborn in an isolette, being cared for by hospital staff amid the mass of technical equipment, you might consider your presence to be unnecessary, at best, or even a hindrance to him. Get to know the hospital staff who are caring for your child so you will understand what they are doing for him and participate in his care, talking to your baby, touching and holding him, and, if possible, feeding him.

One father shared with me that he felt distant, unconnected to his baby at the birth. He was in tears as he described his lack of excitement. I believed he really wanted to feel close. I was baffled until I went back and looked over my notes. I realized that his son had not begun breathing immediately and had even turned blue. To cope with the intense fear that he could lose his child, the father had distanced himself from the event, and in the process cut off his feelings. With support and understanding, this father developed closeness with his baby later on.

If your child is born with handicaps, you might have difficulty becoming initially attached to your baby because much energy will be used up in mourning the loss of the hoped-for "normal" child. Your grief can seriously interfere with the father–child bond. Support groups for parents who have children with handicaps can help you understand that this response is normal. Together you can gain strength from each other as you learn to cope with your anger and disappointment and focus on constructive ways to meet your child's needs. Your tender, nurturing feelings toward your baby will develop as a result of your involvement with him. As your involvement grows, the barriers will break down.

Opportunities for Closeness

There will be many opportunities to develop closeness as your baby grows and develops. When your baby smiles or coos, giggles or laughs, when he sits, crawls, stands, or walks, and when he reaches out to you, or appears to talk to you, mimic you, or say "Da Da," his adorable qualities can reach out and captivate you, almost against your will. By allowing yourself to become fascinated with your baby, and be a part of his ongoing development, you'll find him hard to resist.

Family Bonding

Communication with your wife is essential to ensure that your engrossment in your baby is occurring within the context of a caring relationship. Some fathers are completely unprepared for the way their feelings for their babies sweep them off their feet. While wives are usually delighted that their husbands are so fascinated with their babies, they need to feel important too. After all, the birth was a tumultuous process for her. She's just undergone the severing of the ultimate biological and emotional bond of pregnancy. And she may be going through a letdown, as her physical and emotional condition is now rapidly fluctuating. Your acknowledgment and support are therefore very important. But some fathers, drawn to the baby by forces they cannot control, forget or become unaware of their wives' needs. For example, one overwhelmed father confessed:

> *I just sit and stare at the baby and talk to my wife and comfort her a bit. But the main thing is the baby. I just want to hold the baby . . .*

Some women become angry when their husbands ignore them during their visits to the hospital, spending all their time looking at their new child. But if you are prepared in advance and have some awareness of the amazing power of the newborn, you may be able to respond to your wife in a way that fully considers her and her needs.

For most fathers, the feeling of closeness to the baby includes their wives as well. They have gone through an important life event together. So the moment of birth is not only a time of closeness for the father and mother separately with the baby, but also for husband and wife with one another. It is a time of "family bonding."

Usually hospital staff will allow your family time alone to get acquainted immediately after the birth. This is essential, not only to help you become engrossed in your child, but also to allow you, your wife, and child to bond together as a family. You and your wife can now explore, hold, cuddle, sing, and coo to the baby together. In the solitude, away from the prying eyes of the world at large, the two of you can feel free to release tears of joy and laughter. Some hospitals or alternative birth centers also allow you to bring in your older children, giving them an opportunity to hold and cuddle their baby brother or sister. And you can introduce your baby to his grandparents as well, thus enhancing their own positive feelings toward the baby.

In the calm of the bonding room, all of the surging energy held in check over the past nine months can now be released. The frustration, anxiety, and fears finally burst forth in a flood of relief. Merged with this is a powerful feeling of exhilaration. All has gone well and the baby is here!

Despite these intense emotions, there is also a sense of tranquility in the recovery room. One father shared with me his feeling that this room, protected and undisturbed, was like a peaceful lagoon following a raging hurricane (the birth).

This is a once-in-a-lifetime experience, when you feel incredible closeness to your wife and your child. You feel in touch with yourself and have a heightened sensitivity to everything around you. It is in the peaceful and protected setting that family bonding frequently begins to flower, when you and your wife and child begin to come together as a family.

This time together will be very important in your relationship with your wife. Many women share how meaningful it was to have their husbands at their sides during the pregnancy, labor, and delivery, and in the immediate aftermath of the birth. They feel a new dimension in their marriages, as well as a heightened intimacy with their husbands.

The bonding room has an energy all its own generated by the coming together of your family. The presence of your baby is a confirmation that the two of you have weathered an overwhelming storm, have gone through a unique life process together. The time in the bonding room is a culmination of all that has happened, a bonding not only between you and your baby but between you and your wife as well, leading to an expanded dimension of your marital vessel.

The Letdown

There is a natural sense of isolation that begins to occur for fathers in the weeks after the birth. Even for those fathers who experience the emotional high of engrossment, there may be a letdown as the magic of the birth passes and the realities of parenting begin.

Jealousy

Perhaps there is no more destructive emotion that you will have to cope with in the early months after your child's birth than your own jealousy. It is not jealousy per se that is so destructive, but rather the refusal to acknowledge that it is there. Jealousy inevitably accompanies fatherhood. How we accept and deal with it are the primary factors determining whether it wreaks chaos in its path.

In the next several weeks and months, you may ask yourself, "What is my role now? My wife is close to the baby but where do I fit in?" And if your wife is breast feeding, you may notice the intimate relationship between baby and mother and wonder if there is space for you. Furthermore, as you go off to work every day, you may be aware of increased feelings of isolation and exclusion. You have to leave while your wife still has the opportunity to enjoy the closeness that comes as she develops her own unique relationship with the baby. At bottom, this is a jealousy that comes from wanting to be closer, to be included, to establish contact with your newborn.

Of course there is also the "traditional" jealousy that fathers often experience after the birth—actual jealousy of the baby. As a father you have good reason to feel jealous. After all, the baby is taking up time and attention that was previously available for you. And you may feel pushed out of the picture as this young father who said:

> Before you have a baby it's usually just you and your wife. There's a lot of hugging and holding and kissing and she's really involved with you. After the birth, all of a sudden the baby is involved. It takes up your space. It's hard to have someone take away from that space that you used to have.

Besides having less time with your wife, you feel like your freedom with her is curtailed. You used to have limitless possibilities in terms of intimate time together. Now suddenly the baby is there.

If you are a young father, these struggles will be greatly magnified in intensity, leading to increased frustration, tension, and confusion. You may feel trapped like the father who admitted:

> My jealousy was coming out in all sorts of weird feelings. I would get upset. I'd never felt this way before. You have your baby but he's cramping your life-style. If you wanted to go to the movies, you couldn't go because the baby wasn't feeling good or something like that. You have to get used to that. But I wasn't used to that. I was just really getting wound up.

The birth of your baby also dramatically changes your sexual relationship with your wife. It's likely that your wife's interest in lovemaking diminished during the last trimester of pregnancy and this disruption was further aggravated in the first six weeks after birth, the period in which many physicians recommend refraining from intercourse. Even when your wife's doctor says it's okay to resume sexual relations, it may still be hard to get on track again. Not only is there less time available for intimate moments, but you or your wife may be exhausted and less interested in lovemaking. If you've got a crying baby on your hands, this will affect your energy level in general and your interest in sex in particular.

You may worry about what impact the sight and sound of your lovemaking has upon the baby. This can diminish your spontaneity even further. This leads to a "let's get this over with before the baby cries" attitude, leading to a further loss of the fun and spontaneous quality of sexual intimacy. This continuing disruption of your normal patterns can result in trouble if it is also accompanied by a lack of communication.

You may be jealous if your wife doesn't give you special attention now, doesn't pamper you. At times your wife may have felt like a little girl needing support and love, and you provided this for her. And there were times when you, although a grown man, felt weak and vulnerable, like a little boy, and your wife gave you the extra attention you needed. But now she doesn't, for she already has a baby to care for. She can't handle two of them. This can be seen as a rejection and result in anger toward the baby if it's not discussed and the problem is not faced. One father put it this way:

> Before our son was born there would be times when I'd come home and I'd want to be the little boy. You know, you have a parent–child relationship as well as husband–wife relationship, and I don't mind admitting that at times I liked to be the little boy and just escape that way. My wife used to buy into that. I don't get that anymore.

There is no need to feel ashamed and embarrassed about your jealous feelings. These are universal struggles that we all must work through. It is important, however, for you to talk about your concerns, to help your wife become aware of your needs. Then you can develop a plan to spend more time alone with her and more time alone with your baby.

As you interact with your baby and become aware of his precious qualities and his increasing responsiveness to you, you will begin to establish a vital companionship together. This will go a long way toward tearing down the wall of jealousy.

The Perils of Responsibility

While fathers, at the moment of birth, talk about their intense love for their children, some also express a desire to work harder at their careers for the good of their child. For example, a new father said:

> From the moment of the birth it's been ecstasy with him. He's put years on my life. He's put a smile on my face. He's given me hope. He's made me a better person. I'm not thinking of myself as much as I was before. I'm thinking of him more, of supporting him, of trying to earn more money . . .

These kinds of comments used to baffle me, for by going off to work, the father was leaving his child, being separated from him. But if we understand that the father's expression of his desire to work is, in essence, a desire to protect his child, these comments are less perplexing.

Primitive man, in order to afford protection for his child, had to linger close by, be physically present. If an enemy attacked, he could bash the enemy with a club, pick up his infant, and run with him. As he held his baby, he was in physical contact, and it is likely that he also felt close to him, bound to him. The protection that he provided very likely resulted in increased bonding.

The acts of protecting and nurturing are closely related. Both are instinctual. Among many animals the protection that the male provides often results in bonding and nurturing the infant. Many men, particularly new fathers, see the act of providing (protecting) as an act of love. It connects them to their wife and children, and gives their lives meaning. Here we can clearly see the link between protecting and nurturing. The desire to provide for, hold, and cuddle your own child is, in reality, an explosion into the instinctive, universal experience of men, past and present.

How sad it is that as a man works harder and harder, he is increasingly separated from his child. Physical contact is the single most important ingredient in establishing closeness with his youngster. Many men do not realize that the act of protecting (or providing) is instinctual but has been separated from nurturing in our modern world. Ironically, working makes fathers feel close to their families, yet the harder they work, the less contact they have and the more isolated they feel.

There are a number of resolutions to this dilemma. First, it's important for your wife to be aware of the trap that you're in. Share your feelings of love for the baby and talk about how you feel when you are working to provide for them both. This might give you new insight and your wife increased understanding.

Inevitably, however, the real solution is to have more contact with your child. Your wife may be able to help. If her own work schedule permits, perhaps she can bring the baby to visit you on the job so you can see him during the day. Or maybe the infant's sleep schedule or your work schedule can be changed so that he is awake when you come home. If you can get home from work while the baby is still awake and responsive, this is a wonderful opportunity for contact with him.

It would be helpful if corporations and businesses were more sensitive to the needs of parents and provided time off for paternity as well as maternity leave. In reaching out to fathers and to parents in general, companies would be enhancing their employees' sense of well-being, giving them an increased opportunity to experience the joy of parenting. This would probably result in improved work efficiency and mental health, and therefore fewer sick days.

I don't have an easy answer to this dilemma. Maybe it's sufficient for both you and your wife to be aware of the tendency for you to become increasingly isolated because you want to work for the well-being of your family. Your wife needs to know that your focus on work comes not out of disinterest, but from caring. When you are aware of this yourself, you might reevaluate your priorities.

Those early years move by so quickly. A new father put this in bold relief by stating:

I am bound and determined to share as much time as I can with my baby because I see that these times won't be around much longer. The first year passes very quickly! I would hate to think three or four or five years from now that anything was more important than giving her the quality time that she needs right now!

Coping with Crying

Since your feelings of closeness are influenced by your baby's responsiveness to you, the baby's crying can create real barriers to your relationship. New fathers, especially, see crying as the baby's stamp of rejection. If your baby cries every time you pick him up, you'll feel like you want to run and hide. And, of course, it will certainly diminish your enthusiasm to pick him up the next time.

There is universal chaos triggered by the baby's cry. Even the most experienced parents can be devastated by the shrill howl of a newborn infant. When your baby doesn't respond to your attempts to quiet him, you may feel helpless. His cries are like a loud pronouncement for all to hear. It's as if he is yelling, "You can't do anything to stop me from crying. What an incompetent father you are!"

Claudia and I were invited to a party to celebrate our entrance into parenthood about two weeks after Jonathan was born. At the beginning of the party, Jonathan was very well-behaved, demonstrating to all the world what an expert I was. In fact, he was asleep. How can you go wrong with a sleeping baby?

But his slumber was not to last for long. He gradually awakened, shrieking as he did so. With cocky confidence, I strode over to my infant and whispered to him as I picked him up, "Come on, Jonathan, show everybody what a good father I am." I don't know why it is, but whenever a baby suspects that you're not responding to him with complete spontaneity or that you have a hidden agenda, he smokes it out. Well, Jonathan must have suspected something, because he acted as if I had thrown cold water in his face.

His howls caused at least four people to come scurrying from different directions to his rescue.

"Can I try?" they asked one after another, waiting in line to make their own efforts to calm his cries. But none were successful. Secretly I was relieved! I tried one more time, but Jonathan battered me with his cries. I felt like slithering away, crawling into a corner. I assumed everyone was looking at me. "Some father, and a psychiatrist yet!" they were probably thinking. "He can't even stop his baby from crying."

"Maybe I've made a terrible mistake," I thought. "I wonder if I'm not cut out to be a father. Maybe I'd better reevaluate this whole fatherhood thing." Jonathan finally went to sleep, and Claudia and I took him for a walk along the ocean. But he had brought me hurtling from the clouds back to earth. It wasn't the last time that he'd do it. But at least now it doesn't surprise me as much.

Over the next weeks, as I talked to more men about their experiences, I recognized the universality of many of our conflicts. I learned how vulnerable we men are as fathers, how easily we begin to question our role, how we tend to criticize our performance and assume that others are doing likewise.

My experiences with Jonathan have made me aware of how important it is for parents to develop a productive approach to deal with a baby's crying. I'd like to share some of my "secret weapons" with you here.

Learning what the cries mean. As you spend more time with your newborn, you'll begin to understand his rhythms and learn what works and what doesn't work with him. As this occurs, you'll feel more competent and better about yourself as a father, and better about your baby as well. Now you'll see your infant responding to you and your efforts.

When you become more experienced you'll begin to get some idea of what his cries mean—for they really are a method of communication. Perhaps he is crying because he's hungry or uncomfortable in a wet diaper, because of a rash, or because he is cold. And remember, babies sometimes cry excessively when they are becoming ill. Sometimes normal crying can decrease or disappear as part of the lethargy of illness. If you suspect that your child may be ill, consult your pediatrician.

Babies often cry when they are alone and simply want to be picked up and cuddled. Infants need human contact to grow and develop. Newborn babies will not be spoiled by affection. Babies also are apt to cry when they're overstimulated or overtired and just need to sleep. Some newborns miss the comfort of the mother's womb and feel more secure when wrapped from the shoulders down in a receiving blanket.

Colicky children are especially frustrating to parents because even your most heroic efforts will be unlikely to soothe your child. Babies suffering from colic seem to cry endlessly, usually toward the end of the day. They are generally irritable and often appear to suffer from stomach distress that can become so intense that they pull their legs up toward their chests as they cry out in pain.

Being overly sensitive to stimuli, these babies need a calm, relaxed environment. That's very difficult when you see your child so miserable. Doctors often note that colicky children are more likely to be born to tense parents. It might be more accurate to state that colicky children generally produce nervous parents.

Some doctors think colic is caused by swallowing air, others blame the infant's slowly developing nervous system, while still others see it as the result of milk allergy. Colic is often used as a wastebasket term for something we don't understand. Many treatments have been recommended, but most have uncertain effectiveness.

If you and your wife have a colicky baby, do whatever your doctor suggests to help him reduce his stress and minimize his stomach distress. Some doctors suggest placing a lukewarm hot water bottle under the baby's tummy. If you try this, be certain it isn't too warm and wrap it in a towel to protect his sensitive skin. Laying your baby on his belly across your legs while you rub his back can also be helpful. Often the best treatment is to just let your child cry for fifteen to twenty minutes to release some of his tension. Despite what you do, you'll probably find that this condition usually phases out by the time your youngster is about three months old.

Music and playful rhythmic movement. Babies respond well to music and rhythmic activity. You may be able to quiet your child by calling out his name, by talking to him in a warm, soothing voice, or by singing to him. He may respond well to your bouncing him gently on your knees or swinging him (not too vigorously) or dancing around the house with him. And if you play a musical instrument, you may be pleasantly surprised to find that he stops crying and squeals with delight as he listens.

Movement in general. Virtually anything that provides rhythmic movement is helpful in soothing your baby's cries. A rocking chair is very useful, as is walking while rocking him gently in your arms or holding him in different positions. Taking him for a walk in the front baby carrier or backpack can be a particularly effective technique. Sometimes when all else fails, you and your wife may want to just drop everything and take your baby for a ride in the car. We often did this with Jonathan—an act of desperation that usually worked.

Droning noises. Different babies respond to different activities, and what works one day may not work the next with the same child. Babies are often calmed by the noise of a washing machine, the ticking of a clock, the whistling of a tea kettle, or the motor of a hair dryer. (The gentle rush of air from the dryer may be comforting as well.) Most young children are very frightened by the noise of a vacuum cleaner. Jonathan used to respond to it as if it were a wild beast unless I held him while vacuuming. Then he enjoyed a sense of power over it as we walked back and forth together. It may be that these various noises are reminiscent of the sounds the baby heard in utero—the cushioning waves of the amniotic fluid and the pulsing rush of blood through the body, occurring against the background of the mother's heartbeat. Regular, droning noises often help babies feel secure.

Water. While the bath only serves to increase the cries of some babies, others are calmed by water and enjoy playing in their baths. And many babies enjoy the gentle sensation of water sprinkled upon their bodies in the shower, a unique opportunity for you to have skin-to-skin contact with him as well.

Toys. The movement of a rattle or other colorful toy back and forth in front of his field of vision may capture your child's attention and diminish his tears. As he grows and develops he will increasingly reach out and grab his toys, creating a momentary diversion, and thus a lapse in his crying.

Other acts of desperation. Parents will often do anything to stop a baby's cries. "Can't you give my baby a tranquilizer?" mothers would ask me when I was a pediatric intern. And if the answer was no, they would invariably ask for medication for themselves, anything to shut off the sound of their infants' cries.

One mother shared with me that breathing in rhythm with her newborn baby invariably worked, putting her daughter to sleep within minutes. But that didn't work for me with my son. Before Jonathan could respond to my efforts, I had hyperventilated myself into a state of somnolence.

Companionship

Many fathers experience a closeness with the baby at the birth but then have little contact thereafter. If so, though you may still feel close, you are not communicating your feelings to your baby. Expressing closeness is important throughout your child's development. At this early period, the way you communicate your love is by physical contact. In this way your child perceives his father as a reality. How can he know about your enthusiasm and happiness over being a father? You need to translate your feelings into a physical relationship to make your impact felt.

Your relationship with your child needs a reality base and the reality base is contact. Contact through looking at and listening to him, holding him, cuddling him, and playing with him. Contact through talking and singing to him as you walk with him, diaper him, or put him to sleep. Contact is your total physical experience with your baby as opposed to your thoughts and images of him. The thoughts and images are very important! But it is also important to translate them into reality.

As you develop a closeness and companionship with your baby, you'll

feel less overwhelmed with feelings of jealousy. You'll feel better able to cope with him when he cries. You'll feel less excluded and more engrossed. And your engrossment will help you to cope with many of the struggles already mentioned and others that loom on the horizon.

The key to building a companionship with your baby is to be alone with him, either in the house or on walks together. If your wife is around, you will have a tendency to defer to the "expert." And she will have a tendency to want to rescue the baby every time he cries. In fact, you may welcome the rescue effort. However, the next time you think about being alone with the baby, you may worry about whether you will be able to cope on your own.

When you start taking your little baby for walks, you'll feel closer to him. You're the one in charge. There's something about being the one in charge that intensifies a father's feelings of protectiveness and love for his infant.

The front baby carrier and backpack allow you to walk with your baby, greatly enhancing your companionship. The front baby carrier is a kind of portable pouch—a "portapouch." It allows you to walk with your baby while carrying him close to your chest and abdomen. The backpack, on the other hand, has a cloth seat for the baby and a metal frame; the seat gives him an opportunity to look at the world from your shoulders. Generally you can use the front baby carrier with a very small infant—up to about five months or so. You can start using the backpack when your baby has developed some muscular control of his head and neck, from around four to five months until he is one year or even older.

When you're walking with your baby in a front carrier you feel a sense of closeness. You put your finger in his hand and he grabs it. Or perhaps you snuggle his face against your face. The rhythmic motion of walking together contributes greatly to the sense of bonding.

The amazing thing about the baby carrier is that it has a calming effect on the crying baby; perhaps it's the rhythmic motion transmitted through walking that's the key ingredient. You feel the pride of being able to get your baby to respond to your efforts. You tell yourself, "Now I can do it, now I'm competent as a father." This greatly increases your own sense of confidence and self-esteem. And it adds to your sense of a connection with him.

When you're walking along together, you feel your special relationship. It's just the two of you. You don't have to worry about what others think of you. You can let go of your own critical judgments of yourself.

I used to take Jonathan for walks on the beach in California until he was four months old. I began taking him for walks in the backpack in the forests of Switzerland when he was about four and one-half months old. I looked forward to our special times together. We watched the waves break against the shore and I would talk to him, reaching for his hand as he slowly went to sleep. Our walks together were treasured moments when I sang and talked to

him. I used to sing, "Twinkle, twinkle, little star; how I love my Jonathan Are" and I would make up all kinds of different verses about my feelings for him.

When my second son, Jacob, was born I changed the words of "Michael Row Your Boat Ashore" to "Jacob, row your boat ashore." And I made up other rhyming strains to express my love for Jacob. I decided I wanted Jacob to have his own unique song; that helps give a unique and characteristic memory to each child.

As you walk along with your baby, it's as if you've finally let go. You can allow the playful side of yourself to emerge, the child within. Try singing to your baby as you walk with him. Songs are a special way to communicate for they are words from the spirit, the emotional language of love. I think this is why babies like their fathers to sing to them. Try making up words to capture your feelings for your baby and your song becomes a love song from daddy to baby.

What can you talk to your baby about as you walk along? Tell him about the trees and the sky. Talk to him about the love that you feel for him. Tell him about how much you enjoy your time together. Your baby will be nurtured by your caring words and he will sense the love and tenderness in them. Your words are like a loving caress. But most importantly, as you are walking with your baby, you are creating a companionship with him through your physical contact.

During your walks together some very important things are happening. You suddenly realize that he is now cooing happily instead of crying. And as a result you feel better about yourself as a father and feel closer to him as well. The pleasure in your walks will result in your wanting to spend more time with him because it feels good, because you enjoy it. You'll want to do it for yourself, for "selfish" reasons.

As fathers increasingly fall in love with their children they become more concerned about what kind of world their children are growing up in. They realize, not just intellectually but on a deep emotional level, that their child is a part of their connection to the future, a link in the cycle of life. One father put it this way:

> My grandma used to watch horses and buggies and now here's a guy on the moon. What is my daughter's generation going to see? The same thing I see, until she is grown up and married. And after I die she is going to see even more. It is kind of hard to judge what is going to happen—all the nuclear worries! We are the generation to change it—to keep the cycle of life going. I hope things just go on forever and ever. I hope my child's children will go on. And her children's children and their children's children and so on. I hope it keeps going.

Parents' Need for Relief

The opportunity for parents to have relief from the all-encompassing demands of child care is extremely important. Parents who are alone and isolated, without sources of help or relief, have a difficult time becoming engrossed in their children.

They feel exhausted, depleted of energy. They begin to wonder if they are automatons, just going through the motions. It's hard for them to spontaneously play with their children, to appreciate the uniqueness in their youngsters.

This is why a father's development of companionship with his child can have such vast ramifications in the marriage and family relationship. Most women want their husbands to be close to the baby. Your wife knows intuitively that this is good for the baby, and the pleasure she sees you experiencing makes her happy and increases her tenderness toward you. But beyond that, your relationship with the baby is also a kind of life raft for your wife. Now she knows that the person at her side is capable and can take over in a pinch, and that you even enjoy doing so. This does a great deal to erase her feelings of being trapped by the increasing demands of child care, and eases her sense of stress and frustration.

Your ability to relieve your wife is a real act of nurturing. For that matter, each of you needs relief at times when you are feeling overwhelmed by the stresses of child care. The lack of relief in the face of constant stress can have serious adverse consequences for a family.

A System for Relief

The husband and wife need to be able to acknowledge to themselves, and to one another, that they are not perfect, and that at times each one of them needs relief. I call this relief *spelling*, or giving your partner time off, away from the baby.

Spelling Guidelines

Because parents can have their feelings hurt and misunderstandings often arise, it is helpful to draw up some basic guidelines for spelling beforehand such as the following:

1. Discuss the basic idea of spelling in advance; it is important that each parent be able to admit that he or she is not perfect and may need relief at some point.

2. Spelling should always be nonjudgmental (i.e., without put-downs or critical comments). It should be smooth and matter-of-fact; this is not the time to go into why the caretaking parent is having difficulty.

3. Try to develop a signaling system in advance (i.e., a nonverbal cue, such as a raised pinkie finger).

4. Spelling should always be supportive and encouraging. It should never flaunt success where the other parent is experiencing failure. The tables could easily be turned next time around; in a competitive atmosphere, one parent begins to hope that the other parent will fail so that he can succeed. This is not a healthy situation. Spelling in such a situation is seen as an attack.

Spelling and Anger

The more time you spend with your baby, the more perceptive you will become of when your wife needs relief. You will become increasingly aware of those situations that were most difficult for you, when you hoped and prayed your wife would come to get you off the hook with a shrieking and unresponsive child.

One evening I was at home caring for six-month-old Jonathan while Claudia attended class. Jonathan had been peacefully napping. He woke up about six o'clock in the evening and began to cry fiercely and loudly. Usually when this happened I was able to soothe him, but on this day when I offered him a bottle, he behaved as if it were the ultimate insult and threw it down. I tried to cuddle him, to talk to him. "Come on, Jonathan, poor baby, what's wrong?" I placed him on my shoulder as I tried to reassure him. It was at that moment that I felt a shock of pain go through my body. Jonathan had bitten me!

I was stunned! I abruptly put him down on the bed, saying angrily and sharply, "Jonathan, don't you do that!" I felt a sudden impulse to strike out and at the same time experienced a fear of my own impulse. This was followed instantly by a sensation of intense guilt—guilt over my own anger, guilt over my fear of loss of control. I felt angry at myself and I also felt humiliated. Parents aren't supposed to get enraged at their babies. At that moment, I was not able to distinguish *feeling* out of control and *being* out of control. If only Jonathan would forgive me, I thought. And the only way I could get him to demonstrate that he forgave me was for him to stop crying.

I used one of my "secret weapons"—the football position—where I held him with his legs straddling my forearm and walked with him through the house. Every time I stopped walking he resumed crying, spurring me on to greater effort. It was like a marathon course, carrying him into the kitchen, then the dining room, into the living room, through the hallway and into our bedroom, and across into his bedroom and back through the hallway to start the course again and again and again. Every time I stopped, he would resume his sobbing and my guilt would drive me on further. In this frenzied fashion I carried him for two and a half hours.

I felt a knot in my stomach, a tight band across my head, my shirt was wet with perspiration, and I felt like I was on the verge of tears. "Please come home, Claudia, get me off the hook," I prayed.

When Claudia came home, I felt overjoyed and relieved but didn't show it. "What in the world are you doing?" she asked. "Oh, Jonathan is kind of tense and irritable, and every time I stop he wakes up," I said. I was still feeling ashamed of myself and couldn't admit what had happened.

Up until that time I had merely been fascinated with Jonathan's attractive attributes and had not stopped to think about much else. It was only later, as I described my ordeal at a conference about children, that many of the participants urged me to have the courage to share the experience. They pointed out that dealing with anger was the other side of parenting, and that acknowledging only the joyful aspects of the child neglected the real struggles, the frustration, and the anger that so many parents feel.

I have since come to realize that anger and the fear of losing control is a universal struggle among all parents. As we come to accept that we are not perfect and can experience anger and yet still love our children, I think we become more human, more caring parents.

An Aside to Mothers: Helping Your Husband Hook Up

Many a new father will not make the effort to get involved with his baby until he is invited by you, his wife. It's not that he is uninterested, but rather that he sees this as your domain.

It's absolutely essential that you provide "space" if you're going to help your husband become engrossed and develop a companionship with your child. You are the catalyst, that special ingredient that can encourage your husband to experience his feelings for the baby and thus to become engrossed.

You can create a space by simply *stepping back,* by offering the child to your husband and letting him know how much you enjoy his contact with the baby. You create that space by getting out of the house, by leaving your husband alone with the baby, and by not immediately rescuing him every time the baby cries.

You can also draw your husband in by praising his efforts. Comment on how effective he is at soothing the baby's cries. And when he gets discouraged, say something supportive like "She'll settle down; she did that with me too. You're doing fine." Let him know how important it is that he spend time with the baby, how proud it makes you feel that he's increasingly developing a relationship with "our" child. You can reinforce him when you see the baby responding to him or smiling at him or mimicking him. My wife used to say things to me like "Look at how he loves his daddy." And "Oh, look how he loves to walk with you, Marty," as Jonathan would reach out his hands in anticipation of going for a walk with me. These words of support were very important for me in my efforts to establish a relationship with both of my children.

Guidelines

Here are some summary guidelines that may help you draw your husband in to hook up with his child:

1. Be patient and understanding.

2. Compliment and encourage.

3. Attempt to point out those obvious positive aspects of the bond between your husband and the baby.

4. Attempt to make him aware of exciting changes as the baby grows and develops—how the baby smiles or coos, laughs, and giggles; how he sits or crawls, stands or walks. And point out how he mimics his father or appears to respond to him.

5. Describe the unique ways in which the child looks like him.

6. Indicate how good you feel about him in his involvement with the baby.

7. Reinforce him with enthusiastic approval when he plays with the baby, holds him, smiles at him, and cuddles him.

8. Encourage him to talk and sing to the baby and even dance with him.

9. Invite him to participate in the baby's visits to the doctor with you.

10. Encourage him to take walks with the baby.

11. Emphasize how important his care of the baby is to you, how it gives you not only relief but also great pleasure to see him enjoying the baby.

12. Use supportive comments. When your husband feels discouraged, say something supportive like "He was cranky with me this morning too. Don't worry, you're doing fine."

13. And most importantly, try to keep your sense of humor and ability to laugh at yourself. Remember, this is a unique and exciting period. The time passes very quickly, so enjoy yourself. And you'll become more accepting of your husband in the process.

The Marriage Relationship

Breathing Time

Husband and wife need to pay attention to one another and to their marital relationship. The baby is so fascinating that he sweeps everybody into his focus; he draws you both in as if he were a magnet. He can disrupt your lovemaking, your intimate patterns. His cries can seem like bombs exploding overhead and make you feel you want to escape and hide.

Before your baby was born, you and your wife could pretty much come and go as you chose. You had unlimited time together; you could spontaneously go out to dinner or even go on vacation on the spur of the moment. Now suddenly this is changed. *Breathing time* is the answer to your new feeling of claustrophobia. You need time for one another, time to share your feelings, your thoughts and aspirations, to laugh, to talk, to cuddle and hug. You need intimate time together, time away from the baby and time to take care of your own individual needs.

If there is a loving grandparent nearby, then you can be assured that the baby is with someone who really cares about him. But even if this is not the case, perhaps you can leave your baby with a friend or neighbor or an older nurturing woman whom you both trust.

Sanctuary at Home

Even if one or both of you don't feel good about leaving the baby yet, you can still set up a special time together, a kind of sanctuary within your home. To make sure your sanctuary is protected against intruding influences, it helps to:

- Put distracting things aside (including newspapers, magazines, mail, and bills).

- Take the phone off the hook or unplug it or put on the answering machine (if you weren't home, you couldn't answer the phone, so pretend you're not home).

- Let your friends, family, or neighbors know when you are not available. You don't have to apologize for your need for privacy.

- Try to set up a special time each day when the two of you are together. If you're able to do this for one or two hours a day, this will be a remarkable potion for your marriage.

Importance of Other New Parents

Having an opportunity to be with other new parents is also helpful. You have a chance to share your struggles with one another and commiserate about some of the difficulties you've experienced. You can laugh together about events that at the time seemed frightening, almost overwhelming, but in retrospect seem amusing. This sharing together will give you a sensation of renewed energy and revitalization.

Finding a Sense of Meaning

Humor

Your sense of humor is particularly important in helping you survive the early days of parenting. It adds a sense of vitality to your marriage as well. Once you learn to laugh at yourself, you'll also be learning to laugh with one another. Taking yourself too seriously can be deadly. Sometimes you just have to laugh, and laughter is like a healing salve.

I have often seen the way in which laughter can heal. I remember an incident that occurred when our son was about eight months old. We had been traveling all morning, about four and a half hours. I was exhausted. We were driving in our Volkswagen bug, which was fully laden with cargo—diapers, car seat, portable tables, and suitcases. As we pulled off the road for a brief moment, my wife said to me, "Can you change Jonathan?" I replied, "Is it pee-pee or poo-poo?" It was not that I refused to change the diaper depending on the contents, but I always liked to know what I was getting into. "Pee-pee," my wife replied without blinking. Without further ado, I opened Jonathan's diaper on my lap, only to notice a small round brownish object zooming out from the diaper and rolling around as if it were a ball on a roulette wheel. I followed it as if hypnotized. It finally rolled to a stop, lodging itself against my favorite beige sweater. At first I was stunned and said nothing. Then when I caught my breath, I looked at my wife and shouted, "Claudia, you told me there were no poo-poos!" My wife, attempting to stifle her response, had her fist in her mouth. I became increasingly angry as I heard nothing but a muffled noise or two coming from her. "Claudia," I yelled. "You told me there were no poo-poos!" My wife was no longer successful in stifling the flow of laughter that was seeping around her fist. The more she laughed, the angrier I became. Finally, glaring in rage and frustration, I started the car and headed down the road. "Dammit," I shouted. "It's not funny. That's my favorite sweater." (I think I was probably more upset about the idea of this earthy deposit being on me than about my sweater.) "You did it on purpose!" I screamed.

"No, I didn't," Claudia protested, now laughing more than ever.

During the next thirty minutes I uttered not a sound, alternately glaring at my wife and then the road until the complete ludicrousness of the situation finally hit me. Suddenly I began laughing so uncontrollably that I had to pull off the road.

"Hon, you looked so funny with that poo-poo in your lap," Claudia said, and this caused me to laugh even more.

Jonathan, sensing something amusing going on, added his own laughs to the shared mirth. Although he didn't know why we were laughing, there was something in it that related to him that made him feel good. We all hugged as a family and I felt an intense closeness that enveloped all three of us.

The opportunity to laugh at our struggles gives us a sense of meaning, even as it helps us to go beyond the frustration and pain. It's not that it gives us *the answer*, but it allows us to cope, to pass beyond. What you might have viewed as a failure in your efforts, you can see simply as a sharing of your humanness. It's as if having tripped and fallen, splat! . . . you suddenly see the world from a new vantage point and can now view the joy, spontaneity, and humor of it all.

Storytelling

It's wonderful to be able to share the stories of your child's birth with him. We started telling Jonathan the story of his birth when he was about two years old. I remember watching my wife and son together in fascination and amazement as she would say to him, "You grew and grew and grew inside Mommy's tummy, and then you were born!"

Later I talked to him about how "I used to carry you in the baby carrier first against my tummy and then on my back as we walked together in the forest. I would talk to you about the sky and the trees and the woods and the birds and you used to love to take a walk with Daddy. You would reach out your hands, all excited, and I would pick you up and take you for a walk."

I still have many vivid memories of my own father, and I share these stories with my children. A particular memory stands out. I was seven years old and living in Long Beach, California. My father was teaching me how to ride a bicycle. He was pushing my bicycle down the alleyway, huffing and puffing as he raced along beside me while I struggled to keep the bicycle upright. There came a point when it seemed that his presence and my union with the bicycle had become one. I assumed that my father was still pushing me when I heard his voice from about fifty yards back. "You're riding, Marty!" he shouted. "You did it."

"But I'm afraid!" I shouted back.

"You can do it," he cried back. "You don't need me anymore. You can do it on your own." And his voice trailed off as I left him far behind.

This memory captures a theme that is important in our lives and our children's lives. We run alongside our children, trying to keep them upright, helping them get on the bicycle, on the cycle of life. We continue to race alongside them until finally we are forced to let go as our children become older and stronger—and are setting out on their lives on their own life cycle, leaving us behind.

We experience sadness and loss in being left behind; but what is not left behind are the stories of our children's lives. These stories now make it easier for us to let go, and they give us something in the present to hold on to. They fill us with happy images. These memories are our connection to the past and they allow us to reach out to the future. They give our lives and those of our children a sense of meaning and vitality. Now we have stories of our children's present and future to look forward to, stories that we will pass on to our children and grandchildren and stories that they will pass on and share with their children and their children's children, and so on, as we, through our stories, add to the everlasting pattern of the life "cycle," the circle of life. These stories fill us with tears and laughter and make us realize how rewarding it has been to fall in love with our children, to be born as parents, as fathers, and in a sense as human beings.

By the Author

The Birth of a Father. New York: Continuum, 1985.

References

Greenberg, Martin. "The Birth of Fathers." Special issue on *Fathering in Nurturing News,* Vol. VIII, No. 2, June 1986.

Greenberg and Morris. "Engrossment: The Newborn's Impact upon the Father." *American Journal of Orthopsychiatry,* 44 No. 4, 520–531, 1974.

Lamb, M. *The Role of the Father in Child Development.* New York: Wiley, 1976.

RICHARD FERBER

Meet the Author

Dr. Richard Ferber is generally accepted as the nation's leading authority in the field of children's sleep and sleep disorders. He is Director of the Center for Pediatric Sleep Disorders at Children's Hospital in Boston. This center, which he cofounded in 1979, is the first of its kind anywhere in the world. There Dr. Ferber has personally worked with over 800 families, studying the origins of childhood sleep disturbances and developing new approaches to therapeutic intervention.

Dr. Ferber graduated magna cum laude from Harvard University. He received a Doctor of Medicine degree from Harvard Medical School and is currently a member of their faculty. During his pediatric training at Children's Hospital in Boston, he studied under pediatrician and child development expert Dr. T. Berry Brazelton. Dr. Ferber was awarded a two-year fellowship at the National Institutes of Health in a laboratory partially devoted to the Study of Child Development in Primitive Cultures. There he worked under the guidance of Nobel laureate D. Carleton Gajdusek.

Following his residency, Dr. Ferber spent several years working with the noted developmental psychiatrist and psychobiologist Peter Wolff. For one year he was the resident pediatrician in the Psychosomatic Unit at Children's Hospital, and he received special training in the field of sleep disorders at the Sleep-Wake Disorders Unit at the Montefiore Hospital in New York. There he trained under the neurologist Eliot Weitzman, a pioneer in the field of sleep disorders medicine and chronobiology.

Dr. Ferber also directs the Sleep Laboratory at Children's Hospital. He is certified as a Clinical Polysomnographer, is Board Certified in Pediatrics, and is a member of both the Nosology and Examination Committees of the Association of Professional Sleep Societies.

In the field of pediatric sleep disorders Dr. Ferber has lectured widely and has authored many articles and chapters both for lay and professional audiences. His book Solve Your Child's Sleep Problems *has been acclaimed as the most useful treatise of its kind.*

Dr. Ferber is married and has two sons.

3

THE CHILD WHO DOESN'T SLEEP

RESOLVING COMMON SLEEP PROBLEMS
RICHARD FERBER, M.D.

Your eight-month-old son wakes up two or three times each night and won't go back to sleep without a bottle or a hug from you. Your two-year-old daughter has gotten into the habit of staying up until eleven or twelve o'clock and she never seems sleepy—but *you* are! Your one-year-old screams in her crib every time you leave the room at bedtime. Your nights are no longer your own. The amount of sleep you get, the likelihood of your sleeping through the night, even your privacy are being controlled by a young child!

Having a youngster who has trouble sleeping can have a serious effect on the way you live day to day, and on the way you feel about yourself. You may start to question your ability as a parent. Is your child waking because you are doing something wrong? Should you be feeding him more? Should he be on solids? Are you not meeting his emotional needs? Is he suffering from separation anxiety? Is something seriously wrong with him?

Your child's sleep problems can also be a source of continual disagreement between you and your spouse. You wonder which of your approaches to child raising and putting the baby to bed is better. Is one of you too easy ("spoiling him") and one of you too tough ("causing emotional trauma")? Which parent should get up with him? Arguments abound as you and your spouse grow more and more tired, short-tempered, and overwhelmed. You may decide not to have that second child you wanted—taking care of *this* one is more than you bargained for. And for all this, you blame your child.

Rationally, you may decide that your child's sleep difficulties are not his fault—it's probably just a stage. Besides, a good parent should be willing to get up with a child if he can't sleep through the night. And yet, no matter how you try to convince yourself, you can't help feeling resentment toward your child. It's infuriating not to get a good night's sleep! But even if you don't let your anger show, your ability to have fun with your child, to be

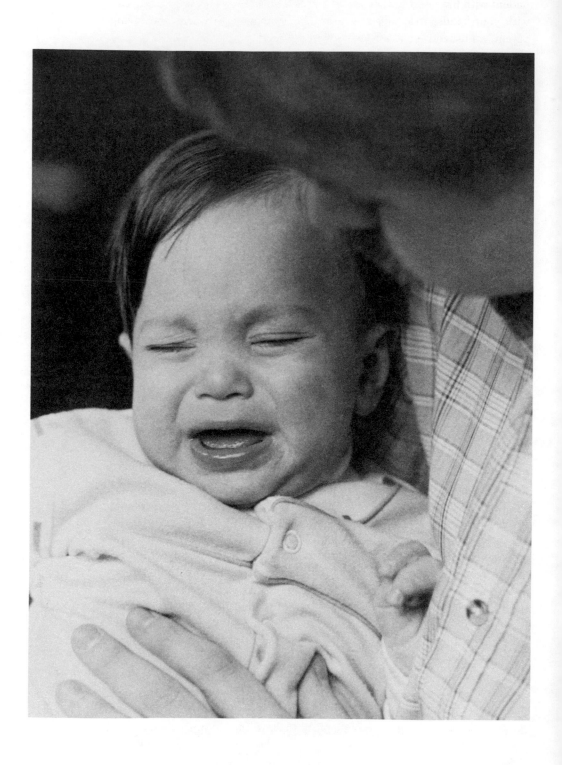

patient with him, and to take joy in him will all suffer—and your relationship with your spouse may suffer as well. You cannot be as warm and loving a parent, a husband, or a wife when you are tired.

As time goes on, getting your child to sleep becomes the focus of your life. You try to go to bed early to get in a few hours of sleep before the wakings begin. You become tense in the evening just thinking of the night ahead. You ask anyone and everyone for advice. At this point you're desperate, willing to try any remedy to help your child fall asleep at a reasonable time and stay sleeping through the night.

Once you're in this state, it's hard to sit back, calmly and rationally, and survey the situation, sort out possible causes of your child's difficulties, and plan a reasonable course of action. But it is not impossible. And with a little help in knowing what to look for, you should be able to do just that.

Adults tend to think that their children's sleep is very different from their own—the way they go to sleep, why they wake up in the middle of the night, and how they get themselves back to sleep after waking. As a result, many causes of sleep difficulties that should be easily identifiable in children are often overlooked.

One reason for this is that it's easy to confuse a child's needs with his habits. Something that has become a habit or custom may take on the appearance of a true need in the physical and psychological sense. And once behavior is viewed as representing a need, adults may feel that changing their response would be wrong and possibly harmful. Who would think of not feeding a two-week-old in the middle of the night just to see if he would sleep better? We all agree that such a young baby, who nurses eagerly after waking at 2:00 A.M., needs a feeding at that time. But what about a child who is two months old or six months old or twelve months old? They all might wake and nurse eagerly. Does this mean that they all have such a "need"? No, probably not by three to four months of age, and certainly not by six months.

Another reason that adults don't identify the causes of children's sleep problems is that their expectations for children's sleep are often arbitrary. For example, parents may decide that a three-year-old should go to sleep at 7:00 P.M. and wake at 8:00 A.M. It may be unreasonable to expect a child to sleep that long, especially when nap times are considered. And there are individual differences to take into account as well. Not all three-year-olds need exactly the same amount of sleep. Remember, some adults require eight hours of sleep, others five. And just as adults may adjust to odd sleeping hours if their work requires it, children, too, may adjust their waking and sleeping hours if parents permit them to. When a child "has his days and nights mixed up," parents may not realize that by continuing to let him sleep during the day, and by playing with and feeding him at night, they are doing little to help him switch to a day/wake, night/sleep schedule.

Without an understanding of the causes of your child's problems, you may unwittingly be creating or intensifying his sleep difficulties. While it is often hard to understand the causes and possible treatment of sleeplessness in young children, they are usually readily apparent when you picture them occurring to an adult. Therefore, I'll describe the three most common causes of sleeplessness in children as if they are happening to you. The hypothetical situations dealing with difficulty going to sleep, staying asleep, or falling back to sleep after normal wakings will help you better understand the most common causes of sleep problems many infants and toddlers face night after night. Once you learn to identify the reasons for your child's sleeplessness, you will be able to help him learn to sleep.

Example 1

After a long, hard day you wearily settle into your comfortable bed and quickly fall asleep. Several hours later you turn over, half awake, and prepare to go back to sleep again. But something is wrong. You are not in your comfortable bed or even in your bedroom. You are lying on the floor in the living room. You are still sleepy, but you cannot go back to sleep there. You want to return to your bedroom, but the door is locked. You become angry and scream for the door to be opened. Only when someone unlocks your door can you return to your room, settle back into your familiar bed, and go to sleep. Two hours later you awaken and again find yourself on the living room floor.

It's Easy to Fall Asleep— If Conditions Are Right

If your child falls asleep easily but wakes up crying repeatedly during the night, you should pay close attention to what actually happens when he falls asleep. In the example above, you fall asleep each night in the same setting, and you wake several times during the night. We all wake at night, although we are not always aware of doing so. These wakings are part of the normal cyclical process of sleep. After each of these wakings, you would go back to sleep quickly—if you were still in the same familiar setting you were in at bedtime. But you are not. Everything is different. You are used to sleeping on your bed in your bedroom, not in the living room on the floor. So you stay awake.

Your child may have many things that he associates with falling asleep, such as being in a swing or car seat, sitting in your lap, being rocked, having his back patted, using a pacifier, or sucking at your breast or on a bottle. He may be used to going to sleep in the living room or your bedroom, perhaps with the lights and television on. You may put him into the crib only after he is asleep. When he wakes up there is a problem. None of the conditions that were present when he fell asleep exist for him anymore. He becomes as frustrated in his crib as you would be if you woke up on the living room floor. He cries, you come in, pick him up, rock him, give him back the pacifier, or do whatever is necessary to return his environment to the one in which he is accustomed to falling asleep. Then he goes back to sleep quickly, and you put him back into his crib. But before the night is over, he may wake one or two more times, and each time he does, you have to repeat the process all over again.

The problem here is not that your child is waking abnormally—he isn't. The problem is that he has difficulty falling back to sleep after waking normally. And the reason he has trouble returning to sleep is not because he has any inherent inability to sleep well. It is because you are putting him to sleep under certain conditions and letting him wake up under others. If you continue to go back in during the night to reestablish the conditions he has come to associate with falling asleep, it may take him a very long time to learn how to go to sleep by himself. And until he learns, the problem may continue.

The solution is to ask yourself under what conditions your child will awaken during the night. Then help him learn to fall asleep in that setting. Once this is accomplished, he will be able to sleep well. He will still wake at night, but when he does, the conditions around him will be right for him to go back to sleep easily. He will not require your help to bring him to a new place, to rock him, to give him something, or to take him for a ride around the block. He will have learned how to fall asleep by *himself.*

Assuming that you don't want to have to get up at night, be certain that the final routines your child uses to fall asleep do not include you. Usually when a child wakes during the night, he will be in his crib alone, in a dark or dimly lit room; without anyone to hold, rock, or nurse him; without a bright light or television on; and without a pacifier in his mouth. Your goal then is simply to help him learn to fall asleep in this setting.

Begin by putting your child down in the crib at bedtime after reading a story, singing a song, or following any other quiet bedtime routine appropriate for his age. Then leave the room and wait long enough for him to fall asleep. This will be his first practice session as he learns how to go to sleep in a way that, for him, is completely new. When he wakes during the night, wait again, this time long enough for him to go back to sleep. This will give him even more practice. Most children have some difficulty the first night, but the second night is usually easier, and by the third or fourth night they have usually mastered the task of falling asleep on their own.

Since your child has become accustomed to having you nearby at bedtime, and to having you come quickly when he wakes at night and cries, simply refusing to respond at all would be confusing and upsetting. You are not trying to punish or frighten your child. His waking is not misbehavior. Take the attitude that his waking is normal, that his difficulty falling back to sleep is based on habit, and thus is understandable. He needs you to teach him new habits. Therefore, it seems most reasonable to go in and reassure him. At the same time, however, give him continually greater opportunity to use the new skills that he is learning.

On the first night it makes sense to go back in after only five minutes of crying (even less if you find that difficult). Reassure him briefly, show him that you are still there, that you love him, and that you are taking care of him. But then leave again, even if he is still crying, or even if his crying increases as you walk back out of the room. The second time you might wait a bit longer before going to him, perhaps ten minutes, and the third and subsequent times, wait even longer than that, perhaps fifteen minutes, before going in. Continue this until he finally quiets and goes to sleep during one of the periods when you are out of the room. If he wakes later in the night, do the same thing: wait five, ten, and then fifteen minutes between brief reassurances.

Each successive night, it's important to handle things in exactly the same way, only increase the waiting times progressively. On the second night you might start by waiting ten minutes and work up to twenty, and on the third night wait fifteen minutes and work up to twenty-five.

Since it is not the crying that helps your child learn to sleep better, it doesn't do any good to let your child cry for a period of time and then rock him back to sleep. As long as he falls asleep the old way, he won't learn the new one. It's difficult to listen to the crying, but understand that it's his way of expressing his frustration as he gives up one well-established habit and learns another. If you had to learn to sleep on the living room floor, you might be quite angry for a number of days or even weeks until you learned to adapt.

Most children start to stretch out their nighttime sleep considerably by three months of age, and all healthy, normal infants have the ability to sleep through the night by six months. Therefore, although the routines described above may work before six months, I would not be in too much of a hurry to try them in a younger infant unless the sleep disturbance is quite marked. While it is especially painful for parents to postpone their response to their crying child when he is very young and helpless, by the time he is six months old, most parents find this task somewhat easier.

If the nighttime wakings are not a severe problem, you may feel less urgency to eliminate them, even at six months. But keep in mind that changing sleep patterns is easier during the second half of the first year than it is at younger or older ages. If your child can climb out of his crib, or if he is already in a bed, matters can be more difficult. First of all, he's stronger, can cry longer at night, and is more resourceful. You need to be able to "set limits" and keep your child in his room if you want to teach him better sleep habits. This can be enforced with a gate for some youngsters; other children need to have their doors closed for progressively longer periods of time until they agree to stay put. If the door must be closed, doing so without frightening your child is vital. Therefore, start by closing it only for a very short period, such as a minute, and stay right on the other side to be as reassuring as possible. With determination, most problems can be resolved within three or four nights.

Example 2

Because of an intestinal disorder, your doctor has recommended that you get up twice each night for a glass of milk and a small snack. This has become quite routine. But now she says that the disorder is cured and asks you to begin skipping the nighttime snacks altogether. This sounds great—at first. But you can't sleep through the night. Instead, you wake up at the same time that you used to. And not only do you still wake, but you wake up hungry. Going back to sleep without a snack now seems impossible.

More Wakings and the Need to Nurse

If your child wakes frequently at night, it is likely that he is being fed at these times, whether he is nursed at the breast, given a bottle in your arms, or handed a bottle in the crib. Very few other conditions can cause such severely and chronically disrupted sleep.

Most likely several factors underlie the sleep disruption in this situation. First of all, as discussed above, your child may fall asleep in your arms while nursing but always wake alone in his crib. Therefore, he would find it difficult to fall back to sleep without nursing, even after normal wakings.

Second, your child may have "learned" to be hungry at night. As in the example above, if you are used to eating at night, you will regularly get hungry at night, whether your body actually needs the food or not. That was obvious in the adult, but it is not as obvious when the same problem occurs in a child. These periods of "unnecessary hunger" at night are an outgrowth of periods of "necessary hunger" that are present in the smaller infant. Young babies certainly have to be fed at night as well as during the day. But generally by three or four months, and certainly by six months, this nutritional need is no longer present, at least not in otherwise healthy youngsters. If your child has grown accustomed to having a significant amount of his daily calories at night, he can easily learn to transfer this caloric intake into the daytime. It is not difficult for your child to change the times at which he becomes hungry, but again it is up to you. As long as you feed him during the night, he may well continue to get hungry then. If you change his routines in favor of daytime feedings only, he will soon change his hunger patterns accordingly, and his nutritional needs will still be met.

The third problem is a bit more complicated. It has to do with internal daily cycles or rhythms. All aspects of body function are under this type of control. That is why we don't sleep randomly throughout the day but concentrate our sleep into the nighttime hours, why we can't sleep for eight hours when we take a daytime nap, and why we get hungry at our regular mealtimes. It's also why our body temperature rises and falls, why our hormone levels show regular fluctuations, and why our intestinal function changes in predictable ways throughout the day.

In a newborn, the hours of sleeping, waking, and eating are much more random. But as the child grows, these rhythms begin to mature and should be fairly stable by three months. As he matures, the longest period of sleep begins to occur at night, and the periods of hunger become more predictable.

Most infants eventually settle into a pattern typical of all older individuals. Nighttime is not only associated with sleep, but the gut is at rest, the stomach is not contracting, and there are no feelings of hunger. However, if you continue to feed your child at night, you stimulate his intestinal and endocrine systems, disrupting his sleep pattern. That keeps him on a routine more like that of a younger infant, breaking the nighttime sleep into multiple short periods and distributing the feedings around the clock. As a result your child doesn't move naturally onto a more mature pattern. He needs your help.

It is important to understand all of this if you are to be able to take the next steps. Your child wakes at night crying and seems hungry. You take him to your breast or give him a bottle, and he takes the milk or juice eagerly, settles down, and then goes back to sleep. Each time you do this, it seems as if you are doing the right thing. It seems so right that it may be hard to see why it is wrong. But what you are doing is reinforcing his broken sleep pattern. In this setting, "hunger" does not imply "need." Your child may feel hungry at night because he is accustomed to being fed then, but nutritionally no such need exists. By continuing the frequent nighttime feedings, this apparent "need" will only continue.

The solution is to help your child learn to expect his feedings during the daytime and not to expect any at night. He is faced with the same task as you were in the example above. As long as you kept up your middle-of-the-night snacks, you would continue your nightly hungry wakings. If you stopped eating at night, you would stop getting hungry then and those wakings would cease. But it would take a while. Fortunately, a child adjusts to new patterns much more quickly than an adult. If you eliminate his nighttime feedings, the wakings usually disappear within a week. If he cries, continue to respond to him, but only after progressively longer periods of time, as already described.

However, if your child has been fed large amounts of fluid (at least 8 oz.) during the night, it's reasonable to taper the amount gradually. Mothers who are breast feeding can make a judgment based on the amount of time spent nursing. A child whose soaked diaper must be changed two or three times a night is clearly getting too much liquid.

If your child is drinking large quantities of fluid, gradually eliminate the bottle at bedtime and after nighttime wakings. Begin by putting one ounce less than usual in each bottle and be sure that your child is never given a bottle more frequently than every two hours. Every night or two you can reduce the amount in the bottle by another ounce and increase the minimum time between bottles by half an hour. This way the nighttime feeding can be eliminated over one to two weeks. If you are breast feeding, you may decrease the amount of time at the breast during each nighttime nursing session by one minute each night or two, and increase the minimum times between nursing in the same manner.

If nursing your child to sleep is particularly important to you, continue the nursing at that time and try eliminating only the feedings later in the night. But if problems persist, you may have to forgo the bedtime feeding as well, replacing it perhaps with another feeding earlier in the evening, before he is ready to fall asleep.

You should be aware that there is nothing inherently wrong with rocking or nursing your child to sleep if you can transfer him to the crib easily without his waking and if he sleeps through the night. When what you are doing is not creating problems, there is no urgent need for you to stop. You should keep in mind, however, that as your child gets older, this bedtime ritual may become progressively longer and it may be harder to break. Also, if your child needs to be nursed to sleep, you may have a problem leaving him with a sitter or even with his father.

Example 3

You usually sleep from 11:00 P.M. until 7:00 A.M. But one day you have an early morning obligation that will require you to get up at 4:00 A.M. So, wanting to have a full night's sleep, you go to bed three hours early. But at 8:00 P.M. you do not feel sleepy. You toss and turn, but no matter how hard you try, sleep does not come. In fact, despite all your planning, you still do not fall asleep until nearly 11:00 P.M.

You Can't Fall Asleep
If It's Too Early

The answer to this third example is obvious. You cannot go to bed several hours before your usual bedtime and expect to fall asleep for the night. Your body becomes ready for sleep at a certain hour and ready to wake at another. If you stay on a regular routine, this usually does not pose a problem. But if you try to go to bed several hours earlier than usual, you will have trouble. The same problem would exist if you flew to New York from California. After the trip you might try to go to sleep at 11:00 at night New York time, but it will feel to you like 8:00 P.M., since you are still functioning on California time. The result is that you'll end up watching the late movie.

If every night you put your child to bed at 8:00 P.M., but he won't fall asleep until 10:00 or 11:00 P.M., he is likely to be coping with a similar situation. That is especially true if he also sleeps late in the morning, until 9:00 or 10:00 A.M. You may let him sleep late because he fell asleep late and you want to let him catch up, or perhaps you want to sleep late yourself. In any case, as long as he regularly falls asleep late and wakes up late, his internal clock will continue to operate as if it were two or three time zones to the west. There is nothing you can do to "make" him fall asleep earlier at night, but you can wake him up earlier in the morning. Eventually this will make it possible for him to fall asleep earlier at night as well.

Most people know that it is easier to adjust after going from New York to Los Angeles than the reverse. The reason is that it is easier to stay up later and sleep later than to fall asleep earlier and get up earlier. This is because our internal biological clock actually tends to run on more of a twenty-five-hour cycle than a twenty-four-hour one. Given the opportunity, it will let your hours of sleep shift in the late direction. And it is given this opportunity when regular morning wakings are not enforced. Some people shift their sleep patterns every weekend and during vacations. That is, they start going to bed later and waking later, and then they find they have difficulty going back to their old routines at the start of the week or the end of vacation.

The problem is called "Late Sleep Phase." It is a very simple concept. Your child is not ready to fall asleep until an hour that is later than you desire, and he is not ready to wake until relatively late in the morning.

The solution is easy. Pay attention to how much nighttime sleep your child needs. Decide what time you want him to fall asleep at night and then figure out what time the morning waking would occur. For example, say your child regularly sleeps for eleven hours, from 11:00 P.M. to 10:00 A.M. You want him to fall asleep at 8:00 P.M. That would mean his waking up at 7:00 A.M. in order to get eleven hours of sleep. To accomplish this schedule shift, start by setting a late bedtime. Set it at the time your child usually falls asleep. Since he doesn't fall asleep before then anyway, nothing is lost, and by allowing a late bedtime, he can become accustomed to going to bed without a struggle. Then wake him thirty minutes earlier than usual. Every day or two after that, move the bedtime and time of waking up fifteen minutes until you reach the calculated time of morning waking. Continue advancing the bedtime until it reaches the desired time and the problem is solved. During this period, don't allow any napping beyond the usual. And be sure to enforce the morning waking every day, even on weekends, at least until the sleep pattern seems stable.

If your child already gets up early five days a week for day care, for nursery school, or to go to a sitter's home, you may decide that a late sleep phase may not be his problem. But even if he only sleeps late on the weekends, that can be sufficient to keep his sleep phase shifted late. In fact, even if he gets up early on the weekends but goes back to sleep for an extra morning nap (which is unusual much beyond the age of one), or watches several hours of cartoons curled up on the sofa in a half-asleep state, you may be seeing the same effect.

It is also important to understand what may be happening during the period from the bedtime you set to the time your child is ready to fall asleep. If you try to put him to bed at 8:00 P.M. and he is not ready to fall asleep until 11:00, you may have three hours of problems. This is especially true if he is out of a crib. There may be repeated "curtain calls" as he asks for extra stories, drinks of water, trips to the toilet, or to have his light turned on. There may even be complaints of extensive fears. Any child who is asked to lie in bed quietly for several hours in a dark room is unlikely to be able to do so comfortably and calmly. His mind will be wide awake and active. He will begin to think and fantasize, and eventually he may start scaring himself. In fact, the same thing can happen to adults, but they will usually get up, turn on the lights, and watch television or read. Adults have ways to provide their own distractions. Young children usually don't have the same opportunities. (Specific ideas on how to understand and help children cope with their fears will be covered in the next section.)

Although a late sleep phase is certainly not the cause of all, or even most, children's nighttime fears, it should be considered as a possibility. When your child expresses fears and has trouble falling asleep at the usual bedtime, but not after a late bedtime or during the middle of the night, it is important to take a careful look at his sleep schedule.

The examples just discussed describe three of the most common causes of sleep difficulties in young children.

1. The conditions a child associates with falling asleep at bedtime are not present after normal, spontaneous wakings during the night. A child may have difficulty falling back to sleep after these wakings, at least until the usual bedtime conditions are reestablished.

2. A child who is always fed when he wakes up at night learns to expect these feedings. Now he wakes "hungry" and cannot return to sleep until this "need" is met.

3. Most nights, despite the good intentions of his parents, a child is put to bed before he is ready and able to fall asleep. As a result, he resists bedtime, stalls, and only goes to sleep quickly on those rare occasions when he is allowed to stay up late.

Other Causes and Other Ages

Insomnia and nighttime wakings can affect children of all ages. The first two examples above (regarding bedtime conditions and nighttime feedings) apply mainly to the infant and toddler years, when being rocked or nursed to sleep is still common. A late sleep phase, as described in the third example, is common at all ages, especially in adolescence when weekend schedules may have a bedtime delayed until the early morning hours and a morning wake-up time not until noon.

Anxiety and fears can also cause bedtime problems for toddlers, older children, and adolescents, and they may lead to nightmares with nighttime wakings and difficulty returning to sleep.

Although not a form of insomnia, sleepwalking and sleep terrors disrupt the continuity of sleep and may be perceived by parents as another form of nighttime wakings. They are common in toddlers but may persist, or appear anew in older children or adolescents. Despite a common misconception, they are neither caused by nor reflect bad dreams or nightmares. Sleep terrors and nightmares have different causes and significance and should not be dealt with in the same manner.

Anxiety, Bedtime Fears, and Nightmares

Children easily become worried, concerned, apprehensive, or frightened. This may be a reaction to an inherently upsetting event (such as the death of a family member). Or it may be a response to an event of particular significance because of the child's current developmental stage (seeing a movie in which a child loses control and attacks a parent or sibling). Or it may simply be a direct reflection of current developmental struggles (toilet training, separation).

An upsetting event can happen at any age. Developmental struggles are usually most apparent during the preschool years; nighttime fears and nightmares occur less frequently in school-aged children. Significant problems persisting in older children may imply that developmental hurdles of a younger age have not been successfully negotiated. Adolescence, a time of rapid physical and psychological change, is also a time for the resurgence of anxiety. School, peer, and sexual pressures are just some of the causes.

Children tend to be busy and active during the day. Most of these concerns can be held in check, but at night, when a child says good night to his parents, goes to bed, and has the light turned out, the concerns may become magnified and harder to control. An adult may avoid the silence and the necessity of "listening to" and "dealing with" his own thoughts by reading or watching television until falling asleep. Many adolescents listen to the radio in bed for the same reason. Younger children are not usually allowed these diversions. This is one of the reasons they often stall. But, whereas bedtime fears might seem alleviated by letting such a child fall asleep in front of the television or listen to the recitation of endless stories, these approaches are not helpful in the long run. The cause of the fear would still be present and would likely show up in other ways. Furthermore, with a late bedtime, the children might end up with too little sleep. And they may still wake at night and be unable to handle the dark, the quiet, and the task of going back to sleep by themselves any better than at bedtime.

By adolescence many nighttime anxieties directly reflect the concerns themselves ("Did I study enough?" "Will she go out with me?"). At younger ages children are unable to think about these matters so directly (a four-year-old would be unlikely to ponder: "Do I have enough control to keep from hurting my new baby sister?"). Instead, they feel the anxiety but have to search around for an explanation. What they come up with are monsters, shadows, robbers, and the dark. So, when your child says he is afraid of monsters, it is your job to try to figure out just what it is he is really afraid of. Searching the room with him to "prove" that there are no monsters about will not be all that helpful, since the "monsters" causing the fear are inside of him.

To deal with these concerns successfully, most children need parents who are nurturing, protective, firm, and controlled. Your child needs to see that you will protect him from internal impulses as well as external threats. So, this is not the time for long searches, conversations, diversions, or fights. Firm, consistent reassurance and setting of limits without losing your temper are the best approaches. Let your child know you are nearby.

In the long run, the daytime is when you set about working on longer-range solutions. This is when most of the conversations should take place.

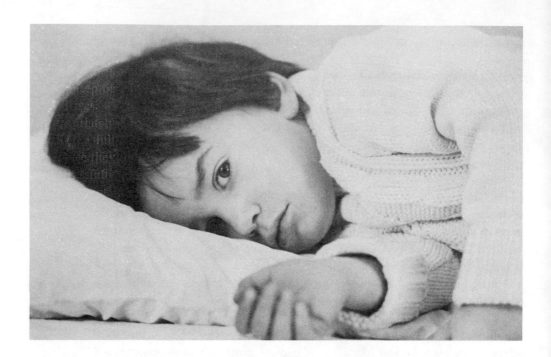

You may help your child learn just what it is that frightens him; that angry feelings toward a sibling are normal, as are pleasurable feelings from masturbation; that identity struggles are part of adolescence, and that you had similar struggles when you were his age.

Some nighttime "fears" should be handled differently. Not all youngsters who say they are "afraid of monsters" are afraid at all. They may have run the gamut of stalling tactics ("I want a glass of water," "I have to go to the bathroom," "One more story") and have discovered that the "monster" one works best. You should be able to distinguish a child who is really frightened from one who is "testing limits." The latter simply does not look frightened. He may walk calmly down the hall to your room and in a very controlled voice tell you about the "robber outside his window." The less you are able to set limits firmly for such a youngster, the less he will see you as powerful and protective, and the more likely he is to develop real fears. By letting him come into your bed against your wishes and perhaps even kicking one of you out, you are likely to exaggerate these fears even further. It is much more helpful to insist that he remain in his room.

Some youngsters are genuinely afraid, but only because they have too much time to lie awake in bed at night. These are the children who are put to bed too early, or who have a late sleep phase. Lying awake for several hours in the dark allows too much time for fantasy. Correcting the bedtime, and the sleep phase if necessary, will quickly solve this "fear."

Finally there are some youngsters whose fear is unbridled. They become truly terrified each night. Their fear may begin and increase as bedtime approaches, and they may beg you not to send them to bed. Their crying takes on a different quality from that of children testing limits. Their appearance is different, too. They are in a panic. Strictly enforcing limits on such children may only make them more hysterical. The causes of these fears (internal or external) are usually the same as discussed above, but for some reason they have gotten out of hand, have never been satisfactorily resolved, or represent a major new stress.

Frequently such panic occurs transiently after a scary movie or event but with parental support usually resolves itself within a few weeks. Over this time it may even be reasonable and necessary for you to sleep in your child's room, or for him to sleep in a sleeping bag in yours. When such major fears persist, however, they should be dealt with differently. They should not be ignored even though the cause is not always clear. Understanding is required, for anger only makes matters worse. Professional help at this point may be needed. As progress is made, you should be able to move back into your own room or your child should move back into his.

If your child has become so frightened of his room that he will not spend any time there alone even in the daytime, spend time with him there. Gradually he may be willing to spend longer and longer times there alone as he feels progressively competent. If he is not comfortable in his room in the daytime, he is unlikely to be at night.

Nightmares represent nighttime fears as well, but these arise during a dream rather than during wakefulness. Nightmares are anxiety-laden, frightening dreams that occur during REM (Rapid Eye Movement) sleep (the sleep stage in which most dreaming takes place). Although some nightmares occur in association with high fever or as a side effect of certain medications, most are psychological in origin and reflect the same type of anxieties that cause fearfulness at bedtime. In the young child, both bedtime and dream-associated fears may appear symbolically, for instance, as monsters. But actually the younger the child, the more likely it is for scary dreams simply to recreate recent scary events. On the other hand, the older the child, who in waking has increasing ability to think about his concerns directly, the more complex and symbolic the dreams may be. Thus, if you can get your two- or three-year-old to describe his dream, you will probably understand the reason for the fear. That is not necessarily true for the adolescent.

On the other hand, on waking, the adolescent will immediately recognize that he just had a nightmare. Usually that is sufficient, and after a while he will be able to go back to sleep. Only occasionally will he need to wake you for reassurance. The young toddler, however, still has difficulty distinguishing dreams from reality. He is just as frightened on waking as he would be if the events in the dream had actually happened. You cannot relieve this fear simply by telling him that "it was only a dream." Here is one time your child really needs your presence at night. You should hold him and be in no hurry to leave. It might be best for him to spend the rest of the night with you. The preschool and school-aged child falls somewhere in between the toddler and the adolescent. He can recognize a dream for what it was, but the attendant fear seems so real that he may still be awake for some time and need your full support.

Thus, it is not a time to be extra firm or angry when your child wakes frightened from a nightmare. It is a time to be lenient and loving, to say "I'm here as long as you need me."

Nightmares occur in everyone, but most frequently in the younger age groups. Even at that age they should happen only occasionally. Frequent nightmares persisting more than several weeks should be cause for concern. Again, efforts at understanding and dealing with the source of these fears should be made in the daytime and may require professional help. But you should be sure that what your child is seeing really are nightmares, true scary dreams. Nightmares tend to occur when REM sleep is the most plentiful and most intense, and this is near morning, not within the first few hours of the night. While your child is having a nightmare, you will be unaware that anything unusual is happening. During REM, a person is mostly paralyzed except for eye and breathing movements. A child having a nightmare looks little different from a child having a happy dream. It is only when the child wakes from the dream and calls out that you will know anything happened.

At that point your child will be completely awake. He will be frightened and will want to be held tightly. He welcomes your presence and is comforted by it. Although very young children may remain somewhat confused for a while, not being clear that a dream has ended and that the imaginary threats are no longer present, children will generally be rational. If the child is old enough, he should be able to describe the scary dream to you. And because the memory of the dream is still so intense, the child may be very reluctant to go back to sleep (and risk another dream). Understanding this is very important because parents often confuse sleep terrors with nightmares.

Partial Wakings: Sleepwalking, Confused Thrashing, and Sleep Terrors

Early in the night there is another type of event that may interrupt sleep, but instead of occurring in REM sleep, it occurs during a partial waking from the deepest phase of nondreaming non-REM sleep (stage IV; delta sleep).

And instead of becoming aware of this event in your child after it terminates (as is the case when your child wakes *after* having a nightmare), you are aware *during* the event itself. In fact, after full waking is reached, your child appears perfectly calm and sleepy. Instead of being too frightened to go back to sleep, he will have difficulty keeping awake. And instead of describing a dream, he usually remembers little or nothing at all of the event.

Your child cycles through various sleep stages during the night. During the first two to three hours of the night he is mainly in deep stage IV. He is not dreaming and it is very hard to wake him. If he falls asleep in the car on the way home, you may be able to bring him into the house, change him into his pajamas, and put him to bed without his fully waking. After sixty to ninety minutes in this stage, he will have a partial waking. He'll move about, turn over, perhaps open and close his eyes, and possibly mumble before descending back into another deep sleep cycle. Sixty to ninety minutes later the same thing will happen again, except he will go into a REM period and have his first (very bland) dream of the night. Most of the rest of the night is spent cycling between REM and light non-REM.

The events discussed here most often occur during the partial waking after the first or second period in stage IV. But instead of a brief episode with minimal nonspecific body movements, the transition between sleep stages may become extended in time and be associated with more intense behaviors. There is actually a spectrum of possibilities. Your child may simply talk (sleep talking), he may sit up briefly and stare blankly, or he may get out of bed and begin walking about (sleepwalking; somnambulism). Or he may thrash about bizarrely while crying. There may even be a "blood-curdling" scream, and he may get up and run wildly.

Sleepwalking in young children is usually calm. They walk to whatever room the parents are in (or where lights or television are on) and may stand there staring. Calm sleepwalkers will usually let themselves be led back to bed, possibly with a stop in the bathroom. If you talk to them, they may reply, but in single words, usually "yes" or "no." Occasionally they may urinate inappropriately during one of these jaunts, in the closet, corner, or hall. Older children may walk about in a more agitated fashion, appearing somewhat anxious but not really terrified. Still, they pull away if someone tries to hold or direct them, and the agitation may intensify. Eventually they, too, will calm down enough to be led back to bed, or they will wake fully and go back to sleep on their own.

A sleepwalker does not usually injure himself, but it is possible. He is less observant than usual, and a skate left on the stairway, for example, would be a major hazard. Occasionally a child will walk outdoors, where risk of injury is great.

More intense arousals are also common. Episodes of partial waking with confused thrashing occur frequently in toddlers and preschoolers. These usually start with a period of moaning or whining progressing over a number of seconds or even minutes to a mixture of crying, calling, and screaming. A child in the midst of such an arousal may begin to thrash about, rolling all over his bed, even banging into the walls. These events typically last five to fifteen minutes, but may be shorter or last as long as thirty to forty-five minutes. The child may seem "unreachable" during these spells. His eyes are open but they seem to "look right through you." Parents often say that during such episodes their children seem "possessed" because of the strange sounds they make, their strange behavior, their seeming lack of awareness of the world about them despite the fact that their eyes are open, and their apparent lack of recognition of even their parents despite the fact that they may be calling them. Generally the child looks more confused than frightened, but the appearance of fear may be present as well. Unlike what happens *after* a nightmare, the child *during* such an episode does not want to be held.

If you try to hold and comfort him (which is only natural), your child will only arch, twist, and push you away. Frustrating though it may be, there is little you can do to make matters better during such a partial arousal, but there is much you can do to make it worse. The more you try to hold, comfort, or restrain your child, or the more you try to wake him fully (shake him, put cold water on his face), the worse you can make things. Your child does not recognize you at this time and he derives no comfort from you. He is not fully awake but is caught somewhere between waking and sleep. It is as if deep sleep is trying to continue but another system is saying "It is time to wake to start the next sleep cycle." A "battle" between the sleep and arousal systems is taking place and you are witnessing the disturbing result.

During a confused thrashing period, your child may look as if he is suffering, but there is no evidence to suggest that is the case. During the "battle," the nervous system fires the part that would be active if he were frightened. Hence, your child appears upset. But few if any frightening thoughts seem to accompany this. Thus, no matter how intense the thrashing, and no matter how long the event takes, when it ends, your child is not at all frightened, he has no memory of a dream, and he only wants to go back to sleep. You should let him. You can wake him completely at that point if you want to, but then he may see you worried, hear you asking him what he was dreaming about, and become so alert or upset that he may have difficulty going back to sleep. Little is gained by discussing the event with him then or in the morning, for it only tells him that he is doing something about which he was unaware and which was outside his control. This can generate anxiety and may make matters worse.

A true sleep terror may also occur, but a sleep terror in the fullest sense seems more common in older children and adolescents. A child experiencing a sleep terror will sit up and suddenly scream in a terrifying manner. His eyes will be bulging, his heart racing, he will be sweating, and he will look terrified. Occasionally he will jump out of bed and run wildly, as if he's trying to get away from something. Screaming may go on for some time but will usually end after one to several minutes. The older child or adolescent may then wake fully and feel the physiological components of fright, such as a pounding, racing heart. To explain that feeling he may generate an "image" but one that is very vague and simple. "It was after me" would be a typical utterance, but the child cannot describe this in any more detail. It is very different from a dream, and it is not a nightmare. Even if a child describes such a "memory," he does not seem all that upset and he has no difficulty going back to sleep.

Thus, in a nightmare there are very scary thoughts but few physical changes to go along with them. In a sleep terror there are few or no scary thoughts, but the physical changes are marked.

When partial wakings occur in a young child, before age six or seven, they are usually considered to be of developmental origin. They reflect how very deep a child's sleep normally is early in the night in that age group. In fact, anything that increases the drive into deep sleep may make these partial wakings occur more frequently and intensely. Parents often note that they are more common when their child is overtired, perhaps after a late bedtime or a missed nap. Therefore, cutting out a nap is not helpful. Also, since the timing of sleep cycles and intervening arousals is so related to these symptoms, it is not surprising to find that young children on chaotic schedules may be particularly susceptible.

Therefore, it is very important to remember to:

1. Make sure your child gets plenty of sleep.

2. Make sure his schedule is regular and consistent.

3. Be ready to respond appropriately when an episode occurs:

    (a) If he is calm, just help him to lie back down or walk him back to bed.

    (b) If he is agitated, thrashing, or yelling, let the event run its course. Do as little as possible, intervening only if necessary for his protection. When he calms as the event ends, proceed as above. Do not try to wake him or to discuss the event. Do not discuss it with him in the morning either unless he asks, and then do so matter-of-factly. Do not make him feel strange or unusual; he is neither.

When these events happen frequently (several per month, several per week, nightly) in the school-aged child or adolescent, psychological factors must be considered as well. Such children typically are very nice youngsters, considered "angels" at home and in school. But under that calm exterior an angry fire is burning, an anger that is kept well bottled up. Sometimes these children are living in environments in which unwanted upsetting occurrences seem to be happening outside of their control (parental separation, multiple moves, repeated surgery). These same factors occasionally are relevant in younger children as well. In this setting, assuring adequate sleep and a regular schedule, although worthwhile, will not have much effect on the nighttime arousals. The best approach is to help the child learn to be better in touch with, and to better express, his pent-up feelings. Psychotherapy is often the best way to achieve this, but learning these new skills often takes considerable time.

In the meantime, it is important that your child be safe. You do not want a young child walking about the house asleep without your knowledge. Fortunately, it will usually occur before you go to sleep. But if it tends to happen later, you might consider a gate at the top of the stairs, a gate in his doorway, or bells hanging from his door to alert you. If he tries to walk outside, an extra chain lock high up on the front door will add sufficient protection.

Occasionally events are so marked, with wild running, falling over furniture, and trying to get out of the window, that other protective measures become important in the short run. Here we must turn to medication. Certain drugs, particularly those such as diazepam (Valium) and related agents, are often useful, especially in the older age groups.

It is worth noting that these events tend to wax and wane in frequency over time, with good weeks and months and bad ones. Trying to correlate these changes with day-to-day events in the child's life is usually a futile task. In fact, except as described above, looking for causes is generally unrewarding. Most parents at one time or another look for dietary explanations ("food allergy") and try to identify the offending food product. Such searches are almost invariably frustrating, difficult on the youngster, and may provide an excuse for not providing needed therapeutic help.

General Sleep Requirements

You cannot rely on your child to tell you what his own sleep requirements are. Infants will usually get the number of hours they need, though not always at night. Toddlers may not always get enough sleep, but instead of looking sleepy, an overtired two- or three-year-old may show an increased activity level, decreased ability to attend, and increased irritability and tantrums. Sometimes the symptoms of insufficient sleep are subtle and only become obvious when you see the improvement that follows increased sleep time. In older children, sleep loss may easily be associated with suboptimal school performance and social difficulties.

Although the actual number of hours required by each individual for normal performance varies considerably among children, it is good to keep some general guidelines in mind.

A newborn generally sleeps sixteen to seventeen hours a day, with sleep divided into a number of periods lasting two to six hours spaced throughout the day and night. By three months he should already be adjusting to the day-night cycle, getting most of his fifteen hours of sleep at night and having his longest single sleep period of five to nine hours at that time. During the day he should still be napping three or four times and have one predictable period of prolonged waking. By six months, total sleep time will be about fourteen hours, daytime naps will be decreased to two, and nighttime sleep should be stretched out to ten to twelve hours. He should be sleeping through the night by now (he certainly is able to).

Between one to two years sleep time decreases to about thirteen hours. Soon after the first birthday, naps decrease to one per day, usually in the early afternoon after lunch. From that point on, sleep requirements gradually decrease to just over eight hours by the end of adolescence (see Table I). Most children stop napping before age four, although some continue until the start of kindergarten. Most do not stop before the age of two and a half or three, and many children who "stop" before that would continue napping in a proper environment (for example, at a well-structured day-care program).

The values given in Table I are averages. Most likely your child will fall within one to two hours of that. If he gets over two hours less, you should examine his behavior closely for signs of sleep deprivation and you should examine his schedule and nighttime habits closely to see if more sleep might be possible. If he gets over two hours more than listed in the table, you should be sure that your child is growing well and is normally alert and active when awake. If this is the case, it may just be that he is a long sleeper. If you have any concerns, you should discuss them with your pediatrician.

TABLE I

HOURS OF SLEEP

1 week	16½
1 month	15½
3 months	15
6 "	14¼
9 "	14
12 "	13¾
18 "	13½
2 years	13
3 "	12
4 "	11½
5 "	11
6 "	10¾
7 "	10½
8 "	10¼
9 "	10
10 "	9¾
11 "	9½
12 "	9¼
13 "	9¼
14 "	9
15 "	8¾
16 "	8½
17 "	8¼
18 "	8¼

Summary

The purpose of this chapter has been to present the most common causes of sleeplessness in childhood. This has included causes of bedtime difficulties and nighttime wakings with behavioral-, habitual-, and sleep-schedule-related bases. These all may be treated rapidly, by the parents themselves. It also included nighttime fears and nightmares, occurring as either reflections of normal developmental struggles or abnormal psychological conflict. And finally, it discussed sleepwalking, confused thrashing, and sleep terrors, as normal physiologic occurrences reflecting developmental aspects of sleep or as reflections of certain styles of coping with strong psychological drives.

The aim has been to educate. All too often parents react inappropriately to their children's sleep difficulties because they have not been given a full understanding of what is actually occurring and what is best to do. Once they possess such understanding, most parents are able to deal quite successfully with the problems discussed or know to seek other help when they cannot.

By the Author

Solve Your Child's Sleep Problems. New York: Simon & Schuster, 1985.

References

Cuthbertson, Joanne, and Schevill, Susanna. *Helping Your Child Sleep Through the Night.* Garden City, N.Y.: Doubleday, 1985.

Ferber, Richard. "Sleep, Sleeplessness and Sleep Disturbances in Infants and Young Children." *Ann. Clin. Res.* **17**:227–234, 1985.

Richman, Naomi. "A Community Survey of Characteristics of One-to-Two-Year-Olds with Sleep Disruptions." *J. Am. Acad. Child Psychiatry* **20**:281–291, 1981.

Richman, Naomi, and Douglas, J. *My Child Won't Sleep.* London: Penguin, 1984.

An Explanatory Note

The way we perceive children determines, to a large extent, our style of parenting. Theorists range on a continuum from the behaviorists Watson and Skinner to the developmentalists Gesell, Ames, Ilg, Erikson, and Piaget.

The behaviorists believe that all behavior is learned. They view the newborn as a mass of clay and the parents as its sculptors. In fact, Watson stated that a person could teach any skill to any child at any age, if the teacher used effective teaching methods. (That philosophy puts an incredible burden of guilt on the parent of a child with learning or behavior problems.)

The developmentalists, however, believe that the child grows according to an inner timetable. Though they recognize that environment does impact the child, they do not see it as accelerating the maturational process.

The following two chapters both reflect the developmental point of view, but from different perspectives. Dr. Ames sees the child as an unfolding flower that follows its own physiological schedule, needing only routine maintenance to allow its potential to unfold naturally in predictable, patterned growth.

On the other hand, Drs. Meyerhoff and White believe that the quality of the flower can be enhanced by special care of the root system at the early stages of the plant's development. Once the roots have been stimulated appropriately, the plant will be rooted firmly and will then mature according to its own natural schedule with only basic care.

All three researchers believe that pushing a child to learn skills that he is not equipped to process takes its toll on the child's well-being.

Allow yourself to challenge your thinking as you consider the implications of each of the following two theories—both backed by years of research.

MICHAEL MEYERHOFF   BURTON WHITE

Meet the Authors

DR. MICHAEL MEYERHOFF

Dr. Meyerhoff, the Associate Director of the Center for Parent Education since its inception, is a specialist in early childhood and parent education, a field he has been involved in for close to fifteen years. After working at various day-care centers and preschools in his native New York, he attended Harvard University, from which he received his doctorate in Human Development. While at Harvard, his primary interests were the application of Piagetian theory to early social development and Dr. White's studies of parent–child interaction during the first years of life.

Dr. Meyerhoff has been a staff member at the Barnard College Infant and Toddler Center and the children's ward of McLean Psychiatric Hospital; a researcher with the Harvard Preschool Project; and a consultant to Missouri's New Parents as Teachers Project. His various articles, including "Parenting Information: How to Survive in the Jungle" and "Choosing Toys for Young Children," have appeared in numerous publications for parents and professionals, and he is a frequent guest on television programs.

Although he is admittedly "bananas about babies," Dr. Meyerhoff has no children of his own, claiming, "I'm still trying to figure out what my own parents did wrong."

DR. BURTON WHITE

Dr. White, Director of the Center for Parent Education, is regarded as the country's foremost authority on the educational development of infants and toddlers, a subject he has been studying for almost thirty years. A native of Boston, he received his doctorate in Psychology from Brandeis University, where he studied under Abraham Maslow. He acknowledges that Maslow's philosophy, along with the work of Jean Piaget, have been the major influences on the direction and style of his own research.

Dr. White was the Director of the Harvard Preschool Project during its thirteen years of existence, the first Director of the Brookline Early Educational Project, and was the senior consultant to Missouri's New Parents as Teachers Project (a model parent education program developed, supervised, and implemented by the two authors). The success of these programs has been so remarkable that the Missouri legislature has made the availability of parent education mandatory everywhere in the state.

In addition to his book for parents and textbooks for educators, he has written numerous scholarly articles. He is also the host of a television series, The First Three Years, *produced by the Westinghouse Broadcasting Company.*

Dr. White is the father of four grown children, all of whom have turned out rather well—much to his surprise. As he is fond of saying, "When we had ours, my late wife and I didn't know what we were doing either!"

Through the Center for Parent Education, a nonprofit agency based in Newton, Massachusetts, Dr. Meyerhoff and Dr. White publish a bimonthly newsletter for professionals, conduct workshops on "Educating the Infant and Toddler" all across North America, and provide consulting services to a wide variety of programs for parents and young children.

4

NEW PARENTS AS TEACHERS

NURTURING YOUR CHILD'S INTELLECTUAL
AND SOCIAL DEVELOPMENT DURING THE
FIRST THREE YEARS
MICHAEL MEYERHOFF, ED.D.,
AND BURTON WHITE, PH.D.

Through our research of the last twenty years, we have learned a tremendous amount about early development and how parents can help their children to the best possible start in life. Between 1965 and 1978, we conducted the Harvard Preschool Project, the most extensive study ever done of children who, by their third birthdays, had achieved outstanding success in intellectual development while retaining delightful, unspoiled personalities. We acquired a great deal of information about how such children develop during their early years and about what goes on in these children's homes on a day-to-day basis. Since founding the Center for Parent Education in 1978, we have continued to study young children and their environments. Working with professionals throughout the United States and Canada, we translate the results of our research into educational and support programs for young couples starting to raise families.

Based on our research, we believe that the experiences in the first years of life have unparalleled consequences for lifelong educational development. If children are performing at above-average levels in intellectual and social development by their third birthdays, in all likelihood they will continue to do well in nursery school, kindergarten, and elementary school—even if the schools they attend are mediocre. On the other hand, if children are performing below average at this point, it is unlikely that they will ever attain even average levels of development, regardless of any remedial programs they may be enrolled in later on.

Therefore, parents are not only their children's first teachers; they are their children's most important teachers. Unfortunately, since our society does not routinely provide reliable information about parenting, many parents must face this task unprepared, or at least ill-prepared. As a result, only about ten percent of our children receive the kind of early education that will enable them to make the most of their natural potential.

This dismal percentage is not inevitable. With adequate preparation, parents can have a stronger and more beneficial influence on their children's early development, and can avoid much of the needless anxiety that is often associated with raising children.

In this chapter we will offer you the sort of suggestions we give mothers and fathers in our "New Parents as Teachers" programs. These ideas are intended to help you achieve the very best possible results with your children, and have the most pleasure in the process.

General Guidelines

What do we mean when we say we want children to get a good start in life? In our study of outstanding three-year-olds from a broad range of ethnic and socioeconomic backgrounds, we discovered that all of these children shared certain key aspects of behavior. In their daily activities they tended to exhibit the following abilities more often than the other children:

Intellectual Abilities

- Being able to think abstractly and use ideas to solve problems.
- Being able to notice small differences when things or events are not as they were before.
- Being able to make use of imagination to produce interesting new ideas and make associations.
- Being able to plan and carry out complicated activities.
- Being able to use resources effectively and improvise when necessary.
- Being able to understand another person's point of view.

Social Abilities

- Being able to get and hold the attention of adults in a variety of socially accepted ways.
- Being able to express affection or mild annoyance to adults and age-mates when appropriate.
- Being able to use adults as resources after determining that a task is too difficult to handle alone.
- Being able to show pride in achievement.
- Being able to engage in role play or make-believe activities.
- Being able to both lead and follow agemates.
- Being able to compete with agemates.

If children have acquired these abilities by the age of three, we believe that they have had a superior education during their first years. This educational foundation will go a long way toward ensuring that they enter school well prepared for future development.

How can parents help their children achieve these abilities? In order to do a really good job as your child's first teacher, it's important to remember that, in contrast to adults or even older children, the educational needs of young children change rapidly and repeatedly during the first three years of life. Your child will have very different needs at each stage of development. For example, a toy for a six-month-old won't make any sense for a two-year-old. It's as if you were a teacher in a school and in September you were teaching seven-year-olds; in November the seven-year-olds left and you now were dealing with twelve-year-olds; and in February the twelve-year-olds left and you now were facing sixteen-year-olds. Presenting the same material throughout the year just wouldn't do.

To get a better grasp on the quickly shifting interests, abilities, and needs of very young children, it helps to see the first three years of life in seven different periods, or "phases." Our ideas about parents as teachers will be presented by these phases, and we will concentrate on what is generally true about all children for each phase. Of course, you will have to use this information as a framework for understanding, rather than as a precise description of your child. While all children are similar in fundamental ways, each child is unique, and your child will exhibit his own individual pattern of development as time goes by.

Phase I: Birth to Six Weeks

What can you teach your newborn baby? The answer to that question is "not much," mainly because newborn babies are not very good students. They do come equipped with a few simple and very useful skills, such as sucking, swallowing, grasping, and even the ability to glance at people and things. But these activities are reflexive in nature, and they do not involve any conscious thought or decision on the part of the baby. A newborn's capacity to perceive things is rather crude at this point, and the capacity of his mind to process what he does perceive is almost nonexistent.

There are people in the fields of psychology, education, and medicine who would disagree with us. They claim that children are capable of understanding, retaining, and communicating a great deal right from birth. Consequently, such people suggest that the circumstances surrounding the birth of your child, the things you say or read to him, and the way you hold and look at him while feeding and diapering during these first weeks are very significant and will leave lasting impressions. They could be right, but most of us who have studied early development extensively feel that it just isn't so.

That is not to say there's nothing important you can do for your baby during this phase of development. In fact, the single most important contribution you can make to your new child begins in the first weeks of life. On this point virtually everyone is in agreement: During the first weeks a baby needs prompt comforting when he is distressed, and parents should respond naturally to their child's cries.

Frequent discomfort is inevitable during a baby's first weeks, no matter how healthy the baby is or how attentive his parents are. However, this difficult situation serves a useful purpose. Newborns are not great students, but they do "learn," not by thinking about problems but through conditioning. Each time a crying, uncomfortable baby is picked up, held closely, rocked, fed, or comforted by whatever means a parent uses, the baby unconsciously begins to "learn" to associate the parent's arrival with feeling better.

Little by little over the first months of life, the parent's face, voice, smell, and characteristic way of holding the baby come to mean relief from distress. Such experiences constitute one of the major ways in which babies acquire the foundation for healthy lifelong interpersonal relationships. Nothing you could do for your child is more fundamental or more important.

There are a couple of other factors that deserve mention during this phase. One is the baby's emerging sociability. Newborns are not sociable in the usual sense of the term, but two simple signs of sociability become evident during the first six weeks of life. One is a tendency for the baby to look toward the eyes of the person who is holding him. The other is the appearance of the first "smile" when doing so. It seems that one of the universally inherited human behaviors is this inclination to smile at human faces, particularly those that are about twelve inches away.

The other factor is the baby's innate curiosity. All healthy babies begin to show a deep curiosity about "what's out there" during the first month of life. They also begin to show some interest in their own hands, which they will look at and suck on from time to time. It is in the innumerable activities involving their hands, eyes, mouths, and nearby objects that babies start to move from helplessness to a partial understanding and control of their world. This type of activity is one of the major foundations of intellectual ability.

With this in mind, should you be concerned about providing a great deal of social and intellectual "stimulation" for your Phase I child? Despite what you may read or hear on occasion, special activities and equipment are neither necessary nor appropriate at this point. Your baby will be spending much of his day asleep, and when he is awake and alert, what he will need and appreciate does not require extraordinary effort or expense on your part.

With regard to social development just about every parent we've ever observed has done an excellent job of "teaching" without having had any formal training. Responding naturally to the baby's cries when he's distressed, or simply making a big fuss over the precious new addition to the family, gives him all he requires—a feeling of being cared for and loved. This is a task that new parents not only do well, they do it better than anyone else.

With regard to intellectual development just about every crib or bassinet we've ever seen has contained ample material to feed a newborn's budding curiosity. In addition to the baby's own hands, there are bedclothes, blankets, railings, and other interesting objects to observe. Given the baby's limited ability to interact with his environment, rattles, stuffed animals, and other traditional "first toys" simply do not make sense at this point, and they will be largely ignored.

One type of toy that does make sense for a Phase I child is a mobile. A properly designed mobile can be something interesting for the baby to look at during his first periods of alertness. Unfortunately, while toy stores carry a wide variety of mobiles, very few meet a newborn's interests and abilities. Rather, they are designed to appear attractive to an adult entering the baby's room. Therefore, you'll probably be better off making a simple mobile yourself, using cardboard, magic marker, string, and other household items.

A mobile is best for the baby who is between three and nine weeks of age. Since four out of five babies at this age look to their right most of the time, the mobile is best positioned off to the baby's right side (or off to the left if your baby is one of those who prefer the left side) rather than directly overhead. Also, since babies between three and nine weeks of age do not focus well on objects that are closer than eight or nine inches or farther away than sixteen to eighteen inches, the mobile should be positioned somewhere in the middle of this range.

As noted earlier, newborns like to look at human faces, so the design of the mobile should reflect this preference. They do not appreciate fine detail or subtle colors, but instead respond best to bold colors and areas of high contrast such as eyes, noses, and hairlines. The target should face the baby, and since babies do not follow moving objects well, the mobile should not "flutter in the breeze." We have dubbed the simple homemade mobiles produced by the parents in our programs "stabiles" for that reason.

Phase II: Six Weeks to Three and a half Months

Toward the end of the second month of life, rather abruptly, babies become much more alert and interested in looking at the world around them. While your Phase I child slept most of the time, your Phase II child now will be awake for approximately one third of the day. During these increasing periods of alertness, he will show more curiosity about his surroundings and more interest in looking into your eyes. His visual abilities will develop to the point where he will be comfortable looking at small, nearby objects.

Sometime between eight and twelve weeks of age, children begin to stare steadily at their own hands. This signals a new stage of development wherein they are no longer content with just looking at what's out there, they are now interested in touching as well. This desire to touch is part of the process that will lead to the ability to reach later on. But in the beginning, since their fingers remain fisted during most of this period and they cannot yet use their fingers effectively for exploration, "touching" consists primarily of striking or batting objects with a closed hand.

With regard to intellectual development, you can help your baby practice his new skills as well as satisfy and expand his curiosity in several ways. Now, instead of a well-designed mobile, he will appreciate a good-quality unbreakable mirror placed on the side of his crib or over his changing table. Looking at his own face has a special appeal because, unlike someone else's face, his image will move in a manner that is determined by his own actions. A stainless-steel mirror about five or six inches in diameter, positioned approximately six or seven inches from his eyes, is ideal.

The provision of a few simple objects to bat is also a good idea. Since your baby will not yet be adept at using his hands under the guidance of his eyes, and since he will not have the mental or physical capacity to retrieve something that has moved away, any objects placed in his crib or on his blanket should be basically immobile and they should be within easy striking distance.

With regard to social development, your major task remains the same—giving your baby a feeling of being cared for and loved. This continues to be of fundamental importance, and it becomes easier to do during this phase. First of all, your normal anxiety will have subsided a bit, and you now will be more adept at comforting your baby. Then, by the end of the second month, he probably will be sleeping through the night. Finally, he will begin to smile more regularly and generally look more attractive.

There is one more important point to consider during Phase II, and that concerns talking to your child. Although babies cannot understand the meaning of words until they are six to eight months old, it is very important that you begin talking to your baby long before that. Get into the habit of talking whenever you are with him, and the more the better. Also get into the habit of talking about what your baby is attending to at the moment—this is when he will learn best.

Phase III: Three and a half Months to Five Months

Toward the end of the third month, you and your child will enter into a remarkably serene and enjoyable period. By now your baby will be an established member of the family, and you will have overcome almost all doubts that you could ever succeed at being a parent. Your baby will continue to smile, and he will usually be in a good mood. Of course, there are exceptions. All babies get cranky at times, and some tend to be uncomfortable and unhappy throughout the first six months or so. But on the whole, most Phase III children seem to be highly contented and sociable.

This sharp increase in sociability is accompanied by the emergence of delight and giggling. In addition, experimenting with sounds (an important activity) surfaces during this period. Now that their hearing has become more acute, babies begin to be interested in variations in sounds, especially their own, so they start to make a variety of wonderful little noises. Also, their physical appearance tends to improve dramatically as their heads fully recover from the distortion typically experienced during the birth process, and hair grows.

Apparently this is the crowning stroke in one of Mother Nature's master schemes. In order to survive and thrive, it is imperative that a baby form a strong attachment to some adult. Conversely, it is necessary for some adult to fall head over heels in love with the baby. Babies are well-equipped to encourage this. In the beginning it is their helplessness and their plaintive cries that bring nurturance. This can get a bit tiresome after a while, so the first smiles arrive just in time to renew the adults' flagging spirits. Then, as if to make sure that attachment will be complete, four-month-old children look and act in such a way that makes them totally irresistible.

Therefore, your primary task with regard to your child's social development is to give in to his charms and give way to your natural inclination to adore him. Along with lots of affection, you probably will be talking to him more, and as noted earlier, the more talking you do, the better. Also, the more enthusiasm you demonstrate, the better. Excitement and warmth are contagious, and if you express them to your child, he will respond in kind.

Abundant attention, affection, and enthusiasm are absolutely necessary, but they are not sufficient for optimal development during this period. With regard to intellectual development, there is much to be done in the areas of eye–hand skill and satisfaction of growing curiosity. By about four months of age most children have acquired mature visual abilities. They are able to track objects that move toward or away from them. They can also follow moving targets in all directions. Their eyes turn smoothly toward approaching objects; and consequently they can appreciate three-dimensionality. With a few minor exceptions their ability to use their ears is now about as fully developed as their ability to see.

Mature visual abilities lead to the development of a key visual motor skill—reaching. It is through the use of the hand as a tool that each early exploration proceeds. And it is largely through eye–hand activities that children enter the world of problem solving and the investigation of small objects.

You can identify visually directed reaching by offering a small object to your child about five inches away from his eyes and off to his favored side. If he brings his hand directly to the object and begins to open or close it just before contact, he has acquired the skill.

If you ignore your child's eye–hand behavior, he will still learn to reach before he is six months old. Like most of the basic skills that babies acquire during the first year or so, development will take place without much help from adults, as long as adults do not actually prevent development. However, if you want to help your baby learn, you can get him the kinds of crib toys that can be placed overhead in such a way that reaching is encouraged.

A good crib toy of this sort can be suspended over the baby while he is flat on his back so that small, attractive, and safe objects are within reach of his hand. The objects should not be suspended by strings, and they should not swing freely when hit. The best arrangement is a semirigid mounting so that the objects yield when struck, but then return to place. If a small noise can be produced when contact is made, the results will be even better.

Once your child has learned to reach, his interest will shift to using his hands for exploring objects, picking them up and releasing them, and making things happen. Without special materials and assistance, however, he will not be able to engage in much activity of this sort for a while. For example, if you offer him a rattle, he will reach for it and take it. He then will bring it closer for inspection by his eyes, mouth, and his other hand. But when he drops it (and he soon will), he will not be able to retrieve it or even show that he misses it. Therefore, suitable eye–hand play for a Phase III child involves a few differently shaped, safe objects for handling, along with the opportunity to create simple effects by eye–hand action. Placing your child on a blanket that has several such toys within reach, and being prepared to retrieve them regularly, will provide him with a great deal of appropriate activity.

Phase IV: Five Months to Eight Months

Throughout infancy two powerful forces are at work within children—curiosity and the need to gain complete control over their bodies. All healthy babies have a strong desire to explore their world, but that desire is restricted by their limited physical capacities. As the months go by those limitations are shed, and each time they are discarded, their urge to explore can be satisfied more fully and in more diverse ways.

Phase IV is the final period of frustration for babies. Children at this stage want very much to get around and into their environments, but since they will not acquire the ability to move about on their own until the end of this period, they're really stuck. To make matters worse, they spend a lot of time observing their surroundings, and with their fully developed vision and hearing, they now can be enticed by a multitude of temptations—all beyond reach.

Until he is able to crawl, scoot, drag himself along, or even roll over to get from here to there, you might consider a walker for your baby. With his new capacity to be comfortable in a vertical position and with his powerful leg extension reflex, he will be able to maneuver a well-made walker before he can crawl. Children in walkers can enjoy themselves tremendously, but they also can reach innumerable dangerous objects and get their fingers caught in places such as doorjambs. Be sure your child is carefully supervised whenever he is in a walker. Also, many people in the medical field agree that the use of a walker should be terminated as soon as the child can get around on his own.

What else can you do to encourage development in your Phase IV child? Not much, directly. You can continue to provide materials for eye–hand practice as described earlier. Exploration of small, safe objects still will be fascinating for him. Ideas about the world of objects grow during this period, so that gradually his focus will begin to shift from the act of merely dropping objects to the motion of objects as they fall. He will release an object, and then decide he wants to take a look at the consequences.

New toys can be introduced to feed your child's interest in making all sorts of things happen. Once he can sit well, around seven months of age or so, bath toys that encourage him to explore the infinite variability of water become appropriate. Toys that can be operated with the light push of a button or lever also can be enjoyed during the latter part of this phase. The more dramatic the effect that is caused by his action, the more likely the toy will hold his attention.

That's about it. Phase IV is a comparatively uneventful stage of development. However, it can more accurately be described as "the lull before the storm." Between eight and thirty-six months, several fundamental educational processes will move into high gear, and parents should use this comparatively quiet and easy period to prepare for the critical developments of the coming months. At this point in particular, there are three vital tasks for the parent: see to it that your child can hear well, plan to redesign your home, and begin to concern yourself with the subject of discipline.

Few parental activities are more important in raising a child than regular testing for hearing losses. Your Phase IV child is about to enter a crucial learning period, and should he fail to hear well for long periods of time, he will fail to learn language as well as he might. To the extent that language learning is negatively affected during the first years, so, too, is the development of higher mental abilities. To the extent that both processes suffer, your child also will be hindered with respect to social development.

While babies with profound hearing loss usually are identified very early in life, those with mild to moderate losses often are not identified until they enter school. Parents can be on guard for warning signs throughout their child's early years. The following chart, prepared with the help of the Alexander Graham Bell Association for the Deaf, will aid you in monitoring your child's progress.

Age	Danger Signals
Birth to 3 Months	Baby is not startled by sharp clap within three to six feet; he is not soothed by mother's voice.
3 to 6 Months	He doesn't search for source of sound by turning his eyes and head; he doesn't respond to mother's voice; he doesn't imitate own noises such as "ooh, ba-ba," etc.; and he doesn't enjoy sound-making toys.
6 to 10 Months	He doesn't respond to his own name or to telephone ringing or to someone's voice when it is not loud; he is unable to understand words such as "no" and "bye-bye."
10 to 15 Months	He cannot point to or look at familiar objects or people when asked to do so; he cannot imitate simple words and sounds.
15 to 18 Months	He is unable to follow simple spoken directions; he does not seem able to expand understanding of words.
Any Age	Baby does not awaken or is not disturbed by loud sounds; he does not respond when called; he pays no attention to ordinary crib noises; he uses gestures almost exclusively to establish needs rather than verbalizing.

If you suspect that your child does not hear everything he should, insist on an examination by a pediatric audiologist, if possible. Or for information on the nearest appropriate resource, write to the Alexander Graham Bell Association at 3417 Volta Place N.W., Washington, D.C. 20007. Whenever a sign of hearing loss is detected, careful diagnosis and follow-up are imperative.

The second vital task for parents of Phase IV children is redesigning the home. There are two parts to this job: making the home safe *for* your soon-to-be-crawling child as well as protecting the home *from* your soon-to-be-crawling child. One of our key recommendations for the next three phases of development is to provide interesting experiences for your child, and the easiest way to do that is to give him extensive access to the home. Once they can get about on their own, babies love to move from room to room, and in the process, they find an infinite number of new objects, situations, and challenges.

But homes are designed for adults, not babies, and the typical home is quite hazardous for very young children. Accidental poisonings are very common with newly crawling babies, so all potentially dangerous materials (such as cleaning substances) must be placed out of reach or in locked cabinets. Electric cords and fixtures need to be made safe or inaccessible (it's a good idea to get safety plugs for outlets). Plants should be moved out of reach, and knives and other sharp utensils must be stored in safe places. It's important to examine floors closely for small items such as pieces of broken china or cigarette butts.

As for protecting the home from your baby, remember that anything breakable is fair game for a newly crawling child. If you treasure it, put it away, at least for the next couple of years. If you do not baby-proof your home, your newly crawling child will be a regular source of stress for you. Many parents don't do enough in this regard, and then find that they're working too much at control. An occasional "no" is more likely to work with very young children than constant prohibitions—and it is much less effort.

And finally, the third task for parents is discipline. From about seven months on, parents should employ discipline in the form of clear and consistent limit-setting policies. If such actions are begun as soon as your child begins to move about on his own, they usually are effective. Furthermore, both you and your child will become accustomed to basic ground rules.

Your child will not feel less loved when he learns from his very first excursions around the home that he can't always go where he wants to go. When he decides to visit the part of the floor where you're sweeping up broken glass, or when he journeys to the top of the stairs where you've forgotten to close a gate, you won't think twice about the issue of control.

On the other hand, you should be just as forthright when his travels are likely to destroy part of an unread newspaper or interfere with someone else's game, nap, or housework. Though the child may not be in danger in such cases, by allowing him to ruin someone else's possessions or activities, you are neglecting to teach him to respect the rights of other people. Many children thus learn that no one in the world is quite as important as they are. This is of minor consequence when a child is eight months old, but it can become a major problem when that child is two or three years old.

Phase V: Eight Months to Fourteen Months

The onset of Phase V is a key transition point for both children and their parents. By seven or eight months of age your child has come a long way, but he still has a long way to go. If you think back to the first weeks of your child's life and compare him then with what he is doing now, you can't help but be impressed with his growth in social interest and responsiveness, the increase in his alertness, the development of his looking and listening skills, and the progress he has made in his ability to control his body.

However, a great deal still lies ahead for children at this stage of development. They may or may not have begun crawling, but they probably have not begun pulling to stand, climbing, and walking. It is a rare child who speaks at this point, although a couple of words may very well be understood. There is no reason to believe that seven- or eight-month-old children have much thinking ability or intelligence of consequence. The most complicated problems such children can solve involve pushing aside an obstacle in order to get to a desired object. They have very little memory or understanding of the world around them, hardly any social skills (except for crying to get attention), and their personalities remain rather simple, although each baby is unique.

In other words, those human activities that most clearly distinguish us from other animal species are still relatively undeveloped at this time. The abilities that children have acquired thus far are very basic and, with regard to learning, very likely to be acquired except under unusual child-rearing conditions. That is, most parents, whether they are well-informed or not, usually end up with "well-educated" babies at the beginning of Phase V.

If you follow the suggestions we've offered, your child may be a bit advanced, but even if you knew very little about raising a baby, he still would learn most of what could be learned during the first months of life. You could interfere with the development of vision by keeping your child in a dark room all day, and you also could teach your child not to cry for attention by ignoring him completely. Of course, most parents treat their babies more kindly. By simply acting naturally, they usually provide their babies with a fine basic education during the first seven or eight months of life.

As children move into Phase V, however, the story can change quite dramatically if parents continue to rely solely on "instinct" and "common sense" as their primary guides. This is a time of life when the healthy development of curiosity, language, intelligence, and social skills is very much at risk. There is a great deal that parents can do to either help or hinder development in these areas.

Nothing that lives is as eager to learn about the world as a newly crawling baby. Then again, few things are as troublesome. Crawling babies can get hurt, and as noted earlier, most homes are full of hazards for such children. These active youngsters are clumsy and inexperienced. They don't know what's safe to lean on, and they don't know how doors work. The list of dangers is long. And that's not all. Crawling babies are also messy and destructive. They don't clean up anything, and they seem to enjoy creating and wallowing in litter.

The danger and damage together mean stress and work for parents. Many parents respond to this situation by using playpens or other restrictive devices for long periods of time, to keep the newly crawling baby in one small space. While such methods do reduce the aggravation and effort, they also seem to interfere with the child's optimal development. Curiosity is the major force behind early learning, and as your child's first teacher, it is very important that you preserve and expand it, not discourage it.

Fortunately, it is easy and fun to nurture your child's curiosity. If you've followed our suggestions and have made your home as hazard-free as possible, you now can give your Phase V crawler a wonderful gift simply by turning him loose. By offering your home to your child, you have instantly provided a vast number of interesting things for him to do. And with a little extra thought and effort, you can provide many more hours of accessible and appropriate activities.

First of all, your crawler will enjoy just getting around. For many weeks he's been looking and listening, but he has not been able to get to the many attractive places and things that all homes have. A kitchen cabinet is a wonderland for a nine-month-old. Playing with canned goods, plastic containers, pots and pans is great fun—and anything that is fun for a baby usually is educationally appropriate. As he gets a bit older and can stand and climb, the opportunity to look out the window will be appreciated.

Water is endlessly fascinating at this stage. Providing an inch or two in a wading pool or other suitable container, along with plastic cups or pitchers for pouring, will entertain your baby for quite a while (be sure to supervise). Simple mechanisms are very appealing, too. The action of a light switch or an instant-on radio or television set will capture and recapture his attention. And provided that it is easy to work, simply flushing the toilet will give him hours of pleasure (note: bathroom activities should be closely supervised).

Your Phase V baby will also be fascinated by hinged objects that he can swing back and forth. They can be as large as full-sized doors or as small as a two-inch lid on a small toy. He will get a kick out of the motion as well as practicing the skill involved in producing that motion. Balls of various sizes and shapes will be appropriate and appreciated as well. They move a great deal with very little effort, and playing with them often results in social interaction with an adult.

At this stage of development, your baby will love playing with collections of objects in containers and covering containers with lids, providing that the covering task is not too difficult for him to perform. He will enjoy fitting objects into each other as well as onto one another. In fact, just about any small object (but not small enough to be swallowed!), window, hinged object, simple mechanism, and place to go in and out of will feed your Phase V child's curiosity.

Most of these materials and mechanisms are readily available in most homes, so no expense is involved in providing such valuable experiences for your child. There are also a few commercial toys that can be useful, especially for those inevitable times when your baby seems bored or must be confined for any length of time, such as a car trip or a visit to a home that has not been safety-proofed. A surprise busy box,* bath toys for water play, books with stiff pages, a toy telephone, or a large inflatable plastic beach ball will be

---

* Such as "Disney's Busy Poppin Pals," as opposed to standard busy boxes.

genuinely appealing during these times. However, you should remember that manufactured toys cannot compete with the many wonders that your child will find while crawling around the home.

While all these things are helpful, there is another ingredient that is absolutely essential for the healthy development of curiosity in your child—you. Babies develop best when there is someone who is totally involved with them and who is nearby for many hours each day to share their excitement, help them when help is needed, and especially to talk about what's happening. You can expect to be approached by your Phase V child at least seven or eight times each hour, and we recommend that you employ the following style during your interactions with him.

When he approaches, respond quickly. If he approaches at an awkward time, respond quickly but tell him he'll have to wait to get your full attention. Look to see what's on his mind. Talk in ordinary, full sentences, using a simple vocabulary. Be spontaneous with related ideas such as "Yes, you have a blue shirt—and Daddy has blue pants and brown shoes" and don't hold on to him when he wants to leave to do something else. Such behavior on your part will lead to deeper curiosity and more pleasure in exploration.

It also will lead to good language learning. Language is one critical ability that should be learned well during the first years of life. By the time he is three years old, your child should be able to understand and communicate effectively, and the extent to which he can will depend directly on you. We don't mean to alarm you, but it is a fact that parents are the key to early language learning. By his third birthday, your child should be able to handle about 1,000 of the most common words.

During Phase V, he may or may not be able to say a few words. He is likely to understand simple words such as mommy, daddy, bye-bye, ball, no, and names of family members and pets. Since most parents don't talk to things that don't talk back—chairs, trees, and babies—parents often miss out on months' worth of teaching language. Remember that this is a crucial time for language development, and the more you do at this stage to encourage it, the more your child will learn.

As your child's first and most important language teacher, you have several tasks. First of all, make sure that he continues to hear well. If he regularly becomes congested because of allergies, colds, or infections, his language learning may be adversely affected. Keep him as healthy as possible, and follow up any concern with a visit to a pediatric audiologist.

Next, follow our advice on nurturing curiosity, because it is the interested, involved child who is the best student of language. Then use the response style we have described above. Be careful to use language in relation to the here and now. Phase V children are concrete thinkers, and they will process information best when it relates to what they are focusing on at the moment.

You can begin to use picture books with your child when he starts to show interest in the illustrations as well as in turning the pages. Until the latter part of this period, you can expect that he will be more interested in practicing his finger skills than in labeling exercises. And don't expect him to show much interest in story lines until he is well into the next phase and his thinking and memory processes have grown to the point where he can appreciate and retain characterizations and themes.

Good language learning along with the stimulation and satisfaction of curiosity are major parts of the foundation for the development of intelligence. You will see a fair amount of progress in the growth of your child's mental capacities during Phase V. Perhaps the most remarkable phenomenon will be the expansion of his memory. Early in this period your child's memory will be very short-lived and he will be easily distracted. Within a few months, simply putting him in another room for five minutes, unfortunately, will no longer wipe out the memory of an interesting but forbidden activity.

On the other hand, you still will not see signs of higher mental abilities or real "thinking" emerging at this point. Problem solving will remain rather simple during this stage of development, consisting for the most part of trial and error behavior as opposed to the comparison and judging of ideas. Moreover, it is generally recognized that the basic mental abilities that evolve during the first year and a half or so of life are not particularly at risk, and they will develop quite adequately without special input from parents.

We do feel that parents should provide their children with ample opportunities to play with a variety of objects and mechanisms, and should expose them to a great deal of language during Phase V. But the reason for doing so is a motivational one. In the opinion of many people in the field of early child development, the more opportunities of this kind children have during this stage of development, the better they will learn later on. It provides children with a great deal of enjoyment, and it seems to heighten their need to know.

There are some who would suggest that you should do much more about encouraging the development of your child's intelligence during this period. We will concede that if you put enough effort into it, you may get him to learn some things a bit faster than he otherwise would. However, our preference is that you refrain from any special "educational" programming at this point. It is important to remember that there is more to a Phase V child than budding intellect. This is a special time of life for social development. Too much attention to intellectual goals can adversely affect the attainment of interpersonal goals. This is also a unique time for parents to enjoy their baby, and vice versa, and lengthy training sessions can spoil much of the fun of early parent–child relationships.

Phase V is the beginning of the period when children receive most of their basic training about people. By the time they enter this stage, they have already learned that the arrival of an older person usually means that discomfort will be reduced or pleasure will be increased. They also have learned that crying will often be followed by the arrival of an adult. Over the next year to year and a half, learning more about other people and learning some things about themselves will be their highest priorities. It's easy to see how important parents are with respect to the healthy development of social skills.

For example, the ability to use adults as resources is a significant social skill that surfaces shortly before the first birthday. Crawling and climbing babies need help at times. They get themselves into places and situations that can frighten or frustrate them. They can't express their needs in well-developed speech, but they can draw attention to themselves with crude vocalizations and then use simple gestures to indicate what's on their minds.

Under these circumstances it is the most natural thing in the world for adults to want to help a child, and routine assistance teaches a child that adults can help when a situation is beyond the child's capacity. However, this natural chain of events is not guaranteed. It depends upon the ready availability of a concerned grown-up for lengthy periods over many weeks. Sadly, we have seen some children who have learned *not* to ask for help during this stage.

Another social skill that emerges toward the end of the first year of life is the expression of anger directed toward another person. In contrast to the undirected expressions of rage that are common to all babies in distress, Phase V children will make it clear at times that they are angry with you. Your child might not get to this behavior, but you should be prepared for it. Consider it a sign of healthy development—provided that such moments are less common than expressions of affection.

Shortly after the first birthday, as a result of mental development, children begin to engage in make-believe or pretend episodes, commonly featuring imitation of their parents' telephone conversations, kitchen chores, or housekeeping activities. The sight of a baby, barely able to talk, mimicking adult behavior is great fun, and we urge you to enjoy and encourage it in your child. If a loving adult spends enough time with a Phase V child, reinforcement of such behavior is almost inevitable.

At about the same time, children begin to show pride in their achievements. Beginning at about eight months of age, they become very interested in the responses of other people to their own behavior. The dramatic motor achievements of Phase V are very exciting to parents, especially with their firstborn baby. First the baby learns to pull himself to a sitting position. In the weeks that follow, he begins to crawl, to pull to stand, to climb up stairs and onto furniture, to walk while holding on, to climb down stairs and furniture, and then to walk unaided. This progress in mastering the body has enormous importance for the child, and it is a source of great pleasure for both him and his parents.

The child's joy in genuine achievement, his parents' natural response to his achievement, and the child's rapidly increasing concentration on the reactions of the adults close to him combine to create an air of excitement and pleasure with the appearance of each new skill—however imperfect it may be at first. Shortly after the first birthday, through the long process of conditioning, the child will come to anticipate attention, excitement, and compliments whenever he does something new or difficult. After having done such an activity, he will immediately turn toward his parents in anticipation of praise. This is the beginning of pride in achievement, and once again the magic ingredient is the presence of at least one adult who has a special feeling of love for the child.

Phase VI: Fourteen Months to Twenty-four Months

During Phase VI, you will begin to marvel at the accomplishments of your child. You already have been impressed by his many achievements in the first fourteen months, but what surfaces during the balance of the second year of life is more dramatic for three reasons. First, the development of speech opens up communication. You now actually have access to your child's mind. Second, that mind is becoming much more active and interesting than it has been in the past. Signs of imagination and originality start to blossom. Third, the crystallization of a complex personality proceeds rather quickly. Your simple, lovable one-year-old evolves into a complicated two-year-old at a very surprising and exciting rate.

The Phase VI child has the same major interests as the Phase V child. He is still very concerned with mastering his body, satisfying his curiosity, and coming to terms with the primary people in his life. Whereas the first two interests were probably a bit dominant before, social interest now becomes stronger. As your child's teacher, your three fundamental tasks at this point are: to provide new and interesting experiences for him, to serve as his personal consultant, and most importantly, to introduce him to the rules of civil behavior.

With regard to intellectual development, the first order of business is the completion of the development of the basic mental abilities that children acquire before they become real thinkers. This includes many understandings about the world of small, movable objects. Unlike a one-year-old, a two-year-old realizes that objects have an existence of their own, whether he is playing with them or not. He knows much about how they move when they are thrown or dropped. He has learned a fair amount about causes and effects as well as the sequences of activities. His memory, the capacity to retain mental images in the absence of the actual objects, has grown considerably.

As noted earlier, these abilities are usually acquired without any special efforts on the part of parents. However, during this stage of development, parents can be extremely influential in two other areas of their child's intellectual growth. One is motivation—nurturing the interest in learning. The other is the acquisition of higher mental abilities—the capacity to use ideas to think about the world and to solve problems. Since interest in the person around whom the day revolves will affect many of his activities during this period, helping your child move forward intellectually is relatively easy and very enjoyable.

The more things a Phase VI child has seen and played with, the more he wants to see and play. This process can be helped along if parents participate by providing a new toy or situation when the child seems bored, by sharing the excitement he experiences in play and discovery, and by aiding him when he is stuck or needs other assistance. The role of the parent, quite simply, is to design an interesting environment, allow the child access to it, and then move back, letting the child choose his activities himself. In the meantime, the parent should be available to assist and encourage him.

The best mental development rests upon healthy intellectual curiosity about objects, their movements and qualities, and about how things work. In addition, it depends upon the ability of the mind to cope with ideas and language. During the early part of this period, language focused on the here and now is the primary route to good mental development. Gradually, children reveal a new capacity to deal with chains or sequences of ideas, and simple stories become interesting. Toward the end of this period, simple conversations become possible, and they can be helpful in stimulating intellectual growth. Encouraging role play or pretend behavior is especially recommended.

Helping your child acquire excellent language skills—the key to the growth of higher mental abilities—is easy. It is important to remember that, at this stage of the game, excellent language skills do not necessarily include excellent speech. A two-year-old usually is far more accomplished in receptive language than in expressive language. Though speech ordinarily blossoms during Phase VI, in some well-developed children, it may be slow to develop until the third year. Furthermore, we never have figured out how to help a child begin to speak. If your child does not say much during this period, you need not be concerned. In any event, if he is physically healthy, there probably isn't much you can do about it. On the other hand, he should be able to understand a few hundred words and phrases, and in this area there is a great deal you can do.

If you've seen to it that your child hears well, language teaching is simple and fun. Just watch to see what he is interested in, and get into the habit of talking about that subject. When he approaches you, it usually will be for help, for comforting, or to share an exciting discovery. At times, it may be merely to be near you. In most cases, it will not be difficult to tell what's on his mind. Try to identify that interest, and then respond to it by using ordinary language. You may be a naturally quiet person, or you may not be inclined to talk to your child until he talks more. But if you can overcome any tendency toward silence, you'll go a long way toward encouraging your child's linguistic and intellectual capacities.

With regard to social development, parents have an altogether different role. Phase VI is perhaps the single most difficult period of a child's early years as far as his parents are concerned. The most striking qualities of this stage are the growth of individuality or personality and the struggles with authority that normally occur. Along with rapid growth in intelligence and language, this is the time in life when children first become aware that they have power in their dealings with other people.

One sign of this new awareness is the use of the pronoun "mine." The clearest sign of this period, however, is the child's growing tendency to resist suggestions and directives through the use of the word "no"—in other words, negativism. This preview of adolescence, although annoying, is a normal part of the early attachment process. Under most circumstances, children work these issues through by their second birthdays, and they then turn their attention to other matters such as social life with peers.

During this stage your child will probably start testing wills with you. Children who have been accustomed to occasional control and who are dealt with sensibly, firmly, and lovingly during Phase V become used to the fact that they can't always have their own way. The result is that when normal negativism and testing of wills surface during Phase VI, such children are easier to live with than overindulged children who have learned to ignore half-hearted prohibitions. Children who are used to reasonable limits also tend to leave negativism early, having had less difficulty resolving interpersonal conflicts. They usually return to smooth social relations by the beginning of the third year.

When conducting research on children in their own homes, we paid special attention to discipline. We found that regardless of the family's income, cultural background, or educational level, warm but firm discipline tended to accompany good intellectual and social development. From the time the child began to crawl, his parents made sure that when a behavior was unsafe or unacceptable for other reasons, the child received a clear and persistent message to that effect. In homes where children were developing well, telling the child not to do something was ordinarily not repeated more than once.

Many parents, when noticing a behavior they disapprove of, say something to the child but fail to make sure that he really has stopped the behavior. A momentary interruption can be counted on, but very often, as soon as the parent turns away, the child returns to the forbidden act. It takes real effort to follow through on each occasion, yet all successful parents we have studied did so. Furthermore, as the weeks went by, such parents had an easier time of it than others because their children gradually came to understand that their parents' words really had meaning. With less effective parents, the children learned that if they waited a few moments until the message was finished, they could go back to what they were doing.

The social needs of Phase VI, which are visible in clinging, testing, and other stressful behaviors, tend to interfere with the child's other interests. With those needs satisfied, the child enters into a more mature and easier style of relating to his parents. At the same time, he begins to show genuine interest in children his own age. If control has been loving but firm during this period, the child will rather quickly figure out that his parents are in charge of the home, and he will be free to move on to other pastures. This is a particularly trying age for parents, and few get through it without a great deal of work and attention, but firmness, consistency, and persistence pay off now and later.

Phase VII: Twenty-four Months to Thirty-six Months

As with each of the preceding stages, you will find yourself dealing with yet another type of student in Phase VII. If all has gone well during the first two years, your child should be a remarkable person. First of all, he should have an impressive and complicated mind. Whereas younger children act out most of their experiences, Phase VII children can think—they plot, plan, and

reason. There will be times when such skills will make your child more difficult to handle, but these new capacities also open up many teaching opportunities.

At this stage of life, your child's memory will be quite well-developed. He will be capable of insightful solutions to problems. He may come up with the wrong answer occasionally, but he will no longer have to rely solely on trial and error. Although he still will do better when dealing with the here and now, his capacity to think about the future and the past will begin to grow.

Helping your child anticipate consequences by pointing out the next few events is a good idea during this period when his grasp of time and sequences is expanding. Regular story sessions make sense now, and there are many first-rate books available for children of this age (consult your local librarian). Stories that capture imagination and encourage fantasies are just as valuable as realistic ones, since our research has indicated that the ability to engage in make-believe activity is one of the distinguishing characteristics of well-developed children. Another characteristic is good observational ability, and your child will spend a fair amount of time simply staring steadily at objects and scenes. Commenting on similarities and differences, therefore, is a beneficial teaching habit.

In addition to stories, you can use toys, television, and outings as valuable educational aids. Toys that feature settings such as houses, farms, and stores, along with the associated people, furniture, and animals, are especially appropriate, as are puzzles of increasing difficulty. Television shows like *Sesame Street* may help your child learn numbers, colors, and other simple information. However, we don't believe that any television show provides important educational experiences that will have a lasting impact on your child. *Sesame Street* is witty, entertaining, and informative, but in no way can it substitute for a loving human being who actually shares experiences with a child. We simply recommend the program as one of many ways to broaden your child's interests.

Trips out of the home will also broaden the scope of your child's interests and experiences. Fortunately, a trip to the supermarket with your child will no longer be a threat to your sanity. He will be growing more civil by the day, and will not be as inclined as he once was to attack the contents of the store. He probably will be a delightful companion, eager to hear your comments on all the brightly colored items and fascinating people you both encounter. By the way, your child will still be interested in the home, but events and activities rather than things and places will now be his primary focus. He will want to learn about gardening, cooking, fixing things, and cleaning. He will welcome new challenges like learning how to ride a tricycle, how to handle crayons and tools, and particularly "how to do things himself."

Most parents find it easy to keep a Phase VII child interested and active.

Compared to dealing with a teen-ager, it's simple, because a young child is not yet jaded about very much. Learning to operate a child's phonograph, going to the zoo and seeing the animals up close, or simply watching an adult bake a cake, all still have a freshness about them, and they all can be absolutely fascinating to a Phase VII child.

Throughout this period, we urge you to remember that it is not necessary to smother your child with your teaching. These suggestions about teaching are meant to describe an effective style but not to imply that a parent should hover over a child or insist on many daily learning episodes. Most of the "teaching" we have observed in parents who were doing an exceptional job with their children has consisted of brief episodes that come up naturally as part of normal routines in and out of the home. If you find yourself spending more than two hours of undivided attention with your child in the course of the day, you're probably overdoing it.

You also should be careful not to neglect social goals. If you follow our advice about setting limits and maintaining firm but loving discipline during Phase V and Phase VI, your child will probably be through the trying period of negativism at this point, and you won't have to suffer through the tantrums so often found in "terrible twos."

However, there will be times when he demonstrates that he still has much to learn about living with other people, so it is important to keep setting limits and maintaining discipline. This will be especially obvious when he begins dealing with agemates. Although he no longer will treat other children like inanimate objects (as Phase V and Phase VI children often do), he still will not be adept at taking the perspective of another child or putting his own needs and desires into the context of a group situation or experience. One of your key tasks during this period, therefore, will be to teach him how to "hold his own" while maintaining respect and compassion for others.

We believe that placing your child in a nursery school or play group at this stage is a good idea because it will provide opportunities to practice and refine his interpersonal skills. But you should be aware that research suggests that the most effective teaching about relating to other people takes place in the home. Children tend to learn social behavior through the process of modeling. Loving adults make much better models than other children. The abilities to express emotions to agemates, to both lead and follow agemates, and to compete with agemates—all of which are characteristic of well-developed children—seem to have their roots in what the child is exposed to at home.

Common Hazards
to Good Development

Throughout this chapter we have alluded to various factors that commonly have an adverse effect on the development of children during the first years of life. They include undetected and untreated mild or moderate hearing losses, extensive confinement in playpens, cribs, or jumpseats, overindulgence instead of limit setting, and parental silence during the initial stages of language development. In addition to these, we think you should be aware of some other major factors that our studies have indicated work against optimal development.

One is extensive use of poor-quality substitute care. During the last few years there has been a growing trend toward placing children as young as six weeks of age in less than ideal substitute care arrangements for eight or nine hours a day, five days a week. While this practice may be convenient for parents who wish to have additional income or pursue certain career goals, we do not think it is in the best interests of the children. All our research points to the notion that optimal development is more likely when children receive a tremendous amount of personal prompt attention and affection early in life. This requires that a child have ready access to someone who has a kind of irrational love and commitment to the child. It is difficult to find such people in most substitute care arrangements.

Of course there are situations where some kind of substitute care arrangement is absolutely necessary. If parents or grandparents are not available, the best bet is to have a superb person come into your home. Unfortunately, that is prohibitively expensive for most families. Our next recommendations, in order of preference, would be to have a similar person care for your child in her home; an especially qualified person caring for no more than three children in her own home; a carefully selected nonprofit daycare center where the ratio of children to staff is no more than four to one and where the number of children per room is less than ten; and a very carefully selected profit-oriented day-care center with comparable standards.

Another hazard to good development is parental stress. Child rearing is an occasionally difficult and aggravating job, and someone who is saddled with it for twenty-four hours a day, seven days a week, is not likely to do it well. In our opinion, parents have a right—if not a duty—to "get away from it all" for a few hours on a regular basis. We strongly suggest that mothers and fathers share child-rearing duties as much as possible. With the exception of breast feeding, we see no reason why women should be considered inherently more qualified than men in this area. Whenever feasible, the grandparents should be involved as well. Furthermore, as long as the child is over six months of age, and as long as the majority of the child's waking hours are spent with parents, grandparents, or someone very close to the child, we think that a part-time substitute care arrangement is an excellent idea.

A third hazard is closely spaced siblings. First of all, our studies have revealed that this is the single greatest source of stress for young families. In homes where children were spaced three or more years apart, we generally found the atmosphere to be much more pleasant and conducive to good child-rearing practices than in homes where the spacing was less than three years. In the latter cases, harsh feelings and even physical violence between siblings were common, and the parents often expressed the feeling that they were acting more like prison wardens than teachers for much of the day.

The difficulties between closely spaced siblings are easy to understand if you consider the normal course of social development. If a one-year-old child is confronted with a newborn sibling, he does not immediately feel threatened. He is still very much concerned with his initial explorations of the home, and the sibling—who spends much of the day sleeping in a crib—does not constitute much of an intrusion. Six to eight months later, however, this situation changes dramatically. Now the older child's primary focus is on establishing his relationship with the key people in his life—his parents. At the same time, the younger child has begun to crawl, and because he now can get into much more trouble, he requires a great deal of parental attention. That attention usually comes at the expense of the older child, and since attention equals love in his mind, intense jealousy is the natural result.

In fact, expressions of dislike for the younger child at this point are healthy signs, because they indicate the older child has been receiving a good amount of affectionate attention and, indeed, has "something to lose." But when he expresses such feelings in the only ways he knows how, he is often castigated by his parents—the very people whose affectionate attention he is desperately trying to win back. This compounds the problem and confuses the older child even more. Under such circumstances, we have seen many delightful, happy-go-lucky one-year-olds turn into rather sad and surly two-year-olds as their once rosy outlook on the world gradually sours.

Meanwhile, unlike the older child—who at least spent the first year and a half or so of life in a very warm and accepting environment—the younger child is exposed to feelings of hostility and is routinely subjected to physical abuse from very early on. The younger child quickly learns defensive tactics, such as crying before being hit, and eventually he learns how to retaliate as well. Now the parents are not only faced with the problem of breaking up fights between the children; they can't even tell who started them. And you can imagine what happens to this already unpleasant picture if a third child is added to the scene at this stage of the game!

Things are very different when the spacing between siblings is three years or more. Under these circumstances, by the time the young child has begun to crawl, the older child has firmly established his relationship with the parents, and he has securely staked out his position in the home. He is now moving on to other interests, spending a great deal of time with other people, especially agemates, and is becoming involved in many more activities outside of the home. Of course, there are still moments when things are not perfect between the siblings, but for the most part, intense feelings of jealousy and hostility are less likely than feelings of acceptance and even affection. This makes life much easier and nicer for both the children and parents, so we urge you to plan your family accordingly, if at all possible.

Final Comments

The goal of our program is to help parents raise each child to be a bright, aware, and confident learner with the capacity to take maximum advantage of whatever formal and informal schooling he encounters in the future. We feel it's equally important to raise a caring and considerate person who will be comfortable with the adults and agemates he meets and interacts with along the way. Life has few rewards as valuable or substantial as a parenting job well done.

When we began the Harvard Preschool Project in 1965, interest in preschool education was booming. Project Head Start was new, exciting, and generously funded. Most of the new sizable preschool research was directed toward the rapid creation of compensatory programs for three- and four-year-old children from low-income families. We, on the other hand, chose to initiate a research project that might ultimately provide guidance in the education of all children starting at birth.

It has been with a measure of satisfaction that we have watched early education research evolve into a more comprehensive, family-based study of the sort we concentrated on and continue to advocate through the Center for Parent Education. Today it has become quite fashionable to talk about education during infancy and toddlerhood, whereas twenty years ago few professionals gave such a radical idea a thought. Similarly, the conviction that the family is the first and most fundamental educational delivery system also has become commonplace. Professionals are now willing to admit to a more limited conception of their influence on a child's educational achievement.

We do not mean to say that there is now a general belief that going to school is of no use, but rather that if a family does not do a minimally adequate job of rearing and educating a child in the first years of life, professional educators usually cannot overcome the resultant educational weaknesses. To put the issue more directly, the results of Project Head Start and its many spin-offs seem to indicate that if a three-year-old child is six months behind his peers in the development of language, problem-solving, or social skills, the chance that he will ever become an average or superior student is rather small.

The widespread ineffectiveness of all but a handful of remedial programs has focused our attention on preventing the buildup of educational deficits; and the belief that early experiences are of central importance to a child's later educational achievement has motivated our research. The success of our New Parents as Teachers programs has sustained our efforts to provide young families with the information and support they desire and deserve in order to help their children to the best possible start in life.

In Summary

Things to Do

- Make your home as safe and accessible as possible for your child so that he will have maximum opportunity to explore and investigate his world.

- Remove sharp utensils, poisonous substances, and breakable objects from low shelves and cabinets, and replace them with old magazines, pots and pans, wooden spoons, plastic cups and bowls, and other materials your child will enjoy playing with.

- Be available to serve as your child's personal consultant for the majority of his waking hours. It is not necessary to hover, just be alert to where he is and what he is doing so you can provide supervision, attention, and support as needed.

- Respond to your child promptly and favorably whenever possible, providing enthusiasm and encouragement as appropriate.

- Set realistic but firm limits on your child. Do not give in to unreasonable requests or allow unacceptable behavior to continue.

- Talk a lot to your child, and try to concentrate on what he is focusing on at the moment. Use simple language that he can understand, but make an effort to add new words and related ideas. For instance, if your child gives you a toy truck, say, "This truck is red, just like my blouse. Our car is blue like your pants."

- Provide new learning opportunities for your child—and remember, letting him accompany you on a trip to the market or allowing him to help you bake cookies will be more enriching and enjoyable than sitting him down for a flash-card session.

- Give your child the opportunity to direct some of your shared activities on occasion.

- Help your child be as emotionally spontaneous as your own feelings will allow.

- Encourage your child's pretend play and fantasy activities, particularly those in which he takes on adult roles.

Things to Avoid

- Don't confine your child to restricted areas, such as a playpen, for long periods of time.

- Don't allow your child to focus his energy on you to the point where independent exploration and investigation are missing.

- Don't ignore your child's attention-getting devices so that he is forced to throw a tantrum in order to attract your interest.

- Don't be afraid that your child won't love you if you say "no" to him from time to time.

- Don't feel that it's necessary to win every argument with your child, especially during the second half of the second year when he is passing through the normal period of self-assertiveness and negativism.

- Don't worry too much about the mess your child makes of the house. It's a sure sign that he's a healthy and curious baby.

- Don't be overprotective, and resist the urge to supervise all of your child's activities. Infants and toddlers learn best when their parents act as consultants rather than instructors.

- Don't bore your child if you can help it.

- Don't be concerned about when your child learns to count or to say the alphabet.

- Don't worry if your child is a little slow to talk, as long as he appears to understand more and more language as time goes by.

- Don't attempt to force toilet training too early. If you wait until your child is two years of age, it will be a lot easier.

- Don't spoil your child by giving him the impression that the whole world and everyone in it exist solely for his needs.

By the Authors

Dr. White's book for parents

The First Three Years of Life, rev. ed. Englewood Cliffs, N.J.: Prentice-Hall, 1985.

Dr. White's Reports on the Harvard Preschool Project Research

Experience and Environment: Major Influences on the Development of the Young Child, Volume I. Englewood Cliffs, N.J.: Prentice-Hall, 1973.

Experience and Environment: Influences on the Development of the Young Child, Volume II. Englewood Cliffs, N.J.: Prentice-Hall, 1978.

The Origins of Human Competence: The Final Report of the Harvard Preschool Project. Lexington, Mass.: Lexington Books, 1979.

Drs. Meyerhoff and White's publication

The Center for Parent Education Newsletter—A bimonthly publication for professionals concerned with education during the first three years of life. Center for Parent Education, Newton, Mass.

Videos

"The First Three Years"—A television series about learning during the first three years of life by Westinghouse Broadcasting Company, distributed by the Center for Parent Education.

LOUISE BATES AMES

Meet the Author

Dr. Louise Bates Ames has distinguished herself as the foremost expert in the developmental research of children. She has conducted and published sophisticated scientific and original research for well over fifty years. Her remarkable career has been recognized here and abroad. She received the Bruno Klopfer Distinguished Contribution Award, the University of Maine Alumni Career Award, the Deborah Morton Award from Westbrook College, and was selected by the Ladies' Home Journal *as one of America's 100 "most important, newsworthy, noteworthy" women of 1983.*

Dr. Ames graduated from the University of Maine, where she also received her M.A. She later received her Ph.D. from Yale, an Sc.D. from Maine University, and a second Sc.D. from Wheaton College. After working on the staff of the Yale Clinic of Child Development as Personal Research Assistant to Dr. Arnold Gesell, she became an assistant professor at the Yale University School of Medicine.

Dr. Ames was cofounder of the Gesell Institute of Child Development in 1950. She has served there in a number of roles, including Director of Research, Chief Psychologist, Codirector, and President. She has conducted several television series, written a newspaper column, twenty-five books, and over 300 scientific articles and monographs.

In addition to writing on nearly every aspect of child psychology, throughout her career she has done extensive public lecturing. At an age when most

---

women have long ago retired (she was born in 1908), this seemingly tireless celebrity is as prolific as ever.

She is a dynamic woman who is determined to create a better world for children through her work. Dr. Ames has one child, three grandchildren, and four great-grandchildren.

5

RESPECT FOR READINESS

DON'T PUSH YOUR PRESCHOOLER
LOUISE BATES AMES, PH.D.

The long-suffering parent public has been deluged, in the past two decades, with books that tell them how to improve their children. Among such titles one finds: *How to Raise Your Child's I.Q., How to Raise a Brighter Child, How to Teach Your Baby to Read, Teach Your Baby Math,* and *Blueprint for a Brighter Child.* All of these books imply, or state outright, that if only you start early enough, you can teach your infant or preschooler almost anything you want to at whatever time you choose, regardless of his state of readiness or level of development.

Currently we hear a great deal about the "super baby." If only you start pushing early enough, you can raise a super baby who will, allegedly, outstrip the other babies of the same age. Some unwitting and possibly overambitious parents actually pay rather large sums of money to take courses that will help them teach their children at earlier and earlier ages.

This kind of unseemly effort has always filled us with worry. In fact, we feel so strongly against it that some years ago we wrote a book entitled *Don't Push Your Preschooler.*[1]

It would seem that we are not the only child specialists who fail to go along with the idea that how far and fast your child develops is all up to you. A recent article in the *New Haven Journal Courier* comments on the effort to use flash cards with infants as young as one year of age, to teach math no later than two years of age, and to introduce playing the violin and learning to play chess just shortly thereafter.[2]

The article notes that one mother who made the flash cards realized that "it was the stupidest, most ridiculous thing. I felt so artificial that I threw the cards away." The newspaper notes that "less than a year after super baby first toddled into the national consciousness, a backlash is under way." The article gives the opinion of several outstanding child specialists as follows:

T. Berry Brazelton, M.D.: "I hope there are some laid-back babies and some laid-back mothers, too."

Burton White, Ph.D.: "You can do some of these things, but underlying it must be some pretty intense work . . . You reduce the plain joy and happiness in parenting and in being a baby."

Lee Salk, Ph.D.: "It's a hype."

Nancy Holmes, M.D.: "My gut feeling is that this early education is garbage."

Benjamin Spock, M.D., considers the whole trend to be just one aspect of an unwholesome American drive to compete. He notes that "insecure people want to prove themselves through their children."

So much for eager parents encouraged by those specialists who assure them that their teachings, regardless of timing, will bear fruit. For the most part these parents give up when they find that even quite strenuous efforts (in one instance a group of parents attempted to spend five hours a day teaching math to their two-year-olds) do not bear fruit commensurate with these efforts.

We are less concerned about parents than we are about teachers, schools, and state departments of education, some of whom have joined the bandwagon and support the idea that if only we start soon enough and push hard enough, we can increase and speed up learning. The position of such educators seems to be especially dangerous because so many of them, particularly at the state level, are in a position to determine or at least influence school policy.

When such environmentally oriented professionals (those who believe that the environment can ultimately determine the child's rate and level of learning regardless of the child's own time schedule) combine with overeager parents, in our opinion, much harm can be done to children.

Are Children Brighter Than They Used to Be?

Are children brighter or relatively more mature today than they used to be? Some say they are and give this as a reason that we must provide ever more demanding curricula, or even that we put four-year-olds into kindergarten.

Though it is true that many children today seem more sophisticated than children of the same age a decade or two ago, we have no evidence that

children in general are really brighter or more mature. Certainly we find much evidence of superficial sophistication. One four-year-old of our acquaintance, in listing the bad things he was not going to do—not hit his brothers, not fight with them at the table, not force the pieces in the jigsaw puzzle—added to his list, "And if anybody offers me dope, I'm just going to say 'no.' "

His first-grade brother, when asked if he liked school, said he liked it except that the kids said mean things. Asked what mean things they said, he replied, "They say I'm a retard. And they say I'm gay." Asked what gay meant, he replied, "I don't know but I'm going to find out."

In spite of such seemingly precocious statements, the four-year-old was behaving, in general, just the way we expect of a four-year-old—wild, wonderful, and out-of-bounds—and his brother seemed very much like the more or less typical six-year-old—complex, intriguing, and ambivalent.

Admittedly, in some instances we do see very slight signs of acceleration. We ourselves made a comparison of two- to six-year-olds examined in the 1930s with a second group of the same-age children examined in the 1970s.[3] The two groups of children compared were similar from a socioeconomic point of view. Most were white middle-class boys and girls of a New England background.

Children were compared on the basis of their responses to the various sub-tests in the Gesell Developmental Scale. In thirty out of fifty-one comparisons made, that is, in fifty-nine percent of the measures, *scored behavior occurred at exactly the same time in each of the two groups of children.* Thus, for fewer than half of the measurable comparisons were there differences between the two groups. In eighteen instances the later group of subjects was about six months ahead, in three instances the earlier subjects were more advanced.

This modest amount of acceleration in the later group may be compared to the fact that children on the average are currently found to be somewhat taller than they were in the 1930s. Some attribute this increase in size to improved nutrition, which might also be responsible for this very slight acceleration in behavioral response.

However, our own findings on behavior characteristics of the various early ages do seem to fit with actual real-life findings of parents and teachers just as they did when they first appeared in the 1940s.[4] In any case, our clinical impression is that, with certain exceptions, infants and preschoolers are developing at much the same rate, and through the same stages, as they have in the more than half century during which we have been describing the behavior of young children.

The same thing, in our opinion, holds true for high school boys and girls. However, as young people grow older, though they still develop through fairly predictable stages, the effect of the environment on their behavior becomes increasingly evident. By high school age, the world that the young person experiences is undoubtedly much more complex and demanding than it was for high schoolers even ten or twenty years ago. It is probably true that they go through the same stages as ever, but their lives are different from what they would have been in the past because their worlds are so different.

Kindergarten for Four-Year-Olds

New York State Commissioner Ambach suggested in the spring of 1984 that we start four-year-olds in kindergarten. His argument was that if you start children in kindergarten at four, they would then graduate from high school a year earlier, at sixteen instead of seventeen, and thus would "save" a year.[5]

Such a notion would be ludicrous except that when suggested by a state commissioner of education it takes on serious implications. It implies that we, not nature or the child, decide what any given child is able to do at any given age. It seems to many of us in the field of child behavior that an educator who could propose such a suggestion clearly lacks substantial knowledge or understanding of what young children are like and how they develop.

Typical four-year-olds, as any nursery school teacher can attest, tend to be active. Most are not ready to sit and fill out little workbooks or be subjected to making early efforts at learning to read and print. Most are not ready to meet even the demands of an extremely free-wheeling, nonacademic kindergarten.

Normally, four-year-olds enjoy extremely active gross motor play. They like to climb and tumble, slide and scoot around—preferably out-of-doors. They love the jungle gym and hanging bars. They like to play with large blocks—building houses, stores, boats, and airplanes.

They enjoy imaginary play, pretending that they are mothers and fathers (one little boy we knew, the major family positions having already been taken, asked if he could be "the little dog"). They imagine they are storekeepers and salesmen, pilots and stewardesses, firemen and policemen, nurses and doctors —whatever adult role comes to mind. They love to dig in the dirt. They love dressing up dramatically. And their play is fluid—they can be robbers hiding in a cave one minute and policemen arresting the robbers the next.

Though they like to listen to stories, many four-year-olds are a long way from being able to read them. Our findings are that even young Fives can recognize such words as "stop" and "go" and may ask "What does 'dog' spell?" But most have not come too much farther than that in reading. Though Fours enjoy paint, clay, and other creative materials, many can do little more than make an occasional and random letter—and that one is often upside down or backward.

Though some teachers, in a moment of abandon, might call their four-year-old group a kindergarten, most Fours are light-years away from being able to do kindergarten work. Certainly most would not be ready the following year, when they were five, to move on to even an extremely relaxed first grade.

Even if on rare occasions it becomes possible to teach a four-year-old things that we assume the average four-year-old is not really ready for, some careful preschool teachers have asked the pertinent question, What are the children missing that they normally would be doing when they are being pushed into advanced activities?

All-Day Kindergarten?

One of the most aggressive concepts currently going around in educational circles is the notion of all-day kindergarten. Certainly most kindergartens are not now run on an all-day basis. But some are. And in many communities the debates are heated. The state commissioners of education are conducting formidable campaigns to make their case.

There seem to be three basic notions behind this push of all-day kindergartens that are gaining significance. The first is the philosophical argument that we do not need to wait for a child's readiness or pay too much attention to his ability and stamina—adults should arbitrarily decide what small children will do.

The second argument is that children are smarter and quicker than they used to be. They not only can but should be doing schoolwork that is substantially more advanced than it has been in the past. In many kindergartens the work now offered comes very close to being what first grades offered only a decade ago.

A third and powerful argument is that with so many mothers working, we now need to offer children a safe place in which they can spend their afternoons. And kindergartens would provide that place.

Our own position does not support any one of these three propositions. To begin with, though he may have exaggerated slightly, we do go along with Shakespeare in his comment, "Ripeness is all." In our experience, the best results in working with children of any age come when we respect the child's maturity level and his own timetable. We must make our demands fit each child, rather than make our own arbitrary decisions of what we are going to expect and/or require.

As to the second argument, we have no evidence that children are smarter or quicker than they used to be or that they need more advanced kindergarten work than they have been getting in the past. In fact, we have learned through the evaluation that we've made over a period of years that the standard curriculums that are offered by a majority of schools are too advanced for most children.

First-grade teachers routinely tell us that many of their pupils begin to read sometime during the second half of the year, when they are around six and a half years of age. We have no evidence that in a normal situation the ordinary five-year-old is ready to read.

An interesting exception to this was found in a private school in Princeton, New Jersey. The kindergarten teacher assured us that *all* of her five-year-olds were reading, thanks to an all-day kindergarten. She did not seem to make the connection between this all-day schooling and the fact that some of the second and third graders were sucking their thumbs in school. Pressure expresses itself in interesting ways.

At any rate, it would be our preference that kindergartners be offered *less* academic work than many schools provide. As one knowledgeable school principal remarked, "Keep those workbooks off their desks and those pencils out of their hands for as long as possible." A principal from Pauling, New York, makes the rule that children not be provided with pencils (merely with large crayons) until the middle of first grade.

The third, and perhaps most practical, argument used by supporters of all-day kindergarten maintains that with so many mothers working, children need a safe place to be during the afternoons.

Admittedly, day care for children of working mothers is becoming an increasing problem. Our own position is that the two needs—for schooling and for day care—should not be confused. If children need day care, and many do, this should be provided in some way by each community. But the need for day care must not be misconstrued as a need for longer hours in the kindergarten classroom.

Our chief reason for objecting to all-day kindergarten sessions, aside from the fact that they are not necessary academically, is that many five-year-olds tire unduly if kept in school for so long. It has always been the Gesell position, supported by research carried out by educator John C. Mulrain, that even many first graders fatigue unduly with an all-day session. Mulrain conducted a study of first-grade teachers working in a shortened school day.[6] After two or more years teaching under these conditions, ninety-three percent of the teachers considered that the shortened day resulted in less pupil fatigue and less pupil frustration. They reported that the children's attention span was improved by a shorter day and that work habits improved as well. And eighty-five percent of the teachers perceived the positive effects of the shortened day in the area of pupil enthusiasm.

Furthermore, eighty-five percent of the parents felt that the shortened day had fully met the academic needs of their children. Another eighty-eight percent felt that the shortened day had no negative relationship to the child's

acquisition of basic skills, while eighty-two percent felt that the shorter day met their child's social needs and that the child's attitude toward the shorter day had been positive. A continuation of the shorter day program was recommended by eighty-four percent.

Some communities hold two daily sessions for kindergarten, one in the morning, one in the afternoon, providing some flexibility as to when the children may attend school. The younger or less mature children attend in the mornings so that they can still have their naps in the afternoons.

Two letters sent to us from kindergarten teachers working in an all-day kindergarten speak for themselves. The first is from a teacher in St. Louis, Missouri.

> *Help! I am a full-day kindergarten teacher. This is our first year of full day. I am experiencing so many things I've never experienced before—so many difficulties I didn't anticipate. I seem to have several categories of students: (1) the oldest Fives and young Sixes seem okay; and (2) the young but very bright Fives seem to manage.*
>
> *Only these two seem to hold up to these long hours. Other categories that do not manage as well include: (1) The young Fives; (2) those Fives who are young for their ages; (3) those with social, emotional, and behavioral problems, who are here because their parents want them out of their hair; and (4) those who have been in*

day care because their parents work. For all of these last four groups, every day is a struggle.

A second letter from a Connecticut teacher, also teaching all-day kindergarten, tells much the same story.

> *Presently I am teaching in an all-day kindergarten. Everything people say about how bad these long sessions are is true. A stepped-up academic kindergarten curriculum is neither necessary nor desirable, and five-year-olds absolutely cannot absorb an all-day session.*
>
> *I am teaching twenty-two children. By 10:30 they are finished learning, but our school day, which begins at 8:00 A.M., is not finished until 3:15 P.M. Yet I am forced to keep them occupied until dismissal time. I can truthfully say I am ready to pull my hair out at the end of the day. I am withdrawing from this school in June. I cannot agree with this type of setup.*

A five-year-old boy who attended an extended-day kindergarten reflects the effect of pushing on a youngster's general outlook toward school. This boy had loved nursery school, but when asked in the fall of his kindergarten year how he liked school, he replied vehemently, "I hate it!" When asked what parts he hated, he said, "All of it." Then he added, "But don't worry, because I'm quittin'." When he was asked if he would like to go back to nursery school, which he had enjoyed, he replied sadly, "No chance! Once the kindergarten gets hold of you there's no going back."

A knowledgeable New Hampshire elementary school principal who understands the needs of young children commented recently, "Keeping five-year-olds in school all day violates everything we know about five-year-old behavior."

An admittedly serious problem does exist with regard to underprivileged inner city children. Some people claim that kindergartners in these areas are better off in school buildings than they are on the streets and sometimes even in their own homes. This may well be true, but this is a *very special* situation. It seems unrealistic, impractical, and unfair to confuse the needs of this specific group of children with those of the majority of our kindergartners. Keeping needy children off the streets is indeed a problem that must be solved. But it seems unwarranted to extend all of our kindergarten sessions from a half day to a full day to solve a problem that pertains to relatively few children. Their plight requires a more specific solution.

Developmental Placement

Up until now most of our suggestions have seemed somewhat negative: don't teach your baby to read or do math; don't push your preschooler; try to keep your four-year-old out of kindergarten; and avoid all-day kindergartens.

What, then, do we have to say of a more positive nature? Just this: If parents would take pains to start all children in school, and subsequently promote them on the basis of their *behavior age* rather than their *age in years,* quite possibly one third to one half of school failure might not occur.

Schools and parents all too often make the assumption that by reaching the age of five, every child has automatically reached the behavior level which *on the average* characterizes that age. This obviously is not the case. Some children at five will indeed behave as a typical Five. Some will be a bit ahead of this level. Some will be behind. There are many perfectly "normal" five-year-olds who are behaving much more like four-and-a-half-year-old children.

What this means is that many, if not most, children start school simply because they have had their fifth birthday before some time which each state arbitrarily determines—five years old by September/October/November/December, or even January. Without any evaluation of the child's actual readiness or developmental level, it is assumed that he is "ready" for whatever work the kindergarten curriculum prescribes. Since most curriculums are presumably suited for an *average* or *typical* child, this clearly means that they are *not* suitable for—in fact, they are too demanding of—those many children who are not up to "average."

This can be particularly unfair and, in fact, harmful to many children—especially boys, since on the average they develop at a rate approximately six months more slowly than girls.

Thus a great many children are started in our schools some months before they are ready. As a result, even though many of them are quite normal, with good potential for learning, they fail. It is to prevent such needless failure that we proposed what we have termed *developmental placement.*

The Gesell position has always been that behavior in the human individual develops in a patterned, more or less predictable, way. Though some educators maintain that Gesell, unlike Piaget, does not "believe in" the environment, nothing could be farther from the case. Gesell has stated, early and often, his respect for environmental factors.

Two typical statements define his position. In 1927 he noted:

Growth is a unifying concept which resolves the dualism of heredity and environment. Environmental factors support, inflect, and modify but they do not generate the progressions of development. [7]

In 1940 he elaborated still further:

In appraising growth characteristics, we must not ignore environmental influences. But these must always be considered in relation to primary, or constitutional factors, because the latter ultimately determine the degree, and even the mode, of the reaction to so-called "environment." The organism always participates in the creation of its environment, and the growth characteristics of the child are really the end-product expressions of an interaction *between intrinsic and extrinsic determiners.* Because the interaction is the crux, the distinction between these two sets of determiners should not be drawn too heavily *[emphasis mine].* [8]

Thus Dr. Gesell quite clearly respects the role of the environment, but he does not believe, as do many, that it can make anybody into anything at any time, or even substantially alter or hasten the logical stages of development.

Dr. Gesell had much confidence in the child's inborn tendency to develop to the best of his potential. Though he gave parents a great deal of information about what growing behavior was like, he did not provide any vast amounts of advice as to what they should do. He believed that though any child will benefit from good parenting, most suffer relatively little from a parent's well-intentioned mistakes.

The notion that parenting has to be superb, that you substantially determine your child's personality or potential by the way you treat him, or that it is all over by some arbitrary age unless you have done just the right thing is not supported by parents and professionals who follow a Gesellian point of view.

In her scholarly book *Mother Care, Other Care,* Sandra Scarr notes:

Most Gesellian psychologists, such as Edward Zigler and I, stress the importance of the child's biological organization and the individual differences in developmental patterns that determine most of the ways children develop, as long as they have reasonable environments. We argue that parents can and do have important effects on their children, but that most middle-class families provide adequate care for their children to develop normally, even optimally. [9]

While on the topic of how important the developmental approach is for children, we should consider the question, "Is it absolutely essential for a child's welfare that his mother stay at home and be fully and solely responsible for his care, as some child specialists claim?"

If a mother is financially able and emotionally suited to being a full-time mother, she has much to offer that hardly any other person can or will. However, the many mothers who are not able to provide full-time home care themselves must not be made to feel guilty because they cannot do so.

For any working mothers who cannot be at home with their children, Sandra Scarr's book *Mother Care, Other Care* is an excellent resource. Dr. Scarr provides strong support for the idea that all is not lost and, in fact, considerable benefit may be gained when a mother finds capable, reliable persons to take over at least part of the responsibility for bringing up her child.

Though Dr. Gesell strongly believed that behavior develops in a patterned way and through a predictable sequence of stages, he also gave full respect to individual differences. Thus he appreciated that though the *sequential stages* tend to be much the same for almost everyone, the *rate* at which each child develops is his very own.

If this concept is accepted, then it is quite natural to deduce that our custom of entering children in school based on their birthday age is highly flawed. Dr. Gesell first faced this probability back in 1919 when he stated:

I suggest a psycho-physical [developmental] entrance examination of every school beginner. . . . No feature of public school administration is apparently under less control than that of school entrance.[10]

Two years later he continued with the same theme:

No feature of public school administration is apparently under less control than that of school entrance. . . . The excessive repetition in Grade I (about one out of four first-graders fails of promotion) is itself a sad commentary. We virtually place a premium upon failure by insisting so speedily on academic standards of promotion.[11]

This important expression of the belief that children should be given a developmental or behavioral examination before they start school in order to determine their readiness for starting, was not followed up by Dr. Gesell. In fact, his feelings on the subject were not known to his staff in the 1950s when our interest returned to this special area of investigation.

Gesell staff in the 1930s and 1940s were fully aware of the need for children to be "ready" before certain achievements in eating, sleeping, toileting, and social behavior in general could be expected. But we had not applied this notion to school behavior itself. Rather, like other people, we more or less took it for granted that so far as school was concerned, five-year-olds would be behaving in a manner that was fully five. Thus they should be ready to begin kindergarten at whatever date the law allowed.

When children who were failing or having trouble in school were brought to our clinical service, we—like others—sought the more or less customary possible causes of failure. It was only in the mid-1950s that it struck us forcibly that almost all of these children had one thing in common: nearly all of them had been placed in a grade that was ahead of the one for which they were ready *developmentally*. Thus a large amount of the school failure that we were seeing was caused primarily or even solely by overplacement.

We then asked ourselves if focusing on a population of children who were having school difficulty biased the study. Or if overplacement could be true in the population in general. To answer this question, with support from the Ford Foundation we conducted a three-year study in the Hurlbutt School in Weston, Connecticut.[12]

In the course of this research we gave Gesell developmental examinations to all kindergarten boys and girls, to children in one first-grade class and in one second-grade class. We then reexamined all of these children yearly for a three-year period. This research was aimed at answering three questions:

1. How many, if any, of these children were, in our opinion, overplaced?

2. Do the "unreadies" eventually catch up?

3. To what extent can the Gesell tests predict, say in the fall of any given year, what the teachers will actually say about the children in the spring? That is, do the tests predict which children are unready and will thus eventually fail the grade in question and thus need to repeat?

The results were as follows:

1. Though findings varied slightly from group to group, in general only the children in the top third of any given grade seemed fully up to their age and thus ready for the work of the grade in question. One third seemed to us questionably ready and one third definitely unready.

2. It was only in the very rare instance that any given child caught up. Since our research indicates that a child must grow, in behavior, a full year in any school year to hold his own, he would need to grow more than a year in any given year in order to catch up. Such catching up is theoretically possible, but in the "unreadies" catching up very seldom occurred.

3. To an appreciable extent it was possible to predict in the fall of the year, on the basis of a behavior test, whether or not a child would successfully accomplish the work of the grade he was in, and thus be eligible for promotion to the next grade come spring. The judgments of the kindergarten teachers seemed to support predictions made from the developmental examinations. In one of our original kindergarten classes, the agreement between prediction and teacher's decision was eighty-three percent. The disagreement came only in those cases where we had labeled the children "questionably ready." Teachers did not have this category.

Though this research was continued for only three years, we did check on our original kindergarten children when they were in the sixth grade. We compared their sixth-grade performance with predictions made from our tests given at the beginning of kindergarten. We found that of all those predicted *fully ready,* sixty-five percent ended up in the top third in the sixth grade and nobody ended up in the bottom third. Of those predicted *unready,* nobody ended up in the top third in sixth grade and sixty-four percent ended up in the bottom third. (It is important to add that the teachers were not being influenced by the results of our testing, since our records were not available to the school.)

The research in Weston proved promising. It supported our suspicion that a great many children were not ready for the work of the grade in which the law placed them and might in many instances fail simply because of overplacement. Thus we proceeded to develop norms for our tests and write a book, *School Readiness,* which explained our point of view and presented these norms.[13]

Since that time it has been our privilege to give hundreds of seminars and workshops in this country and abroad. We have taught teachers and psychologists how to give our developmental tests and how to set up what we call developmental placement programs in schools.

The method of setting up such a program is relatively simple. In any school that decides to proceed developmentally, all entering kindergartners are given our test to determine their developmental level. Many of these children whose chronological age is five are also five developmentally. Thus they are suited to starting kindergarten and, presumably in another year, may be promoted to first grade. Others will be on the young side of five and thus suited only for a prekindergarten class. Such children will be expected to spend two years in kindergarten before proceeding to first grade. Most boys and girls, after completing the regular or advanced kindergarten, will then proceed the following year to first grade. Some, however, will not appear to be developmentally ready for first grade even after completing kindergarten. For such children we like to see schools provide a prefirst or readiness class.

It would be the somewhat unusual child who would need these three levels of schooling—prekindergarten, kindergarten, and prefirst before being ready for a full first grade. But if a school system can afford these programs, they serve a very important purpose for those who need either of these extra steps.

Our experience has been that if all children who enter first grade are actually ready for it when the time comes, the number of school failures can be dramatically reduced. In the twenty years or so that developmental placement has spread throughout this country, substantial success has been reported. Probably the most substantial application of our principles has taken place in Fort Lauderdale, Florida, where we have had the privilege of consulting. Nearly all of their over ninety public schools use developmental placement principles in determining the time when children shall start school and be subsequently promoted. A directory that we have put together lists schools throughout the country that are either fully or partially run along developmental lines.[14]

A dramatic breakthrough for developmental placement took place in July 1985. A bill was passed by the legislature of the state of Oklahoma and signed by the government that required, in part, that:

The State Board of Education shall develop and implement a program to screen students enrolled in kindergarten in the public schools of the state for developmental readiness prior to entry into public school first grade.

If funds are made available for the 1986–87 school year, students who are enrolled or who are expected to enroll in a public school kindergarten class shall be screened for developmental readiness prior to entering such a class and prior to exiting the public school kindergarten.

The state of Louisiana is considering the passage of similar legislation.

Studies are showing that children deemed immature who are permitted to proceed against the recommendation of the developmental tests tend to get into more difficulty than those who are considered ready. It also appears that the introduction of a developmental placement program can substantially increase and improve grade averages. There follow single examples of each of these findings.

In a study conducted in Conval, New Hampshire, 300 students in grades four, five, and six were examined to determine whether there is a direct relationship between developmental level at the time of school entrance and subsequent school success.[15] A comparison was made between results and subsequent recommendations from a Gesell examination given prior to entrance into grade one, and the actual need for special services, retentions, and peer and school attitudes as the students progressed into the middle grades.

The developmental examination given to each of these students indicated whether they were ready to enter first grade. Since the school did not have a developmental placement program, these recommendations were *not* acted upon, and the children began first grade at the time the law allowed, ready or not. Results of the study showed that of those children who subsequently needed to repeat a grade, only three percent of the "readies" needed Chapter I help (a federally funded program for children functioning below the level of their peers). This compared to thirty-three percent of the "unreadies." Only six percent of the "readies" were referred to the local Children's Center for special help as compared to thirty-three percent of the "unreadies." Only ten percent of the "readies" were reported to have a poor relationship with their peers, while fifty-two percent of the "unreadies" were shown to have poor peer relations. And finally, only three percent of the "readies" were said to have a poor school attitude as contrasted with forty-five percent of the "unreadies."

It seems quite evident that if school policy had permitted "unready" children to wait an extra year before entering, the number of children in trouble could have been substantially reduced.

A second finding is that when developmental placement is used in a school district, grades tend to go up. One such example was reported by Ben Nelson of Oxford, New York.[16] The first developmental placement of kindergartners in his school occurred in the 1980–1981 school year. Thus 1980 scores reported by him were scores achieved by students *before* there was developmental placement. Scores earned in 1981 and after represent the results of developmental placement.

The following scores are from the Metropolitan Achievement Test and the Otis School Ability Test.

Table 1

Academic Scores Before and

After Developmental Placement

	1980	1981	1982	1983	1984
Second Grade					
Reading	2.6	2.9	2.6	2.9	3.2
Math	2.8	2.8	2.9	3.3	3.5
Language	2.6	2.6	2.9	3.0	3.6
Totals	2.6	2.8	2.6	3.0	3.4
Third Grade					
Reading	3.4	3.5	4.1	3.7	4.0
Math	4.2	4.3	4.1	4.0	4.3
Language	3.6	3.9	4.2	4.0	4.3
Totals	3.8	3.9	4.0	3.9	4.1

A grade of 2.6 means that the child is performing at the level of the statistically "average" second-grade student in the sixth month of the school year.

These reports are, needless to say, only two of the many positive indicators that come in to us from schools around the country. They suggest that careful developmental evaluation, and subsequent placement, *does* improve academic performance and reduce school difficulties. Teachers, especially, report that teaching a class of children who are all more or less at the same developmental level is far more effective, successful, and comfortable.

At Least Have Them on the Old Side

It is clear that we at Gesell prefer to have the time of school entrance determined by the child's behavior age, not his age in years. However, in those schools where some sort of developmental or other evaluation as to readiness is not available, we encourage parents to allow their children to be among the oldest in their classes rather than the youngest. It has been our experience that girls do best if fully five before they start kindergarten. Boys do best if fully five and a half. In first grade children are most successful when girls are fully six before they begin, boys six and a half.

Throughout the country, school teachers and school principals consistently tell us that they find the most failures among what are called "fall babies"; that is, children whose birthdays are in October, November, December, or even January, after starting kindergarten in September.

Recognizing the importance of having children on the older side before they start school, states are moving their cutoff date to or near September. According to the latest figures available, sixteen states have a cutoff date of September first or earlier, and five others have a date sometime in September. Eight more states have an October cutoff date. This makes a total of twenty-six states. Two others have a November date and six a December date. Parts of Pennsylvania and all of Connecticut have a January first date—this means that a child who is only four years and eight months of age is allowed to begin kindergarten.

Some states with late cutoff dates soften the blow by not mandating that a child start school until he is six or even seven years of age. Going in the other direction, Commissioner Tirozzi of Connecticut, one of the strong advocates of all-day kindergarten, has recommended (so far unsuccessfully) that the mandated starting age be five.

It does seem safe to say that in general mandating a later required starting date provides a safety net for the youngest children. And in general, when an entrance date requirement is changed in any state it is usually moved earlier, providing that, for the most part, children will be ever older before they are allowed to begin school.

Results from others' research also support the position that the older a child is, the more likely he is to be up to the demands of whatever grade he may be in. Marie Williams of Annandale, Virginia, evaluated 400 children, half of whom entered kindergarten when about five and a half, and half of whom entered before they were five. Her research demonstrated that the older children, as measured on the Metropolitan Readiness Test, were at significantly higher levels of readiness at the end of the kindergarten year. They also attained significantly higher levels of reading and math in fourth grade as measured on the Science Research Associates Achievement Tests (SRA).[17]

A study, "The Birthdate Effect," by Di Pasquale and others, tested out the thesis that children who begin school together but who differ in age by several months may also differ in readiness for schoolwork.[18] In Di Pasquale's study, 552 children from kindergarten through high school who had been referred for school difficulties to the Psychological Services in Ontario, Canada, were checked for birthday age. The calendar year was divided into six equal parts. The birthdays of the children were compiled to determine in which parts of the year they fell. There turned out to be a direct relationship between birthday month and amount of difficulty the child experienced. For the older children (born January and February), there were only seventy referrals. This number increased as one came to the younger children until there were 110 referrals for those born in September/October and the same number for those born November/December. This relationship was much stronger in boys than in girls.

An unpublished study from the three towns in Massachusetts, Dighton, Berkeley, and Rehoboth, was carried out in 1983.[19] It found that between the years 1968 and 1974, the percentage of schools with a September first dead-line increased in the state from 3.7 percent to 15.3 percent and was still increasing. These three towns compared the number of children under five by September to the number of children already five by September who were referred for special services.

Their finding was that, though certainly *some* of the older children were referred for special services, there were many more younger referrals. In Dighton there were twenty-five percent of the younger children referred as opposed to eleven percent of the older; in Berkeley there were fifty-two per-cent younger referrals, only thirty-five percent older; in Rehoboth fifty-one percent younger, thirty-three percent older. The average of all three towns was forty-three percent younger referrals, twenty-six percent older.

A poem written by Kay M. Innes, of Madison Heights, Michigan, a developmental coordinator at the Edmunson Elementary School, expresses the feelings of a too young boy. He is one of the many so-called fall babies who started school before he was ready to do so:

I'm a bright November boy,
School for me is not a joy.
How I dread to hear the bell,
How I pray for old Gesell.
Dr. Ilg please rescue me
From this shame and misery!

Teacher thinks I'm rather slow.
I just need more time to grow!
Next to me sits prissy Pearl
Teacher's "good" December girl.
Pearl just loves her A, B, C's,
Wants to learn to make her threes.
I prefer the trucks and water,
Teacher doesn't think I oughter.

Johnny's March, he really shines.
Colors well within the lines.
April Smith can print her name
In big round letters, all the same.
Teacher says that I don't try,

All I do is blink one eye.
She thinks that I'm not too bright,
I still mix my left and right!

"Teach" says I should listen more
And spend less time down on the floor.
I can sing, and march, and play,
I can paint, but not her way!
I made a person, red and blue
With lots of hair and buttons too!
It was good, but what the heck
All she said was "Where's the neck?"
Teacher's getting rather riled,
Thinks I am a stubborn child.
Hopes that I don't have a brother
Says she couldn't stand another!
Warns if I don't pay attention
She is thinking of retention.
That threat of hers it thrills me so
Then I would have more time to grow!

Teacher, young as I may be
I do know biology.
Birds and bees aren't celibate,
And as long as people mate
There will be November boys
Who look forward to school's joys.
Teacher, hurry to Gesell,
Don't make all their lives a Hell!

This chapter has covered children of many different ages, from infancy up into the elementary school ages, but the message for every age is the same. Children can function most effectively if parents and teachers are able and willing to recognize and respect each child's level of development, each child's individual timetable.

Our position with regard to human behavior is, as indicated, that behavior develops in a patterned way and, to a large extent, through a series of more or less predictable stages. These stages are highly similar from child to child, but each child reaches each stage at his own individual time. The sequence of stages is more or less invariable; the timing highly individual.

But whatever the timing, it is the person's own and, to a large extent, is biologically determined. To the best of our knowledge, efforts to push children to accelerated performance for which they are not ready, and to effect spectacular increases in intellectual achievement, have not been substantial or lasting.

References

1. Ames, Louise Bates, and Chase, Joan Ames. *Don't Push Your Preschooler,* rev. ed. New York: Harper & Row, 1980.

2. Article in the *New Haven Journal Courier,* November 6, 1984.

3. Ames, Louise Bates, Gillespie, Clyde, Haines, Jacqueline, and Ilg, Frances L. *The Gesell Institute's Child from One to Six.* New York: Harper & Row, 1979, pp. 174–176.

4. Ames, Louise Bates, and Ilg, Frances L. *Your One, Two, Three, Four, Five, Six* and *Seven Year Old.* (A series.) New York: Delacorte, 1976–1985.

5. Campbell, Bertha. Talk entitled "Historical Perspectives on the Issue." First Annual Early Childhood Symposium at Elmira College, Elmira, New York, August 15, 1984.

6. Mulrain, John, and Ames, Louise Bates. "Half Day for First Graders." *The Instructor,* February 1979, pp. 116, 118.

7. Gesell, Arnold. "The Measurement and Prediction of Mental Health." *Psychology Review, 34* (1927): 281.

8. Gesell, Arnold. "The Stability of Mental Growth Careers." In *National Society for the Study of Education 39th Yearbook,* 1940, p. 159.

9. Scarr, Sandra. *Mother Care, Other Care.* New York: Basic Books, 1984.

10. Gesell, Arnold. "Mental Hygiene and the Public School." *Hygiene, 3* (1919): 5.

11. Gesell, Arnold. "Kindergarten Control of School Entrance." *School and Society, 14,* no. 364 (1921): 560–563.

12. Ilg, Frances L., Ames, Louise Bates, and Apell, Richard J. "School Readiness as Evaluated by Gesell Developmental, Visual and Projective Tests." *Genetic Psychology Monographs, 71* (1965): 61–91.

13. Ilg, Frances L., and Ames, Louise Bates. *School Readiness.* New York: Harper & Row, 1964.

14. *Directory of Developmental Placement Programs,* rev. ed. New Haven, Conn.: Gesell Institute, 1985.

15. Unpublished study carried out by an Early Childhood Group in Conval, New Hampshire, 1976.

16. Nelson, Ben. Unpublished study from the schools of Oxford, New York, 1984.

17. Williams, Marie. Unpublished doctoral dissertation. George Peabody College for Teachers, Vanderbilt University, 1984.

18. Di Pasquale, Glenn, Moule, Allan D., and Flewelling, Robert. "The Birthdate Effect." *Journal of Learning Disabilities, 13,* 5 (May 1980): 234–238.

19. Unpublished study by a committee of teachers for the public schools of Rehoboth, Berkeley, and Dighton, Massachusetts, 1983.

By the Author

by Dr. Louise Bates Ames

Is Your Child in the Wrong Grade?, rev. ed. Rosemont, N.J.: Modern Learning Press, 1978.

Child Care and Development, rev. ed. New York: Lippincott, 1979.

coauthored by Dr. Ames

(With Gesell and Ilg) *Youth: The Years from Ten to Sixteen.* New York: Harper, 1956.

(With Ilg) *Parents Ask.* New York: Harper, 1962.

(With Metraux and Walker) *Adolescent Rorschach Responses,* rev. ed. New York: Brunner/Mazel, 1971.

(With Gillespie and Streff) *Stop School Failure.* New York: Harper & Row, 1972.

(With Metraux, Walker and Rodell) *Child Rorschach Responses,* rev. ed. New York: Brunner/Mazel, 1974.

(With Gesell, Ilg and Rodell) *Infant and Child in the Culture of Today,* rev. ed. New York: Harper & Row, 1974.

(With Gesell and Ilg) *The Child from Five to Ten,* rev. ed. New York: Harper & Row, 1976.

(With Haines and Ilg) *The Gesell Institute's Child from One to Six.* New York: Harper & Row, 1979.

(With Chase) *Don't Push Your Preschooler,* rev. ed. New York: Harper & Row, 1980.

(With Ilg et al.) *School Readiness,* rev. ed. New York: Harper & Row, 1981.

(With Ilg and Baker) *Child Behavior,* rev. ed. New York: Harper & Row, 1981.

(With Haber) *He Hit Me First: When Brothers and Sisters Fight.* New York: Dembner Books, 1982.

A Delacorte Publishing Company series with Ilg and Haber, from 1976 to 1985: *Your One Year Old, Your Two Year Old, Your Three Year Old, Your Four Year Old, Your Five Year Old, Your Six Year Old,* and *Your Seven Year Old.*

FITZHUGH DODSON

Meet the Author

Dr. Fitzhugh Dodson is recognized worldwide as one of the leading authorities on child raising, particularly in the area of discipline. His approach is positive, developmentally geared to the stage of the child, and practical.

Dr. Dodson's training reflects his intellect and versatility. He graduated cum laude from Johns Hopkins University and magna cum laude from Yale. Then he did a year of graduate work at the Union Seminary and Columbia University, studying religion at Union Seminary and television and radio at Columbia. He also spent a year at Lewis and Clark College studying "nothing but psychology."

A little-known fact is that Dr. Dodson was a minister for several years before turning to psychology. He has been working in private practice for over twenty years in Redondo Beach, counseling thousands of parents and children, while helping raise three of his own children at home.

Dr. Dodson has written ten books, five of which have been best sellers. Most of them have been translated into a number of foreign languages. He is featured in Who's Who in the West.

The major theorists that have influenced his thinking are Sigmund Freud, Erik Erikson, Carl Rogers, B. F. Skinner, and Fritz Perls. Probably more than any of these, he adds, are the magic three—Robin, Randy, and Rusty, his children.

6

HOW TO DISCIPLINE EFFECTIVELY

STRATEGIES FOR MOTIVATING
POSITIVE BEHAVIOR
FITZHUGH DODSON, PH.D.

Contrary to popular opinion, the word "discipline" does not mean to threaten, hurt, humiliate, or punish. When I hear people say things like "That kid needs more discipline—with a paddle or the back of a hand," I know they just don't understand the concept. Discipline means "to teach," and teaching is something that parents are doing all the time whether they are aware of it or not. When you discipline a child, you are teaching him to behave constructively (to be considerate of others' feelings, to be responsible for himself, to express his feelings assertively) and not engage in unacceptable behavior.

The *main* principle of teaching children desirable behavior is a very simple one, and I have never understood why parents and school teachers aren't given this information as part of their preparation for working with young people. The idea is that whenever you see a child behave in a way that is good—behavior that is not unfriendly or otherwise disagreeable—you reward that child for his good behavior. You praise his actions or give him a smile, a hug, or a friendly pat on the shoulder. You do something to indicate that you think he is a splendid little person.

This simple process does wonders for a child's behavior! For example, let's look at a scene with a mother and two children—a scenario that you will find duplicated in millions of department stores all over the United States. Picture a four-year-old boy, his two-year-old brother, and their mother. First recognize what the four-year-old is *not* doing. He is not running up and down the aisles. He is not pulling toys off the shelves with a crash. He is not kicking or biting his brother. And what is his reward from his mother for his good behavior? Does his mother hug him or kiss him or praise his behavior? No. She ignores him. She goes on with her shopping, grateful for a few minutes of peace and quiet.

Now let's suppose his behavior changes. He argues with his little brother and pushes him. He starts running up and down the aisles, pulling toys down to the floor. His mother immediately gives him some attention. She scolds him or smacks him or gives him some other very negative response. When she does this, without knowing it, she is breaking "The Law of the Soggy Potato Chip."

The Law of the Soggy Potato Chip

The Law of the Soggy Potato Chip is very simple: A child naturally prefers a fresh crisp potato chip to a soggy one. But if the only potato chip the child can get is soggy, he will take it. A soggy potato chip is better than no potato chip.

It's the same with children and behavior. A child ordinarily wants positive attention from his parents. But if the only attention he can get is negative, he will settle for that because even a negative response is better than none at all.

Parents intensify sibling rivalry by offering soggy potato chips when their children are fighting. When siblings play quietly and cooperatively, their parents ignore them, but when they start fighting, the parents are right in there fighting with them to teach them to stop fighting. The logic is incredible when you think about it!

To teach children to get along with each other, ignore them when they are fighting. Ignore the negative behavior unless:

1. It might harm either child.

2. It destroys property.

3. It makes the parent feel unduly stressed.

The Positive Reward System

It's far more constructive to reward children with positive attention when they are behaving well. Parents pay most attention to their children when they misbehave. And that only makes them misbehave more, because they've learned that's how they can get the attention they crave. Positive attention will reverse most misbehavior.

Developing Rapport

In order for the positive reward system to work, rapport is crucial. Rapport is that feeling of warmth and harmony between two people, a feeling that you're on the same wavelength with someone, a feeling of nearness with him.

It's easy for a parent to build rapport with a child from birth, while cuddling, feeding, and talking warmly with him. Then, when the child is past the infancy stage, it's important for the parent and child to spend time doing things together in order for that nice feeling of rapport to continue. Unfortunately, not many parents do that. Too much of the interaction between parents and children destroys rapport. Their conversations aren't conversations at all: "Ruthie, get your hands off that bookcase!" "Mitch, how many times do I have to tell you to stop pestering your sister?" and so on. Their conversations consist of directions, commands, accusations, and other verbal artillery with which the parent pushes the child around.

To maintain a good rapport, the parent can think of things to do with the child that they both enjoy—activities that don't require anything from the child except to have fun with his parent.

When my children were young, I used to take them on little trips around the neighborhood. We went to see things like the fire station, the police station, and a newspaper press in action. The children still remember those trips with pleasure.

Rapport building means relating with the child at his own level. One great way to interact is to have periodic "story sessions" in which the parent and child take turns sharing stories about themselves. The parent can talk about something interesting or funny that happened to him in his youth. Children especially enjoy hearing parents talk about something he did when he was young that wasn't very smart, something the child can identify with and laugh about. That often encourages the child to tell things about himself. Over a period of time, these occasional story sessions can promote a very good feeling between parent and child.

A parent who feels rapport with a child will be much more successful in teaching or disciplining him. Good rapport helps build the child's self-confidence because it helps him to see himself in a very positive light.

Developing Trust

An important aspect of rapport building is creating a sense of trust. Trust comes from leveling with your child, telling him what to expect from you, even if it causes him to be temporarily angry or scared. For example, when you leave your child with a baby-sitter, tell him when and where you are going and when you will be back. You might think that by slipping out unnoticed you're sparing your child trauma. You're only sparing yourself from having to listen to his cries. By being honest with your child, you are trading temporary anxiety for long-term confidence.

When you say something will or won't hurt, be accurate, to the best of your knowledge. If you say an injection will feel like a mosquito bite but it feels more like a hornet's sting, later on your opinions about important issues may not have much credence. Trust also means keeping your word. When you say you will do something, it's important for your child to know that you will follow through if you possibly can.

Setting Goals for Behavior

To make the positive reward system work most effectively, you need to set simple goals for the child's behavior. This means making a list:

1. Actions of the child that you approve of.
2. Actions that you wish he were doing less of.
3. Actions you want him to do more of.

For instance, let's take Erin, a normally active seven-year-old. If she plays quietly with her toys or with her siblings, these are actions to be encouraged. So the parent gives her a pat on the shoulder, a smile, or a word of appreciation for her positive behavior. When the child is whining instead of being cooperative, she does not get that approval. She gets no attention at all, because this behavior is on the "not wanted" list. And if the parent is interested in getting the child to help out more in the house, she watches to see when the child is doing just that, and then gives the child a smile to let her know that she approves of her behavior. It's important to know what motivates each child. There are no universally acceptable rewards for everyone—something that pleases one child will not necessarily please another.

The parent doesn't have to make a big deal out of the process, but it does require forethought. She first decides what behavior is beneficial to the child and reinforces it. Then she decides which behavior she would *not* reward the child for, so that behavior would gradually be extinguished.

Of course, this preparation takes time and effort, but think of all the aggravation the parent saves by not engaging in negative interactions like nagging and threats. Parents generally agree that the few minutes of effort expended ahead of time are worth the positive behavior that's likely to result.

Once the parent gets the hang of this system, it's quite easy. Basically, what she is doing is responding to desirable behavior and giving positive attention as soon as the child is behaving in a way that she wants to reinforce. (It works best when the reinforcement is given immediately after the behavior you want to encourage, but that may not always be possible.)

At the same time the parent is ignoring the undesirable behavior (not the really annoying or *bad* behavior—these may have to be handled with one of the methods described in the rest of the chapter). The parent needn't give a reward for absolutely everything good the child does, but at first the rewards should be frequent.

Very soon the child will need a response only once in a while because he'll have learned to feel good about doing well. He now *knows* his behavior has the parent's approval and the parent doesn't have to reinforce him for it every time. After a while, occasional reinforcement is all the child needs—or even wants. The more effective the positive reward system is, the less negative behavior there will be to deal with.

A parent can set up a regular program of rewards to get things going. Depending on the age of the child, he could earn happy faces on a chart, or pennies, or get to choose the next game to play each time he achieves a desired behavior.

Some people might say that giving rewards for good behavior is bribing the child, but they would be wrong. A bribe is a reward given to influence someone to do something illegal or immoral. Hanging up clothes and putting toys away are not illegal or immoral activities. They are perfectly fine, and you want the child to do them. I like to call these rewards the "Wages of Childhood."

Contracting

Working for wages is a one-way system in which the parent decides what behavior will be rewarded; the child has no say in it. But with young people who have developed the ability to make decisions, you can use an even more motivating technique we call "contracting." In contracting, the child does have a say about what he'll do to get a particular reward. Both the child and parent promise to do one thing in exchange for something from the other. The child is being trained in negotiation, since he and his parent work out a mutual agreement about the contract. It's important to take the time to work out an exchange that seems fair to both of you. When the child has been involved in the decision making and feels that the contract benefits him, he has a stake in making it work, and everyone wins. He won't look for opportunities to undermine the agreement.

For example, a child with behavior problems might be willing to work on a contract to improve them. A child who takes food from other people's plates at the dinner table might get dessert for changing his behavior and eating from only his own plate. A child who clears the table after each meal for a week, without needing to be reminded, could get the opportunity to bake cookies with some friends. Or the child who is cooperative with a new baby-sitter might be reinforced with a special surprise under his pillow the next morning. Contracting is used in addition to the positive reward system.

It's wonderful to begin teaching contracting early because then the child will have facility with the system by the time he's a teen-ager. Contracting is a valuable tool that saves a great deal of arguing, since the participants have mutually agreed on the contract. Just be sure to give the payoff *after* the child has done something positive, not beforehand. (If you give it away ahead of time and your child doesn't keep his promise, where do you go from there?) But don't be thrown by griping. Your child has a right to complain while he's carrying out his part of the contract. He doesn't have to like it, he just has to *do* it.

Sometimes the parent promises a payoff (like going on a trip or getting a bike) that is to be given in the future. Then it's important to use short-term, tangible reinforcers to keep the child aware of his progress. (The same technique works well for a goal that is complicated or difficult to master.) Children often enjoy stickers or coupons that could be traded in for the sought-after reward. Reinforce the small steps toward the goal to help him see his progress; otherwise the goal can seem quite unattainable. This also lessens the parent's temptation to withdraw the reward at the end of a rough day and throw away many days of concerted effort.

For effective contracting, follow the guidelines below:

1. Watch your timing. When family members are angry, suggest waiting until tempers cool down before working out a contract. That helps to make the decision process more rational and less emotional.

2. Stay away from generalizations—be concrete. (Instead of asking your child to "be neater," ask him to "put all of the toys in the toy box before going to bed.")

3. Make a semipermanent record of the agreement. (For young children a tape recording or a picture chart can be very effective. Older children can write down the steps of the plan. Then both of you can sign the contract.)

4. Enhance your chances for success with small steps appropriate to the child's level of maturity. Don't overwhelm him by demanding major behavioral changes. (For example, ask a two-year-old child to put out the placemats each night before dinner rather than ask him to set the entire table.)

5. Stress reward, not failure. Keep the child focused on working *toward* a goal rather than forfeiting points.

6. Follow through on your end of the bargain promptly.

Time-Out

One of the most effective methods of teaching children to avoid undesirable behavior is called Time-Out. When a child is being really disruptive—hitting other children, breaking things, or throwing food—don't bother punishing. Remember, it's a waste of time to punish children and expect that it will do them any good. In addition, punishing teaches children to be sneaky and to retaliate, rather than to cooperate.

A Time-Out is simple but effective. You use it when the child is in the midst of disruptive behavior. Begin by specifying just what it is that is unacceptable. Say something like "Tom, you keep hitting David and you need a Time-Out. I'll set the timer for five minutes. Go to your room until the buzzer rings." The idea is to put five minutes of physical distance between the child and his problem. He can't punch his brother if he's somewhere else. And five minutes of isolation from his family or friends is not the same thing as negative attention. It's definitely not a reward. It's a time to calm down. (In fact,

Time-Out is also beneficial to the parent, giving the adult a chance to gain some self-control before dealing with the child.)

If your child refuses to go to his room, escort him there. And unless he's being destructive, don't legislate what goes on in that room. That could lead to a power struggle. If he complains or whines from his room, ignore him. If you reinforce his bid for attention, you'll negate the purpose of his Time-Out. Just give him time to be by himself.

At the end of the time, don't make a big deal out of it. Simply say, "Time is up" or let your child respond to the ringing of the timer. If he resumes his negative behavior, escort him back into his room for another Time-Out. If your child runs right out again, then you'll have to be very firm with him. You might even need to lock the door to his room for those five minutes of Time-Out.

I know that sounds cruel, but think how much crueler it is to let a child have his own way whenever he wants it, to let him grow up without respect for authority, and to expect that his wishes will be granted no matter what they are. How successful do you think his relationships will be in the future? Remember, I'm *not* talking about isolating him for hours, just five minutes. The beauty of this system is that once a child is accustomed to the routine of a Time-Out, he generally accepts the inevitability of it.

Don't let the presence of other people interfere with your ability to be effective. If your child is behaving poorly when you're at a friend's house, don't let him take advantage of the situation. Find a room where he can be alone and follow through as if you were in your own home. For example, if your three-year-old child keeps pinching his friend's baby sister, first take him into another room to remove him from his audience and then state, "You are pinching Laura and you need a Time-Out. Wait in the family room (hall, extra bedroom) for five minutes. I'll tell you when to come out."

You might have to override some embarrassment in front of others if they disagree with your methods. Their rules might be different from yours, but *you* have a right to follow through with what works best for *your* child as long as you are there to supervise. It might help to remember that people have different ideas about what works for children and that you don't necessarily have to agree with anyone else's. If you are confident that what you're doing is best for your child, you'll be better able to follow through whether you're home, at a friend's home, or at a store.

If the behavior is serious, you might want to remove your child for the rest of the day. If your two-year-old son bit his friend's hand, and after a Time-Out he resumed the biting, take him home immediately. Though you'll have to cope with an unhappy child for a while, you're teaching him that biting puts an end to socializing. That message should have a strong impact!

Reverse Time-Out

For those children who are not mature enough to handle a Time-Out, the parent might try a Reverse Time-Out. That is where the parent puts space between herself and the child by going into another room to get away from the whining, sulking, yelling, kicking, or otherwise disagreeable behavior. Going into your bedroom or bathroom and turning on a radio does wonders to block out annoying noises. The benefit to you is obvious—you're not driven bananas by the behavior, because you don't see or hear it.

When your child calms down, rejoin him. But if the annoying behavior continues, remove yourself again. (Don't *threaten* to leave, just *do* it.) Stay on the premises, though, so he doesn't feel abandoned. You're not rejecting him, you're just refusing to be affected by his negative behavior.

Of course, if your child is in danger of hurting himself or others, physically restrain him. For example, when a child is standing with a raised hand tightly wrapped around a toy truck, ready to throw it at a playmate, remove the truck while saying firmly, "Trucks are for playing, not for throwing!" First stop the damage from occurring. Then discuss his behavior.

Environmental Control

Another approach to disciplining the young child is called environmental control. You wouldn't put a lively Rhesus monkey in a living room full of breakable knickknacks and expect the monkey to stay quiet and not knock anything over. The living room environment isn't suited to a monkey! But often we put our small children in environments that are really suitable only for adults. We leave out fragile, expensive items and then become incensed when toddlers break them.

Too often when dealing with young children we don't give much thought to the size of the environment, the materials in it, or the length of time we expect them to be there.

I recently saw an example of lack of environmental control at a football game that was pretty typical of what goes on in families. A parent slapped his two-year-old because the child was standing on his seat, facing backward, throwing popcorn at the people behind him. Since a two-year-old has a short attention span, and he certainly couldn't understand what was happening on the football field (or even *see* the field), the father set the stage for trouble by taking him to the game in the first place. The father ought to have thought about what the afternoon would be like for his child. He would have realized that he was practically programming his son for boredom and frustration, which would eventually result in disruptive behavior.

After all, would that father have enjoyed being forced to sit behind people who were twice as tall as he was for an all-day technical conference on a topic that was not relevant, understandable, or interesting to him?

Another way to implement environmental control is to prepare ahead of time for periods when your child has low coping reserve. Reduce environmental stress when your child is ill, is suffering prolonged or acute tension, or is overtired (especially when suffering the aftereffects of a sleep-over at a friend's house). In addition, incorporate environmental control into your daily routines. The late afternoon hours are often a period of high stress–low energy where parents and children tend to overreact to each other. Each afternoon fortify your children with healthy snacks, quiet activity, and brief periods of positive reinforcement to help them cope until dinner. (It wouldn't hurt to do the same for yourself.)

Reducing Sibling Rivalry

Environmental control can also do wonders to reduce sibling rivalry in families. If your children have difficulty being with each other for more than two minutes at a time, minimize their time together. Even friends, whose relationships are based on choice and compatibility, often have trouble interacting for long periods. Can you imagine how awful it must be for siblings who don't get along (they're at different life stages and have different personalities and interests) to be subjected to each other for hours on end? When you force them to be together for extended periods, you're intensifying their negative feelings, increasing their opportunities for conflict.

When you want to plan a special family day together but you have kids who spend much of their time teasing, kicking, and name calling, use environmental control to create a positive emotional environment for the family. Even though you might wish that you could spend a blissful day together as a happy family unit, realistically everyone's day might be more enjoyable if you allow each child to invite a friend.

When families go on trips, parents often put kids in the back seats of the car for long hours with the expectation that they'll be pleasant and cooperative. Then when the children begin whining and being generally difficult, parents yell at them for being unappreciative.

It's often easier to take a few minutes to prepare for success than to suffer the consequences of lack of foresight. Before the trip, brainstorm for ideas to break the monotony. You might bring tape recorders and age-appropriate toys. Help the children create visual or word games to turn the drive into an adventure. Give them maps that you've created ahead of time and ask them to help find landmarks to visit along the way. Look at the map together to decide when to take "pit stops." All of these efforts give them a sense of control, excitement, and self-respect.

Basically, what parents want to do is stop the fighting and correct the problems. In doing this, parents often become referees, taking sides and meting out justice. That doesn't give their children the opportunity to learn to resolve their own differences and develop their problem-solving skills. In addition, it often actually ruins their fun. Most of us can remember ourselves, as children, getting upset with a parent for stopping a good fight in process. It's frustrating to be left dangling in the middle of a conflict just because a parent doesn't like the commotion. Even worse, the parents often make arbitrary assumptions about who is at fault during a fight. When a parent repeatedly blames one child, the child feels the pain of the injustice. Remember that both children are usually participants to some degree. The "picked on" child might be using his vulnerability to get the other child into trouble. Keep in mind that under normal circumstances a child has the option to leave if he doesn't want to be part of the action. And, of course, if the parent doesn't want to listen to the bickering, she can ask them to continue fighting in another area of the house or she can remove herself from the chaos.

Sibling rivalry could also be reduced if parents respected each child's need for privacy. If they are fortunate enough to have their own bedrooms, it would be helpful for the older child to have a lock for his door to protect his belongings from a destructive younger sibling. If they have to share a room, you might use a room divider (bookcases or a folding screen) to give them a feeling of privacy. Provide each child with a cabinet or drawer that can be locked to keep his special items intact. Then let them decide which toys are for sharing and which are to be kept under lock and key for personal use.

One common complaint I hear from parents is, "Each of my children thinks I favor the other one. They are jealous about *everything*—who got more dessert, who got served first, or even who got the last good-night kiss." These parents work hard to convince their children that they are loved equally, but their concern tends to escalate their children's demands for justice. The parents don't realize that they're reinforcing their children's concerns by demonstrating that their fears are real. There's an obvious payoff here. The children have the power to keep their parents constantly working at proving equal loyalty and love.

Children need to know that they're loved "uniquely," not "equally." Love cannot be measured and balanced. Sometimes one child's needs are greater than another's at a particular time, but that doesn't mean that he's loved more. Instead, give each child support, love, and attention without associating your behavior toward him with your behavior toward another child. Most important, don't compare children. Respect their uniqueness!

FITZHUGH DODSON, PH.D.   159

When you're first setting out to correct misbehavior, it's important to realize that, for a while, the children will expect that everyone will continue to play their game. The family has established a pattern that will be difficult to break. It's up to the parents to look for creative ways to change the rules. For example, next time a parent is about to serve dessert, she would be wise to announce that she has some cake, but that she doesn't know if she should serve it, because in the past she's realized that giving them cake has created problems. She then might ask the children to decide how to work things out ahead of time so there will be no sad faces, whining, or fighting when the cake is served.

The children could decide that one of them would cut the cake and the other could choose which piece would be his, or that the parent could cut the cake, and they would enjoy it without comparisons. Whatever the decision, she needs to stop giving them soggy potato chips.

Another problem area for parents with more than one child is tattling. The younger one often thinks it's his job to "tell" on his big brother. Parents hear everything from "He didn't take a long enough bath" to "She didn't brush her hair." Parents have traditionally told children that it is babyish to tattle and that they must stop, but that doesn't stop children from reporting stories in minute detail to their parents.

Instead, stop giving children payoffs for their news bulletins. Let them know that unless the event (or nonevent) could be dangerous, you really don't want to hear about it. When the child loses his payoff, he won't waste his effort. Once again, refuse to give him soggy potato chips—don't reinforce the negative behavior.

Of course, if sibling rivalry is severe, it's important to look at what needs of each child are not being met. The constant fighting might be a way of asking for more attention or it may be a symptom of other stresses. Sometimes a younger sibling is just the most accessible target for a child's anger or frustration. In that case, the older child needs to learn more effective ways to communicate his frustrations and concerns so they can be dealt with appropriately.

Getting back to environmental control, you can begin even before your second baby is born to think about creating a healthy psychological environment to nurture a positive sibling relationship. Parents often underestimate the effect of a new baby on an older sibling.

To appreciate the trauma that children go through with the adjustment to a new sibling, picture that you are a wife of fifteen years. Your husband announces to you with pride, "Dear, I love you very much—so much, in fact, that I have decided to share some of my love with a new young bride, Roxanne. She'll live with us and I'll be with her Mondays, Wednesdays, and Fridays, and with you on Tuesdays and Thursdays. Sundays will be up for grabs. When she comes home I want you to treat her nicely, as a mature sister should. Let's go look through your bedroom furniture, clothes, and jewelry to find things for you to give her." You watch your treasures being taken from you to give to an intruder.

Later, when he returns with his new sweetheart, friends and family gather at the house to meet her. He, of course, holds *her* on his lap. After the guests finish "oohing" and "ahhing" over his new wife, giving her presents, they comment on how mature you are becoming or compliment you on your lovely new shoes. Imagine what that would do to your self-concept, your feelings toward Roxanne, and your love for your spouse!

You will not be able to eliminate your firstborn's stress when a newborn arrives on the scene, but you can reduce it.

1. Well before the birth of your new baby, prepare your first child, William, for his new sibling and the changes the birth will make in his life. Let him know that babies take a great deal of time and attention and that you need him to tell you when he is feeling left out. Assure him that he will never lose his place as your first, that he will always be the big brother.

2. If it is necessary to move your firstborn from a crib to a bed or change his room, do it well before the birth of the new baby. He'll have enough adjustments without having to lose his basic security at the same time.

3. Before going into the hospital, buy surprise gifts and hide them all over the house or apartment.

4. When you are at the hospital, phone your older child and announce that this is "William Week," to celebrate his becoming an older brother. To begin the celebration, explain that you have hidden a gift in a specific place, and that you will hold the line until he finds it. After he returns to the phone with his present, talk about the gift, and your positive feelings for him. Continue this each day until you arrive home.

5. Have Dad take home pictures of you waving, blowing a kiss, or otherwise signifying that you still love your big boy.

6. If the hospital allows visits, have someone bring William to the hospital to help him feel a part of the action.

7. When you take the baby home, bring a special gift from the new baby to William to honor her big brother. If at all possible, have help available (not to take care of William, but to take care of the new baby) so you can reassure William with your presence that your love for him is as strong as ever. (It would be wonderful if fathers could get paternity leave for a short while to help ease the transition during this chaotic, exhausting period.)

8. Invite him (don't push him) to help you care for the new baby.

9. Have small gifts available for William so that when thoughtless people come to enjoy your new arrival, he will have a "big brother" gift from each of them as well.

10. Reinforce your son for the grown-up things he can do and offer him big-brother privileges to make the most of his new status.

11. Bring out William's infant pictures to help him understand that he once entered the family as a special baby, too.

12. Allow him to sample baby toys and other paraphernalia—pacifiers, bottles, toys, for example. The novelty will soon wear off.

Sibling rivalry is not a sign of parenting failure. When there is more than one child in a family, it's normal for them to argue, fight, and resent each other at times. In the process they learn to share, communicate, and deal with anger—skills that will help them prepare for other relationships in the future. Environmental control doesn't eliminate sibling rivalry. It helps provide a loving, secure environment for each child to grow in, minimizing conflict.

Securities

Some parents control their children's environment inappropriately. They hide or throw away their child's pacifier, bottle, favorite stuffed animal, or special blanket when it is still a very important part of his life. They see "safeties" as signs of immaturity or emotional weakness, and are embarrassed to have their friends or family members think the child is insecure. These reassurers are a problem only for parents.

Relax. How many adults have you seen walking around sucking on pacifiers, drinking from baby bottles, or carrying stuffed animals? People who grow up with childhood fetishes are generally the ones who suffered denial as children, not the ones who were allowed to satisfy their needs. Your child knows how long he needs his security symbol. When he doesn't need it anymore, he'll give it up on his own.

Offer suggestions for lessening his dependency on objects only when your child indicates that it's a problem for *him* and that he'd like some help with it. After all, in this stress-filled world it would be great if some adults had some "safeties" to hold on to of their own.

Communication

My favorite form of discipline is to teach children to communicate their feelings, both positive and negative, so they won't bottle them up inside. When a child learns to express his feelings verbally, then others know what is bothering him. Once you know what the problem is, you can deal with the issues rather than simply wonder about his moodiness or endure his miserable, aggressive behavior.

Children often fear their own anger because they feel guilty about the intensity of their negative feelings toward people they care about. They hold their anger inside because they're afraid that their parents would stop loving them if they were aware of the strength of their feelings. Children need to understand that love and anger are not opposites. They are both signs of caring.

Teach children how to face anger as a normal part of healthy relationships. Help them talk about feelings and express needs in a way that doesn't hurt them or others. When children aren't allowed to express feelings, the emotions don't go away. They eat at the child, wearing down his vulnerable areas. Children who hold back anger often experience nervous tics, stomach pains, asthma, skin rashes, headaches, or other signs of tension.

First teach children to release negative emotions physically through safe outlets—hitting a pillow or a punching bag, dancing an angry dance, painting an angry picture, or using puppets to communicate angry words. After they learn to acknowledge the anger and release it constructively, it is easier for them to deal with their emotions.

Many adults are just grown-up children who have not yet learned to communicate their negative feelings appropriately. They hold them in and then later nitpick or blow up over something small that has nothing to do with the issue. Or they use passive-aggressive behavior, promising to do something and then claiming to have "forgotten" to do it rather than saying "no" in the first place in order to frustrate a spouse, a coworker, or a friend. Others explode in anger, hitting below the belt as they hurt another physically or emotionally. When people are unable to communicate feelings without attacking, they aren't able to explore and resolve problems.

Feedback

One of the finest gifts we can give our children is teaching them to identify their feelings and express them assertively in a positive, nonthreatening way. The most effective method for helping children get in touch with their feelings is to use a technique called Feedback. When you use Feedback, you listen for the feelings, not just the words. Then you check with the child to see if what you *heard* is indeed what he intended to say.

"Listening" and merely "hearing" what's being said are two different things. A child wants to know that you really appreciate what he is trying to express and that you're willing to look at the problem from *his* perspective, taking his feelings seriously. That doesn't mean that you necessarily *agree* with what he says. It just means that you are willing to get into his world and understand him. And, in the process, you are helping him learn to get in touch with those feelings and express them to others. In using Feedback, do three simple things:

1. Listen carefully.

2. Try to picture in your own mind what it is the child is expressing.

3. Feed back to him, in your words, the feelings you have heard.

Rather than simply parroting back his words, "decode" his message, putting what the child has said into your own words to check out whether your perception is accurate. If you're wrong, he'll correct you. At least he'll know you're trying to understand him. If you're right, he'll appreciate that you're on the same wavelength and he'll feel understood. You avoid a common problem many people experience when they find themselves talking past each other. They fight about separate issues, never quite connecting.

If a child has just flunked a word test and says, "I'm just dumb! I hate it!" don't simply parrot back: "You think you're just dumb! You hate word lists!" Or lecture: "You have no appreciation for the value of education," or push him with "You can do them. You have to study more. Just try!"

Instead, decode his message: "You're feeling frustrated with those long lists of words and you wonder how you'll ever be able to remember them all!" When you empathize with him, he feels that you're on his team and he's more likely to express his feelings to you another time. He'll also be more receptive to any suggestions you might have.

Too often parents jump right in and tell him why he's wrong, try to talk him out of his feelings, or explain that he has no right to them. But they really don't *hear* the feelings behind his words.

The hardest challenge in using Feedback is when the child says those three painful words, "I hate you!" You become flooded with images of the long hours in labor, the nights you paced the floor in worry over him, and the times you put aside your own interests in favor of his. Don't sink to his level and spit back words that are just as hostile. Instead, respond to his sense of frustration: "You are feeling left out because I am spending more time with the baby than I am with you." You're likely to see his body tension melt as he recognizes that you understand his sadness. All feelings (both positive and negative) are okay. It's *behavior* that sometimes requires limiting. For example, it's okay for him to be angry with the baby, but it's not okay for him to kick her.

Feedback is a powerful skill that reduces his tension by giving him a productive outlet for his emotions. Once he senses that you understand his feelings, he'll be better able to listen to what you have to say.

I Messages

There are also times when it's important for you to communicate how *you* feel. When you are upset, you can communicate your concerns, without blaming your child, by using I Messages.

When parents are angry, they usually communicate in You Messages: "You left the milk out overnight again" or "You never come home on time." You Messages are judgmental and lead to defensiveness in the child.

To give an I Message, relate how you feel about his behavior, describing the effect that behavior had on you. Example: "When you . . . (go to your friend's house without calling), I feel . . . (concerned) because . . . (I don't know if you're okay)." I Messages preserve the child's integrity while honestly and openly communicating your feelings.

Note the difference between an I Message, "When there is so much commotion, it is difficult for me to hear Aunt Suzanne on the telephone" and a You Message, "You're being obnoxious and babyish!" By using I Messages, you are teaching your child skills that will help him communicate his own anger without putting others down.

These two discipline techniques (Feedback and I Messages) are powerful tools that strengthen relationships by keeping communication lines open. When I called them my favorite *discipline* techniques, it probably sounded confusing. By now, though, you probably understand the difference between discipline and punishment. The focus is on what the child learns from your method rather than on the amount of pain it creates for him.

Spanking

In some homes parents are still using spanking as their standard child-training method. Those in charge seem to feel that this teaches respect. What it teaches is far from respect—anger, resentment, and even hate.

Hitting might get a child to do what you want him to do. But what is he learning about self-discipline? Nothing very constructive. Since parents are fallible human beings, we can forgive ourselves for losing our tempers and spanking our child with an open hand (never a closed fist, paddle, or belt. That's child abuse!). But we need to recognize that this is not the best way to handle the situation.

Toilet Training

One important issue in discipline is respecting the child's level of maturity in being able to learn a particular task. This is especially crucial where toilet training is concerned. Learning to take control of their body functions is a skill that children can take pride in mastering. Unfortunately some parents turn it into a battle of wills. Timing is of prime importance—not the grandparents' or the neighbors', but your child's. Wait for your child to have the physical maturity to be able to master this complicated task. I'd suggest starting when he is approximately two years old.

The best technique for toilet training is modeling. Take your child into the bathroom with you, and as you go in your "big potty," comment on how big people do it this way.

If you have a little potty nearby, eventually your child will probably want to follow suit and demonstrate his grown-up behavior, too. With a portable potty, the child has a greater sense of control than with the kind that fits on the regular toilet because he can get on and off without help.

Some children enjoy emptying their creations into the big toilet. Be cautious about flushing, though. Sometimes the noise and rapid disappearance of his valued "prize" is frightening. Often children find it easier for parents to do the flushing after they've left the bathroom, while others would rather do it themselves.

When he is just learning his new skills, let him spend time around the house dressed only in training pants and a shirt, so he can react quickly to nature's call without needing your assistance. When you take him out, let him wear clothes that are easy to pull up and down so he can get to his training pants easily. Coveralls are frustrating for the trainee.

A warm, caring, supportive attitude is crucial! Be prepared for mishaps periodically, especially when he is busy, excited, or under stress. He needs to know that you realize that he is making an effort. Treat his feces and urine as natural, not as dirty and disgusting. They are his body's natural byproducts.

Begin by teaching words for what your child is doing. When you watch him getting red in the face, say, "Jerry is having a B.M. in his diaper." Soon he'll tell you when he is "doing it." Finally, he'll tell you that he is about to have a movement so you can help him orchestrate his performance (hold back, run to the bathroom, pull down his pants, sit on the seat, release). It certainly is a complicated skill!

It is only when toilet training is too intense and punitive that it turns into an unnecessary power struggle. Once again, avoid soggy potato chips! Above all, recognize that toilet training is the child's responsibility and that, as a parent, your job is merely to facilitate his learning.

Nighttime Wetting

Sleeping control of the bladder can be established only after two conditions are met. First, your child must have learned through daytime control to respond to tension in his bladder by tightening his sphincter muscles. Second, he must have learned to keep his sphincters closed without waking up. Naturally this is going to make nighttime control more difficult than daytime control, so it will take longer.

What should the parent do to establish nighttime control? Absolutely nothing! The natural maturing of the child's bladder plus the daytime control he has learned will take care of the situation sooner or later. If the child wakes up in the middle of the night with a wet bed, just change the bedding and say to him warmly, "Next time maybe you'll stay dry all night" or "Next time maybe you'll wake up in time to go to the toilet."

At five years of age, approximately fifteen percent of children will have some bedwetting, at six years of age, approximately ten percent will wet some of the time. The important issue is that your child know that you understand that he can't help wetting the bed because he's asleep, but if he wakes up dry, reinforce him for his success.

When your child is interested in staying dry through the night, let him sleep in underpants, not diapers. Diapers make him feel like a baby and they prevent him from feeling himself urinating. (You can protect the bed with waterproof pads under the sheets.)

If the bedwetting persists and becomes a real problem, consult a specialist.

Summary

Being a competent parent means having a number of viable alternative methods for disciplining (or teaching) your child. Effective discipline can take the form of:

- Positive Reward System
- Modeling

- Environmental Control

- Contracting

- Rapport Building

- Time-Out

- Reverse Time-Out

- Communication Skills (Feedback, I Messages)

In making your choice, it's crucial to respect the maturity level of your child.

Before I close, I must describe some fascinating research. A few years ago two psychologists in Tennessee did an innovative school study. They had the school take the really disruptive fifth-grade children and put them all into the same class. Two teachers were assigned to the room, under the psychologists' guidance. Every time any of the students did something well, even if it was only sitting in his chair for six seconds, one of the teachers would say, "Claire, that's wonderful—you sat still in your chair for six whole seconds." At the end of the first week, the teachers reported that class behavior had improved greatly, except for two of the children, Arthur and Alex. "They're such little monsters we couldn't find anything good to say about them the whole week!"

The psychologists said, "Next week don't worry about praising something they've done. When you get a chance, just randomly look over at one of the boys and say, 'It's nice to have you here.' "

Believe it or not, it worked! Just having their presence acknowledged in a positive way calmed them down and improved their behavior. What's just as exciting, the teachers learned to focus their attention on positive behavior.

The results of this experiment have far-reaching implications for parents. When a parent trains himself to tune in to his children's strengths rather than on what needs to be corrected, the child tends to respond positively to the appreciation. And when the child's behavior improves, the parent tends to enjoy him more and interact more positively and lovingly with him. A wonderful cycle is set in motion!

By the Author

for parents about their children

How To Parent. New York: Signet Press, 1971.

How To Father. New York: Signet Press, 1975.

How To Discipline with Love. New York: Signet Press, 1981.

How To Grandparent. New York: Signet Press, 1982.

Give Your Child a Headstart in Reading. New York: Simon & Schuster, 1983.

Your Child, from Birth to Six. New York: Simon & Schuster, 1986.

How To Single Parent. New York: Harper & Row, 1987.

for children

I Wish I Had a Computer That Makes Waffles. San Diego: Oak Tree Publishers, 1978.

The Carnival Kidnap Caper. San Diego: Oak Tree Publishers, 1979.

for parents about themselves

The You That Could Be. Chicago: Follet, 1976.

DON DINKMEYER

Meet the Author

Dr. Don Dinkmeyer, author, consultant, and psychologist, is nationally respected for his practical approach to developing responsibility in children. His name is associated with his former colleague, Rudolf Dreikurs, for their work on the principles of Encouragement and Logical Consequences. His workshops have taken him to forty-four states in the U.S.A. and to Europe, Canada, England, Japan, Australia, and South America.

Dr. Dinkmeyer earned his B.S. degree at the University of Nebraska, his M.A. from Northwestern University, and his Ph.D. from Michigan State University. He has been a member of the White House Conference on Children and Youth and has been honored by the North American Society of Adlerian Psychology for his contributions to Adlerian Psychology through his writing. He was also honored by the American School Counselor Association for developing and editing the Elementary School Guidance and Counseling Journal. *Most recently he won the 1986 American Association for Counseling and Development (AACD) Professional Development Award.*

He is a Fellow of the American Psychological Association. He is also a diplomate in Counseling Psychology from the American Board of Professional Psychology and in Marriage and Family Therapy from the American Board of Family Psychology.

Dr. Dinkmeyer has been featured in American Men and Women of Science, Outstanding Educators of America, Dictionary of International Biography, Directory of Educational Specialists, Contemporary Authors, *and* Who's Who in the South and Southwest.

The theorists who have most influenced his thinking are Alfred Adler and Rudolf Dreikurs and their colleagues, Bernard Shulman, and Harold Mosak. He has also been influenced by Virginia Satir, Carl Whitaker, Albert Ellis, William Glasser, and a number of his coauthors. His ideas about parent–child relationships have been shaped by the parenting experience he shared with his wife, Elvira Jane, their children, Don and Jim, who are now joining him in his work, and in the experiences he shares with his grandchildren, James Drew and Caitlin.

Dr. Dinkmeyer has written over 125 articles. He presently serves as President of Communication and Motivation Training Institute, an organization in Coral Springs, Florida, which has developed CMTI Press and sponsors workshops.

7

TEACHING RESPONSIBILITY

DEVELOPING PERSONAL ACCOUNTABILITY
THROUGH NATURAL AND LOGICAL
CONSEQUENCES
DON DINKMEYER, PH.D.

Motivating children to behave responsibly is one of the most important challenges of parenting, because it's from responsible children that responsible adults evolve. We've passed through a phase of autocratic parenting where children were told what to do and responded appropriately. That produced children who learned to avoid their parents to avoid being yelled at or hit. They were motivated by the fear of punishment rather than self-discipline.

This was followed by a period of permissiveness when children ran the show. Parents were afraid to be firm because they wanted their children to like them, acting more like "pals" than parents. Ironically, the children often grew up angry and resentful because no one had cared enough to stand firm when a loving "no" was in their best interest. In turn, the parents often became angry with their children's demanding, self-centered behavior and angry with themselves for their own ineffectiveness. Neither parenting extreme was rewarding for parents *or* children.

In today's society where people are concerned with equality of the sexes, religions, and races, children also expect to be treated with respect and they demand equal rights. Unfortunately, there has not been an equal expectation for children to demonstrate responsibility. Children are focused on their own immediate concerns and do not realize that they have a responsibility to contribute to the well-being of the family.

Parents and children need guidelines to develop relationships that stress a balance between rights and responsibilities. Children need the opportunity to make decisions, but they must also be accountable for their choices. They deserve respect, but they also need to learn to respect others. We no longer control children, but we have the ability to influence them toward more effective living. First we need to understand the purpose of their behavior and then respond to those needs more productively.

Goals of Misbehavior

Children usually misbehave for a reason. By misbehavior I mean behaviors and words that either disregard or disrespect the rights of others or are self-defeating. The four basic goals of misbehavior were originally identified by Rudolf Dreikurs (Dreikurs and Soltz, 1964). These goals are mistaken because they hinder the child's development in an active and constructive direction.

Once you know what your child is trying to achieve by misbehaving, you are in a better position to deal with the misbehavior effectively. The first step is to recognize your own response to your child's behavior. Your response correlates directly with the purpose of the child's misbehavior. At the point of the misbehavior, be aware of your feelings. Are you annoyed, angry, hurt, or discouraged? Next, look at how your child reacts when you respond to his behavior. Does your child ignore you, become more angry, argue, or stop the behavior temporarily and then begin misbehaving again? By first identifying how *you* feel and then examining your child's reaction, you can identify what your child is seeking.

Rudolf Dreikurs classifies misbehavior under four categories, or goals. Each goal serves a purpose for the child—it results in a specific payoff. By training yourself to look at what your child gains from his misbehavior, you'll be able to respond to his needs more effectively.

Attention

Young children usually seek attention. If they cannot get attention in positive ways, they may try to get it in ways that are disturbing to others, especially to their parents. Children want to be recognized and noticed. A child may try to get noticed by blocking the view to the television, interrupting his parents' conversation, annoying a sibling who wants to be left alone, picking his nose repeatedly in front of "important" company, being noisy when one of his parents is trying to rest, or getting dressed in slow motion so a parent has to constantly remind him to get ready for school on time.

When any of these behaviors happens and you feel yourself getting annoyed, it is most likely that your child's goal is attention. When you ask him to stop his annoying behavior and he ignores you, or he temporarily stops and then does the same thing or something similar to upset you, your assumption that his goal is attention is probably correct. The solution is obvious—ignore the attention-seeking behavior and look for opportunities to offer positive attention.

Power

Power-seeking children challenge the authority of adults and attempt to take control. The power-seeking child looks for ways to be in charge and decides to do only what he wants. He might have a tantrum to get you to let him stay awhile longer at a friend's house, tease an older sibling until the brother or sister retaliates physically (in order to get "the bully" into trouble with their parents), or refuse to eat at the dinner table but demand to be fed later because he's "starving." You will usually know when your child is in a power-seeking situation, because your feeling is anger. If your child does something directly opposed to what you have requested, you will usually feel angry and want to get back into control. If you give in to the power-seeking child, he knows he is in control. However, if you decide to fight power with power, your child will probably be impressed with the usefulness of power and will *intensify* his struggle for control.

Thus the procedure for dealing with the power-seeking child is to disengage from the conflict. It is difficult to fight without an opponent. When you identify power as the child's goal, practice new responses that will not reward the goal. Learn to do the opposite of what the child anticipates and avoid rewarding the misbehavior. For example, the child who refuses to eat with the family during lunch can be told, warmly, "I can see you aren't hungry now. I'll serve dinner at six o'clock and you can eat then." When he demands to eat an hour later because he's "starved," repeat that you are serving dinner at six, remaining friendly but *firm*.

Revenge

When a parent exerts power over the child, the child may decide to retaliate. A child who pursues revenge is convinced that he is not lovable. Since he believes he can't be loved, he works to find his place within the family by being cruel. A child who has lost a power struggle with a parent can still inflict revenge. Examples of revenge include the son who purposely flunks his addition tests to get even with his father (who happens to be a math teacher), the six-year-old boy who cuts his baby sister's curls to get back at his mother for bringing "precious" into the house in the first place, and the eight-year-old girl who shows her big sister's diary to her sister's close friends to humiliate her. When you are faced with revenge-seeking behavior, you usually feel deeply hurt. You may want to retaliate, but if you punish the child, this only provides more fuel for the child's desire to get even.

Giving a child the responsibility for dealing with the consequences of his behavior is far more effective. In the instance of the boy who purposely flunked his addition tests to upset his father, his father would instinctively react with hurt and anger. However, if the father is astute enough to recognize his son's negative goal and is courageous enough to follow through on his insight, he could deny the child satisfaction by refusing to react. Instead, he could be very matter-of-fact about his son's repeated failures, communicating through his lack of concern that the situation is his son's problem.

In addition to allowing the child to suffer the consequences of his actions, you need to look at what the child's needs are and help him find more appropriate ways to meet them. That way you help him develop his sense of inner worth so he doesn't have to demonstrate his power by hurting others.

Display of Inadequacy

A child who seeks pity, protection, and undue service through a display of inadequacy is the most discouraged of all. His goal is to see that others expect nothing of him. He shows his parents that he just can't make friends, entertain himself, perform his chores, make decisions, or meet parental expectations. He believes he lacks the ability to perform competently and tends to have a very low opinion of himself. These children have the mistaken belief that anything less than being the very best means that they are nothing. When they don't think they can be "tops," they give up (Dinkmeyer and McKay, 1982).

Displays of inadequacy include the sixth grader (the twin sister of a male academic achiever) who "can't" do her homework right because she's just a "dumb girl," the obese ten-year-old boy who gets his parents to sign a note excusing him from gym so he won't have to be teased by his peers in the locker room, and the five-year-old girl whose mother has to dress her because she "can't" do it herself. They display inadequacy to be excused from functioning.

The parents of a child who is into inadequacy often feel pity and disappointment. They assume that the situation is hopeless. They secretly agree that the child is not competent and stop supporting the child's effort. Instead, they support the child in his feeling of despair. They make his decisions, excuse his behavior, do his jobs, and take care of his personal needs long after he's mastered the skills. They support him in his belief that he is shy, clumsy, or incompetent.

Discouragement

Children who misbehave are children who are discouraged. They don't know how to be accepted and belong in positive ways. Discouraged people believe they cannot meet the expectations of others or themselves. Discouragement is the basis of most failure to function adequately and cooperatively. It is based upon an assumed inadequacy. Discouraged people have the same desire for success and belonging as others do, but have ineffective and destructive ways of reaching their goals. They believe they can only belong in inadequate ways because they lack confidence and self-esteem.

Very often discouraged people come from situations that they have perceived to be competitive, with standards that seem to be too high for them to attain. They usually believe their parents expect them to produce beyond their interests or abilities. From this setting, the child will often make the decision, "Since I can't be as much as others, I might as well not try!" They experience their parents as being too demanding and overly ambitious. Since they perceive the standards to be beyond their reach, they decide that it's easier to just give up than to make any attempt.

These children lack what Alfred Adler referred to as "Social Interest"— the desire to give and take, or cooperate. They are beset by a belief that governs their movement, that says "I can't" instead of "I can." Their parents, perhaps, have discouraged them through domination and insensitivity; but the child has also made an interpretation that he has no chance to succeed or even any chance to make progress.

Parents discourage in a number of ways. Overconcern with status and prestige and high expectations in a variety of areas, such as athletics, music, dramatics, and academics, tend to make the child feel "I am not as much as I should be."

Encouragement: The Key to Effective Relationships

The solution to discouragement is encouragement. Encouragement is the process of focusing on a person's resources and potential to build his self-esteem, his self-confidence, and his feelings of worth (Dinkmeyer and Losoncy, 1980). The person who encourages intentionally focuses on identifying resources and searching for the positive. Much like Diogenes, who searched for truth, or gold miners who search for gold, encouragers identify an emerging potential in the person. They then focus on the positive and accentuate it, while ignoring the negative. Encouragers never reinforce negative behavior, but approach children expecting realistic success, and they usually get just that. This encouraging attitude communicates "You are capable—go ahead and try."

They help a child understand that mistakes can be growth experiences if we use them to learn. Most important, they encourage the child to move toward his goal at *his* pace, not at their own. Given this freedom, the child becomes a more cooperative, goal-oriented person.

It is important to understand that encouragement means helping our child to meet *his* goals and not *our* goals. We accept attempts, efforts, or any kind of movement toward reaching his goal. This encourages him to accept himself.

In order to be this type of encouraging parent, you need to be self-encouraging. You have to feel positive and encouraged in order to be in a position to be encouraging to others. You also need to be in a position to develop your self-acceptance, and to believe in yourself just as you are.

At times people do not recognize the difference between praise and encouragement. They may even think of praise and encouragement as the same process because they both focus on positive behavior. We need to understand the difference in terms of the effect on the child's behavior. The following chart illustrates some basic differences between the two.

PRAISE	ENCOURAGEMENT
Focuses on desires/wishes of person other than child (parent, teacher, scout leader).	Focuses on *the child's* ability to manage himself.
Focuses on external evaluation (what someone else thinks of child).	Focuses on constructive internal evaluation (what child thinks of himself).
Rewards only well-done, completed tasks.	Provides recognition for effort and improvement.
Focuses on self-elevation and personal gain.	Focuses on assets and contributions.
Teaches child to conform or rebel.	Helps child develop courage to be imperfect and willingness to try.
Reinforces the idea that self-worth is based on others' opinions.	Teaches that self-worth is based on self-evaluation.
Sets unrealistic, unattainable standards.	Helps child to learn to accept efforts of self and others.

(Figure 1. Differences Between Praise and Encouragement.)

Some examples of encouragement are:

"It looks like you've worked really hard on that."

"Thank you for emptying the dishwasher. That made my work easier."

"I can see you put a lot of effort into your science project."

"I like the way you handled that problem."

"You are meeting so many new people during your class election. Whether or not you win, you must feel good about yourself for running."

Encouragement is a skill. The most important skills in the encouragement process are listening, responding, focusing on assets, developing alternate ways of perceiving situations, creating opportunities for humor, and recognizing efforts and contributions.

Listening

When you are listening to a child, concentrate on his feeling and message. Communicate with your very being that you are present and attending. Make contact with your eyes, following him closely without interrupting. Listen to *all* that is said, being alert to the feelings that he is expressing. Communicate both verbally and nonverbally that you are empathically hearing the feelings behind the words.

Responding

When responding, try to be honest and open in communicating how you are experiencing the relationship or the communication from your child. Do not engage in dysfunctional communication. Instead, stay on *his* topic. Be patient and not overly concerned with silence. Attend to what *he* is saying and expressing, helping him to explore his own ideas through open-ended questions (questions that tend to draw out thought-provoking responses rather than one-word answers). For example, rather than ask, "How was preschool?" which will probably elicit an "okay" or "fine," ask instead, "What was the best (silliest, funniest, or happiest) part of your day today?"

Focus on Strengths, Assets, and Resources

Be able to spotlight and magnify your child's positive attributes. Instead of being a "nitpicker" or "flaw finder," always looking to spot a mistake or a weakness, try to be fine-tuned to hearing and seeing resources. How do you usually communicate with people? Are you thinking about faults, places to interrupt, ways to show how you are superior? Or are you truly attentive and, at the same time, absorbed in how their strengths, assets, and resources might deal with their challenges? The person who is encouraging and feels encouraged perceives life more positively. The encourager is a more uplifting person to be around.

Development of Perceptual Alternatives

Perceptual alternatives involve the many potential ways of viewing and giving meaning to a specific situation. An encouraging person will look to find something positive in every situation.

As we become aware that we have perceptual alternatives, we are in greater control of our options. We are able to choose how to interpret events and how to respond to them. Think of all the events that have been going on in your life, perhaps at work, with friends, and in your close relationships. How have you been seeing each situation? Is there another way to view it? Then look at the situation with your children, their schoolwork, their friends, and their cooperation around the house. How have you been understanding their behavior? Is there a perceptual alternative, a different way to understand these behaviors? Learn to develop a more positive perspective on life.

Humor

A person who can see things from a humorous point of view encourages us to reconsider our rigid perceptions of ourselves and others. We are often discouraged as a result of our own self-constrictive behavior. We tie ourselves into knots and then appear to be confused about how we got there and how we can get out. This myopic way of looking at our behavior limits us from seeing ourselves in true perspective.

Humor can have a dramatic and dynamic effect on our physical well-being, as described in works by Norman Cousins in *The Anatomy of an Illness* (1979) and *The Healing Heart* (1983). We can become healthier and happier through the creation of endorphins (hormones produced by the chemical changes that result from exercise, laughter, and positive emotions). Humor becomes a way you encourage yourself and your child to relate to the challenges of life in a more relaxed, more effective way. A person who has a sense of humor is able to see things in perspective. There are fewer catastrophes, because he can see the possibilities of other ways to look at each situation. Humor is a guilt-proof vest against external accusations.

Focusing on Efforts and Contributions

Focusing on efforts and contributions is in direct contrast to focusing on completed products or outstanding behaviors. For example, your child brings home a spelling paper that has five right and fifteen wrong responses. The paper is marked a failure. You choose how to respond. You can either focus on the fifteen marked wrong or the five marked correct. If you respond to the five correct answers, you show creative, spontaneous behavior. You have an opportunity to increase your child's self-esteem and motivation. You might say, "You seem to do very well on certain kinds of words," or "I can see you started out very well." It is important to recognize that it is not only the completed product but any effort, attempt, or movement in the right direction that is encourageable.

Discipline as a Learning Process

Sometimes parents are presented with a situation which requires disciplinary action. Their first thought is how to *punish* or *regain control* over the child. But discipline must be understood in a totally different way. It is a learning opportunity for both parents and child.

Punishment cannot possibly motivate a child to become independent. Punishment does not guide a person to lead a responsible, productive life. It only leaves him in a dependent or power-oriented relationship with those in authority.

When you understand that any disciplinary action should be a learning experience for your child, you have a new way of evaluating your disciplinary procedures. Is sending the child to his room for an indefinite period of time a learning experience? Is spanking a learning experience? What is learned from insisting that the child "shut up"? In fact, there are many undesirable lessons to be learned from all of these experiences. The important issue is, When my child misbehaves, what response will be most valuable in motivating him to act responsibly?

Sometimes adults have a mistaken view of the role of the parent. They see discipline as a way to be in charge or in control. In some instances, they may not be in control at work or in their relationships, so they use their child to help them meet their need for control. If discipline is to be a learning process, it cannot be primarily concerned with control.

As you work intentionally and consistently to help your child feel good about himself and to increase his self-esteem, you will find there is less resistance and rebellion. There is less need for discipline.

Reward and punishment are associated with our autocratic past. They cannot help us guide our children toward independence and responsibility. They demonstrate our lack of respect for them.

Natural and Logical Consequences

A child learns from consequences when his parents allow him to experience the results of his actions. Just as adults who have experienced the inconvenience of running out of gas are more apt to fill their tanks when the marker nears empty, the child who has experienced hunger because he forgot his lunch is more likely to remember to take his lunch bag from the refrigerator before leaving for school.

Consequences are most effective in a relationship based upon equality and mutual respect. A natural consequence is what results if others do not interfere. Natural consequences occur when the child goes against the natural order of events. They can also be a violation of the social order.

For example, if a child goes outside in cold weather without warm clothing, he will experience the cold. If he goes out into the rain without a raincoat or umbrella, he obviously becomes wet. He will learn to dress more appropriately because he was allowed to experience discomfort with his choice. These are the natural consequences of the child's actions. Natural consequences are different from the punishment approach where the parent brings in the child from outside, helps the child into dry clothes, and then forbids the child to watch television for a week. Denying a child television privileges does little to teach him to dress appropriately in bad weather. It simply teaches him to resent the parent.

Logical consequences are used when the parent does not want the child to have to experience the direct consequences of his action or inaction because of concern for the child's welfare. For example, the child does not need to experience the possibly tragic consequences of riding his bike on a dangerous highway in order to learn the importance of driving on safe streets. Instead, the parent could offer a choice: "You may limit your bike driving to the side streets or lose your bike privileges for a week." The child decides by his actions whether or not to experience the logical consequences set up by the parent. If the parent observes the child driving on a busy highway, the parent simply and calmly states, "I see you've decided to walk to school next week," as he removes the bike from the child.

It is important to recognize that there is a major distinction between punishment and logical consequences:

PUNISHMENT	LOGICAL CONSEQUENCE
1. Emphasizes the power of personal authority.	Expresses the reality of the social order.
Makes a demand.	Recognizes mutual respect and mutual rights.
"You took my new dress without asking, and now it's ruined. You're grounded!"	"Erika, how will you replace my dress?"
2. Arbitrary, rarely related to the logic of the situation.	Directly related to the behavior.
"You didn't take out the garbage, so you're not going on your weekend camping trip!"	"I had to take out the garbage for you last night. I'd appreciate your washing the pantry floor today for me."
3. Personalized and implies a moral judgment.	Implies no element of moral judgment. Separates the deed from the doer.
"You are a liar. I can't trust you."	"Since you didn't follow through on your commitment to come home right from school today, you'll need to stay home the rest of the afternoon."
4. Concerned with past behavior.	Concerned with present and future behavior.
"Audrey, you're always playing with food at the table. Stop throwing your food or you'll go to bed without any supper."	"Audrey, after you have eaten your food, you can go into your room to play. Food is for eating, not throwing." (Audrey throws mashed potato at her brother.) "I see you have decided you're through eating" (as you put her dinner into the sink).
5. Threatens to treat the offender with disrespect.	Invoked in a friendly manner, after parents and child have calmed down.

(When on a car trip) "You're acting like a baby. Stop crying or you won't finish this ride with us. I'll take you home and get you a baby-sitter."	Drive to the side of the road and say, "When you've stopped crying, we'll go on."
6. Demands obedience.	Permits choice.
"You stay in the backyard where I can see you or you'll be spanked."	"You can either stay in the backyard to play or you can come into the house." (Your child climbs the fence and wanders off.) "Beth, I see you have decided to stay in the house."

(Figure 2. Differences Between Punishment and Logical Consequence.)

Guidelines in Applying Consequences

As we discussed earlier, there are four major goals of misbehavior. The first step in applying consequences to deal with misbehavior is to identify which goal the child is seeking: attention, power, revenge, or appearing disabled.

Consequences require parents to take an intelligent approach to child training. Consequences are more concerned with the learning that occurs and the maturity of the child than with control. And they put parents in a position where they are treated with greater respect and one in which the relationship improves. The guidelines are:

1. *Determine the Goal of the Behavior.* If the goal of your child's misbehavior is attention, then it is crucial to avoid giving attention for negative behavior. If the goal is power, it is important that your child experience the logical consequence of having no opponent. When you are dealing with a power-seeker, withdraw from the conflict. It is very important that you be careful in applying logical consequences to any kind of power-seeking misbehavior to avoid turning it into a power struggle. Use consequences only when behavior is disruptive and only when it is absolutely necessary.

   In a revenge situation, understanding the child's goal can help you to avoid feeling hurt. Don't try to get even with the child. Instead, focus on building a trusting relationship.

   Logical consequences are not appropriate when your child displays inadequacy. The behavior does not disrupt the family in any way, and it is important not to give up or to criticize.

2. *Determine Who Owns the Problem.* When the child owns the problem, parents need to allow natural consequences to occur. As long as the consequences are not dangerous, do not interfere. For example, if the child stays up too late, he will be tired the next day. When he misses a meal, hunger will follow.

   When parents own the problem, they need to teach the child with logical consequences. For example, if it is a common occurrence in your home to hear someone complaining after you have done the family laundry that something that he *desperately* needs *tomorrow* didn't get washed, you can make use of consequences. Instead of feeling victimized and doing an extra wash for just one shirt, set some new ground rules. Tell the family that you are willing to do the laundry that is in the hamper. Those who decide to empty their soiled clothes there will have their clothes cleaned by you. Those who prefer to leave their dirty clothes elsewhere will be responsible for their own laundry. Younger children can be taught to rinse their clothes out in the sink. Give older children instructions on the use of the washer and dryer so each family member is self-sufficient. The most important factor is to remember that the consequence is the end result of the *child's* decision. Don't turn the consequence into punishment with a harsh tone or an "I told you so," or you'll set the stage for revenge.

3. *Applying Natural and Logical Consequences.* Sometimes parents understand the theory of consequences but have difficulty applying the theory in practice. Use the following goals of misbehavior as a guide when formulating consequences for your child's specific behaviors.

CHILD'S GOAL	PARENT'S USUAL RESPONSE	CHILD'S RESPONSE	PARENT'S POSITIVE RESPONSE
ATTENTION			
example: Child keeps going back to sleep when alarm rings in the morning, takes a long time getting ready, and is often late for school.	feeling: annoyed reaction: coax, remind, nag, to wake up and to leave for school on time.	When awakened, child responds, then goes back to sleep; when prodded, he moves faster for a few moments, then slows down again. He continues to be late for school.	Get child an alarm clock; discuss what time he needs to get up and the time he should leave the house; then let him be responsible for getting to school on time. Don't interfere with consequences imposed by school. Give positive attention for worthwhile behavior.
POWER, CONTROL			
example: Child has temper tantrums to get what he wants.	feeling: angry, threatened reaction: fight, yell, scream, cry	Crying gets louder; child becomes defiant.	Ignore the temper tantrums; refuse to fight or give in; don't reinforce his hunger for control. Help child learn to use power productively.
REVENGE, HURT OTHERS			
example: Child dyes hair assorted colors and cuts it in a punk style to embarrass ultraconservative parents.	feeling: humiliated, furious reaction: yell, threaten	Child shaves his head.	Ignore his hairstyle completely. Avoid punishment and retaliation. Refuse to demonstrate your anger or embarrassment in words, tone of voice, or body language. Reinforce child for positive attitude and behavior whenever possible.

DISPLAY OF INADEQUACY (to get pity, protection, and undue service)

CHILD'S GOAL	PARENT'S USUAL RESPONSE	CHILD'S RESPONSE	PARENT'S POSITIVE RESPONSE
example: Child acts shy, hides behind parents, refuses to speak.	feeling: helpless, discouraged reaction: When introducing child to others, excuse his behavior, explaining that he is shy; when others speak to him, answer for him.	Child decides he is incapable and withdraws.	Allow child to speak for himself. Encourage attempts and partial effort. Focus on assets. Don't give up. Demonstrate confidence in (not pity for) the child.

(Figure 3. A Guide to Responding to Misbehavior)

4. *Offer Choices.* When using consequences it is important to structure the choices to program for successful decision making. For example, if you ask, "What would you like to have for breakfast?" you're inviting frustration, because you'll most likely have to deal with a decision like "candy" or "ice cream." Instead, provide alternatives that are acceptable to you—suggest a variety of healthy breakfast foods from which the child may choose. Once you've offered a choice, you need to be ready to accept whatever the child has decided. Remember, there is no wrong decision, it is just the child's choice.

5. *Choice Stands.* If a child chooses a consequence, the decision stands. He realizes that you will not change the decision. However, after a period of time, he could choose again.

6. *Phrase Choices Positively.* Rather than warn "If you don't clean your room, you're not going out to play," say "As soon as you clean your room, you can go out to play." The actual consequence is the same, but your attitude is positive, not threatening. You have avoided a power struggle.

7. *Focus on Positive Behavior.* Soon after the correction is made, it is important to maintain the relationship with the child. "Catch" your child being good. Tell him something that he has done that you approve of or appreciate.

8. *Negotiate consequences whenever possible.* It is important to have the child involved in making decisions about his behavior.

Ways to Teach Responsibility

You can see that the application of consequences is only limited by your ability to be aware of and imagine the natural and logical ways in which these can be applied. The following are a number of examples of areas in which consequences are effective.

Schoolwork

Parents often see themselves in the role of motivating children to invest time and effort in their schoolwork. It is a common belief that successful people are those who negotiate all the hurdles and hoops of the school system and become academic successes. We hope that academic success will enable our children to win the best jobs, become doctors, lawyers, or bankers.

At the same time, we need to remember that there is a great need in society for people who can work in a variety of skilled trades. These jobs may

not require Ph.D.'s or M.B.A.'s, but they are vital to our society nonetheless. This is not to say that motivation for schoolwork is not important; however, it is valuable to see it in perspective. And there is a great deal of difference between motivation and coercion.

It is my experience that the more parents demand good grades, regular intensive study periods, and a dedication to academics, the more the law of diminishing returns is evident. The child decides that since the parents are so concerned with his academic success, and regularly nag about studying, there is little need for him to worry about academic work. The child believes that one person being concerned is enough, and as a result he lacks a crucial interest in his own education.

Students who become involved with academic work usually become involved because they are in contact with excellent teachers who understand their interests, their feelings, their beliefs, and their concerns—and use these to motivate. These teachers make a connection between the person and the academic material. They do not expect motivation to be an external force. They do not attempt to reward or punish to force the student to comply. Instead, they motivate the child by being sensitive to the internal motivators that already exist.

Each child has many intense feelings about subjects, life events, and relationships. Good teachers discuss these feelings; they value the child's opinions, attitudes, and beliefs; and they work with these factors to create motivation and involvement with the work that is being conducted at school.

You motivate children most effectively when you decide that school is *their* problem. You make them responsible for school while you provide a desk, a quiet room, and sufficient supplies—and you restrict access to external stimuli. In simple terms, you create an environment that stimulates study. You restrict television, permitting only a certain amount. The student has a right to choose what he wants to watch, but there is a limit on the amount of time spent in front of the television. The same applies to listening to records, making telephone calls, or anything else that interferes with studying. You are thereby creating an environment whereby books, intellectual events, and opportunities to learn become more desirable.

You also motivate children to invest time and effort through your own modeling. If you go to Adult Education courses, you study and read books regularly. Are you up-to-date on current events and do you discuss some of your ideas about what you're learning with your children? Do you plan interesting trips to local museums and places of interest that provide stimulation of the learning process?

I see the parent as someone who creates an environment to help motivate the internal beliefs, feelings, and values of the child. The parent does this by being empathic and encouraging, not by demanding that the child study in a specific way.

It is clear that while you can lead a student to academics, there is no way you can effectively and permanently force him to learn. Learning is something that the student has to decide he desires and, as a result, pursues.

Let the child manage his own schoolwork. This way school does not become a weapon that he can use against the parent. When children are aware that school is important to the parents, they often perform poorly just to prove that they can't be pushed to succeed. Letting the child experience the natural consequences of his behavior does not create the negative results that occur when punishment is used. The important thing to communicate clearly to the child is, "I have decided that school is *your* responsibility, so from now on you will be in charge of it."

If a child seems to have difficulty learning, consider having him evaluated. You will want to be certain that he isn't being handicapped by a specific learning disability. Difficulty in learning can lead to poor motivation, hyperactive behavior, and frustration. If he doesn't know "how" to study, offer him the opportunity to take a study skills class. Some children need help learning how to listen, take notes, and organize their work.

Household Chores

From an early age on, children can be expected to be responsible for certain contributions to the family. They can learn to be responsible for picking up their toys or clothes from the floor and cleaning up spills they make. As they mature, you can ask them to do chores that are relevant to their age level, such as setting the table, making a specific part of a meal, washing a bathroom sink, or baby-sitting a sibling.

A weekly meeting of the family offers the opportunity to discuss what people like about the way things are going in the family and what they would like to see changed. This is also an opportunity to develop and consider new chores and to make changes in the assignment of jobs. Frequently resistance to a chore occurs because a child has never had a say in choosing it in the first place. It was "assigned" and is therefore resented. The child feels that he is getting the "bottom of the barrel" assignment. As members of the family take turns in dealing with the responsibilities, there is usually a greater appreciation that this is a family in which everyone cooperates.

If the family system of chores is to be effective, everyone in the family takes responsibility for specific jobs. This obviously includes both parents.

When a member of the family has decided not to cooperate in doing a chore, some type of emergency exists. The emergency action suggested is titled "chore trading." Mother may have some chores she does regularly, such as making meals, vacuuming, or cleaning clothes. She could reduce her frustration and teach her child responsibility at the same time by trading jobs. In this instance, Mother might suggest, "Since you aren't able to take the dishes off the table, and it needs to be done, I am going to take them off myself. During the time I am doing your chore, I won't have time to wash off the countertops. You can do that for me instead."

It is important to understand that this type of chore trading should be done with a cooperative and understanding attitude. It should in no way suggest a power move or a feeling of revenge.

The family system for chores also maintains itself best when the parents regularly recognize the effort involved in the discipline of getting chores done. It is an important contribution to the family. Recognize that effort by saying, "I appreciated . . ." or "I liked . . ." or "That was really helpful." Notes of appreciation for completing chores are also excellent motivators.

Money and Allowances

Money and allowances can be a problem for parents. I believe that money should be given to children to teach them how to manage their finances. They should then be responsible for paying for things like snacks, inexpensive toys, school lunches, or religious contributions, and also for saving for special items they wish to purchase. Money is given with the idea that it helps children learn money management. At the appropriate age they can also learn how to bank and save money.

Children can learn the value of money through allowances and, at times, earn additional money for special chores. An allowance is very important in the training and development of a child. The allowance should not be given for the performance of routine family tasks. These are chores that are done by family members because they all belong to the family. Just as they all receive the benefits from being part of a cooperative unit, they all contribute to its well-being.

When you have a child who is very uncooperative it may be helpful to consider a procedure called the "service charge." When the child does not complete a chore, a service charge is assigned. Somebody else has to take on the chore and is paid for it. This has certain punitive aspects to it as well as being a consequence, so it is important to be sensitive about the way in which it is communicated to the child.

Lying

Often parents see a lie as the sign that the children don't trust them. However, my observation is that lying is often something that is learned at home. Sometimes a child has been told when a phone rings, "Tell them I'm not in." If you are invited to a social event and you don't want to go, the child observes what you tell the person who calls. At other times, parents try to pass their child off as if he were of a younger age (tickets for airlines or the theater). Be aware that practices such as these model lying as acceptable behavior.

It is important to understand that lying, like any other form of misbehavior, serves a purpose. In some instances, it is done to gain the attention of parents or peers. When parents are confronted with a child's lying, they need to recognize that sometimes lies are used to defeat them, to escape punishment, to seek revenge, or to generate some special kind of excitement.

You can help a child to stop the lying by being less impressed. Listen to what is said without acknowledging that you know the person is stretching the truth, without challenging his facts. Later you can give this child positive attention by looking for his assets and by planning ways for him to use these assets as a contribution to family life.

The goal, then, is to help the child see that there is no need to lie in order to impress or to belong in this family. However, when you find that your silence doesn't reduce the lying, you might discuss the situation by saying,

"Could it be that you want to impress me with these stories?" Then discuss why the child feels the need to impress.

When children are young, they often have difficulty distinguishing between fact and fantasy. A child often wishes for something so much he wants to believe it is real. The parent might say, "Wouldn't it be nice if that really could happen?" or "You wish your horse were a real one, not just a wooden one." Rather than label the child as a liar, help him to recognize the difference between wishful thinking and reality.

Whenever the lying actually affects you, then the problem belongs to you. It is at this point that you need to be aware of certain things that could be unproductive or damaging. First, don't set up unrealistic expectations. If you say, "No, you can't ride with Kate!" or "No, you can't play these records," without any explanation, this will often force the child to feel that there is only one way out, and that is to lie.

Children need a certain amount of freedom. They need your trust and confidence. Most important of all, don't overreact if you discover your child has lied. A few lies do not make a person a pathological liar. However, mistrusting, snooping, playing detective, and overreacting will push the lying to continue.

When you are in a situation where your child has lied, use an "I message" to demonstrate your disappointment. For example, state, "When you are not telling me the truth, I feel very disappointed, because I have always been able to depend on what you say and mean." In this way you make your feelings known and appeal to your child's self-respect.

The more accepting, encouraging, trusting, and valuing your relationship with your child, the less likely it is that he will feel the need to lie. Lying may be a signal that there is some distrust in the relationship. If you discover that your child is lying to you, closely examine your relationship and work to open up channels of communication.

Summary

Suggestions can be made for a variety of situations when a child is misbehaving. However, each situation will always be influenced by the dynamics between the parent and child. It is more important to have a personal checklist that helps you cope with each situation.

1. Listen and observe what is being communicated to you through what is said and what is done. Behavior always communicates feelings, beliefs, and the individual's intentions or goals.

2. Determine the goal of the behavior. Your action will be different in a situation that is attention-getting, in contrast to one that is displaying

inadequacy or demonstrating power. Identify the real issue in the relationship, which may be controlling, pleasing, being in a superior position, or seeking to be comfortable at all costs.

3. After identifying the real issue and goal, inventory the individual's assets and strengths, and examine possibilities for dealing with the situation more effectively and productively. Consider ways to change passive and destructive behavior into active and constructive behavior. For example, consider how to help move the power-seeking child to be more autonomous or independent, which is an active/constructive method of seeking power. The revenge-seeking child can be helped to become a child who seeks justice and equal treatment, not only for himself but also for others.

   The child who displays inadequacy can learn to use this withdrawal primarily from conflict situations and, instead, develop a positive orientation to the challenges of living.

   As you become more creative you will learn that there are many challenges of living in which the child is already functioning effectively. Look for places where the child's behavior is adequate, where he handles situations effectively, and emphasize these strengths in your relationships.

   It is important to continuously develop perceptual alternatives—additional positive ways of looking at or understanding the situation.

4. In any conflict situation, work to develop an active/constructive approach to the situation and a specific commitment to change. Through the power of choice and the development of a new goal, help the child to function more effectively.

A Final Word

There is no more important task for parents than that of developing responsible children. The child who accepts responsibility for his behavior is prepared to meet the challenge of living in his work and social relationships and develop his self-esteem and self-confidence.

As we learn to move children from passive/destructive behavior, our goals can be aligned positively. Parents need to recognize discouragement and supply the antidote—encouragement. Because we are not by nature encouraging, we need to develop those skills.

We now can replace punishment and reward—dinosaurs of the disciplinary world—with natural and logical consequences.

By the Author

for parents about their children

(With Rudolf Dreikurs) *Encouraging Children to Learn: The Encouragement Process.* Englewood Cliffs, N.J.: Prentice-Hall, 1963; New York: Elsevier–Dutton, 1979.

Child Development: The Emerging Self. Englewood Cliffs, N.J.: Prentice-Hall, 1965.

(With Gary D. McKay) *Raising a Responsible Child.* New York: Simon & Schuster, 1973. (Paperback) New York: Fireside, 1982.

(With Gary D. McKay) *Systematic Training for Effective Parenting Handbook.* Minnesota: American Guidance Service, 1976; New York: Random House, 1982.

(With Gary D. McKay) *Systematic Training for Effective Parenting of Teens.* Minnesota: American Guidance Service, 1983; New York: Random House, 1984.

"Basics of Adult-Teen Relationships—Basics of Self-Acceptance," CMTI Press, Box 8268, Coral Springs, Florida 33075-8268.

(With Gary D. McKay, Don Dinkmeyer Jr., Jim Dinkmeyer, and Joyce McKay) *Next Step: The Effective Parent.* Minnesota: American Guidance Service, 1987.

for parents about themselves

(With Lew Losoncy) *The Encouragement Book: Becoming a Positive Person.* Englewood Cliffs, N.J.: Prentice-Hall, 1980.

for counselors

(With James Muro) *Group Counseling: Theory and Practice,* rev. ed. Illinois: Peacock Publishers, 1979.

(With Don Dinkmeyer, Jr., and Len Sperry) *Adlerian Counseling and Psychotherapy.* Revised. Columbus, Ohio: Merrill, 1987.

for teachers

(With Gary D. McKay and Don Dinkmeyer, Jr.) *Systematic Training for Effective Teaching Handbook.* Minnesota: American Guidance Service, 1980.

EARL GROLLMAN

Meet the Author

Dr. Earl Grollman is an internationally acclaimed pioneer in the field of crisis intervention. He is the author of sixteen books. Talking About Death *received the UNESCO award of the International Children and Youth Book Exhibition in Munich. His "Talking About" series, which he developed with his daughter Sharon (on adjusting to a new sibling, death, divorce, separation, moving, peer pressure, financial stress, and suicide), is used in schools throughout the United States.*

Rabbi Grollman attended the University of Maryland and received his B.A. degree from the University of Cincinnati. He entered Hebrew College and was ordained in 1950 with the degree of Master of Hebrew Letters. In 1964 he received the Doctor of Divinity degree from Portia Law School in recognition of outstanding spiritual leadership, and in 1975 was awarded a doctorate from the Hebrew Union College. He did further graduate work at Boston University School of Theology and Harvard's Department of Community Psychiatry.

He has been the Rabbi of Beth El Temple Center, Belmont, Massachusetts, since 1951. He has served as a member of the Professional Advisory Board of the Foundation of Thanatology at Columbia-Presbyterian Medical Center of New York, Chairperson of the Massachusetts Ecumenical Council on Health and Morality, and Past President of the Massachusetts Board of Rabbis.

Dr. Grollman is a warm, charismatic speaker who is sought after by universities, clergy institutes, seminaries, physicians' forums, and hospital nursing associations throughout the country. He has appeared on national television and radio on such diverse programs as The Tomorrow Show, Monitor, *and* Mr. Rogers' Neighborhood. *Articles about him and his works have appeared in numerous publications, demonstrating his broad, universal appeal*—Psychiatric Opinion, Newsweek, Ms., New Woman, Time, *and* Harper's.

His greatest joy is speaking to the experts themselves—the children—as he has addressed countless schools throughout the country.

Rabbi Grollman is married to the former Netta Levinson of Pittsburgh, and together they have two sons, David and Jonathan; a daughter, Sharon; and four "brilliant" grandchildren, Jennifer, Eric, Aaron, and Samuel.

8

EXPLAINING DEATH AND DIVORCE

HELPING YOUR CHILD COPE WITH CRISIS
EARL GROLLMAN, D.D.

Growing up is difficult under any circumstances. All children face normal childhood crises: when they first leave their parents' homes to go to school, when they have new baby brothers or sisters, or when friends move to different cities or states. But when youngsters are confronted with the crisis of death or divorce, growing up is even tougher. While death and divorce elicit different reactions, both situations force children to confront the loss of a loved one. And they are both so traumatic!

In recent years, divorce has become more common. In 1950, there were 385,000 divorces, or ten per 1,000 married couples. Currently, it is estimated that well over one third of all marriages will end up in the divorce courts. The increased divorce rate is bringing divorce to a personal level for almost all children. Whether or not their own parents have divorced, they learn about the emotional toll it takes on families from friends who have to deal with its day-to-day realities. Children growing up today are keenly aware of the painful possibility that their parents may not live together " 'til death do us part."

Perhaps more than adults realize, youngsters are also attuned to the reality of death. Even at a very young age, children are confronted with the process when life no longer exists. A pet is killed. A funeral procession passes by. A grandfather dies. A political figure is assassinated. And, of course, there is television with the pictures of death in living color—children starving in Ethiopia and the Sudan, corpses lying in the streets of Lebanon.

Parents too often overlook their youngsters' feelings about death and divorce. They are too absorbed in their own grief to offer emotional support to their children. One study demonstrated that 44 percent of children were not even told of the death of a significant other when it occurred. The youngsters learned about their loss after the fact. Similarly, many children are denied the opportunity to hear firsthand of their parents' divorce. They too often learn the news from the wrong people at the wrong time. One nine-year-old recalled:

> I bumped into the lady next door when I was walking home from school. She patted me on the head and said how sorry she was about my mother and father. I didn't know what she was talking about. I thought maybe they were killed in a car accident or maybe someone tried to rob them, and they got shot. When I found out that my parents were getting separated, I was relieved. After all, they were alive! But I was mad and hurt, too. Why didn't my mom or dad tell me in the first place?

Too often, children hear that their parents are being divorced when in the midst of an argument one parent blurts out, "I can't stand it anymore. I'm leaving!" Sometimes youngsters learn of the impending divorce only after one parent has already moved out of the house.

Why do adults hide these sad truths from their children? For one reason, parents may be too absorbed in the struggle with their own personal grief. Or they may believe that their children are incapable of understanding the traumatic situation. But silence only deprives youngsters of the opportunity to share grief. Secrecy heightens their feeling of isolation and sense of loss. One child recalled:

> I remember going back to school for the first time after Daddy died. It was horrible. None of the kids would talk to me. It was like I had a horrible disease they were going to catch if they even looked at me. My teacher never said she was sorry. She just acted as though nothing had happened. I felt left out and hurt, and I missed Daddy more than ever.

Children can understand the meaning of crises in their lives in their own ways. The words "die" and "dead" are common in children's vocabularies even before they reach the age of three. However, these terms may conjure up different meanings, depending on the age and maturity of the youngster. Small children often try out the words, and roll them around on their tongues. One three-year-old child observed his mother sitting quietly on the couch. He asked her, "Are you dead, Mommy, or are you real?" His mother in turn asked, "What does it mean to be dead?" The child paused for a moment, then answered, "You don't talk. You don't make noise. You don't sing." The mother assured her child that people can be quiet and be "real" at the same time. Once the mother began to talk, the child shook his head and said, "You real now, Mommy." This young child exemplified the first level in Maria Nagy's stages of death awareness.

By studying Hungarian children in the late 1940s, psychologist Nagy discovered that children between the ages of three and five often deny death as a regular and final process. To these children, death is like sleep; you are dead, then you are alive again. Or it is like taking a journey; you are gone, then you come back again. During the course of a normal day, young children could experience real aspects of what they consider "death"—such as when their mother or father goes to work, to the supermarket, or to the movies. It is like playing "peek-a-boo" (from the Old English, meaning "alive or dead"). One moment you are here. Then you are not.

The media contributes to their confusion. Children watch cartoon characters blow each other up with dynamite and then see the victims miraculously bounce back to life. Actors are shot and killed on one program, then appear healthy and well on the next.

Children play cops and robbers: "Bang, Bang, you're dead!" and then brush themselves off and resume their play full of enthusiasm. Death is perceived as temporary and reversible.

The second stage of children's awareness of death occurs roughly between the ages of five and nine. At this time, they are better able to accept the idea that a person has died. However, youngsters may conceive of death as a physical manifestation in the form of a person or a spirit. One seven-year-old girl, upon learning that her uncle had died, begged her father to let her sleep with the lights on. The father was taken aback, as his daughter had never needed to use a night-light. When questioned why, she confessed: "The bogeyman took Uncle Max to heaven. Maybe if the bogeyman sees the lights in my room, he won't try to take me, too."

At about the age of nine, youngsters may enter the third stage of death awareness as they begin to recognize death as an inevitable experience that will happen even to them. Death can then occur by natural as well as accidental causes. Death is no longer embodied in human or supernatural form. Death is an end of bodily life. It is final and universal.

While children may develop concepts of death at an early age, the words "separation" and "divorce" are not often part of most young children's vocabularies. Yet children are acutely aware that something is wrong when their parents do not get along. They listen to their parents yelling at each other. They "hear" the silence at dinner. They witness how mother and father look at each other when they are angry, or when one storms out of the room. Studies indicate that children, even under the age of two, respond to moods and feelings of significant others. One eighteen-month-old child watched her father as he hid his face in his hands and sobbed. She walked up to him, hugged his leg hard, and begged, "No cry, Daddy. No cry." Unhappiness cannot be hidden from young children or old.

Some older children were not surprised when told that their parents were planning to get divorced. As one fourteen-year-old boy said, "Mom and

Dad couldn't be in the same room together for more than three minutes without fighting about something. I guess I was waiting for them to just turn to me and say they couldn't make it anymore living together. I was really sad when they told me that Dad was going to move out. But I wasn't shocked." Some are even relieved when one parent moves out of the house: "I couldn't stand it anymore. All the yelling—like our house was filled with hate. Whenever I was home with Mom and Dad, I was nervous. I was always waiting for someone to explode, and someone always did. At least now that they are separated, the house is quiet."

Since the crises of death and divorce cannot be concealed from children, how then should children be told? With both divorce and death, it is important that children be informed immediately. It is advisable to relay the sad news in familiar surroundings, preferably at home. Delay makes it all the more likely that they will be told of the death or the divorce by the wrong person, at the wrong place, and in the wrong way. Adults should proceed gradually, according to their children's intellectual and emotional capabilities. Parents should speak simply, honestly, and tenderly, without overwhelming their youngsters with too much detail.

When explaining death to children, theological abstractions should be avoided. Telling youngsters that a grandfather died because "God loved him so much" only serves to heighten children's fears. They may express their anxieties in a hostile way: hitting their siblings, starting fights at school, or talking back to their parents and teachers. One child spent a year seeing a school psychologist before she admitted the reason for her behavior: "I was mad at God. He took Grandpa away from me. But I was afraid of God, too. If I was good, he would love me. Then he would make me die, too." A child who is told "The good die young" would be likely to have the same concerns and might look at the surviving parent and wonder: "Then what does that say about *you?*"

Children become confused when death is explained in terms of euphemisms and fairy tales. To say to children, "Your grandfather went away on a long journey" does not ease the strain of Grandfather's absence. Children do not understand why their home is suddenly filled with weeping adults. "Last time Grandpa went to Arizona, everyone thought it was great. How come this time everyone is crying?" When Grandfather does not return, children feel hurt and angry. Grandfather's trip might be interpreted as a kind of desertion. They wonder: "Why didn't Grandpa even say good-bye? Why doesn't he come back? Doesn't he care about me anymore? What did I do wrong?" Another euphemism that causes problems is, "Dad is in a better place." The child can't help but wonder: "Then why didn't he take me? Maybe I should find a way to join him." Others use the expression "He expired." Drivers' licenses expire, not people! People die.

Some parents explain death by saying, "Grandfather died because he was sick." While people do become sick and die, most individuals who become ill survive. When learning that a grandparent died after an illness, many youngsters equate death with common physical ailments and hospitals. They become terrified that they will develop the same illness that "took" their loved one: "I think the doctor is wrong about me. It's not just a cough. My heart hurts me just the way Grandpa's did before he died." Parents must make a distinction between a very serious illness and a simple one. They should repeat again and again, "Even though Grandpa died, you are well. You have a bad cold, but it will go away soon and then you'll be fine. We expect you to live for a long, long time."

It is natural to draw a parallel between "death" and "sleep." Homer in the *Iliad* alludes to sleep (Hypnos) and death (Thanatos) as twin brothers. The two words are often linked in religious prayers. A prime example is the familiar bedtime rhyme:

> Now I lay me down to sleep;
> I pray the Lord my soul to keep.
> If I die before I wake,
> I pray the Lord my soul to take.

(That one has caused its share of insomnia!) Linking death to sleep can be dangerous to a child's mental health. When learning that "Grandma is asleep forever," some youngsters develop a pathological dread of bedtime. They toss about in their beds, fighting to stay awake for fear of falling asleep and never waking up again. Some youngsters are convinced that God "kills" people during their nightly sleep. Some funeral directors have contributed to the confusion between sleep and death by calling a room in the funeral parlor a "slumber room." Slumber means that the dead person will wake up—death is final!

Parents may say, "Death is hard for me to understand. How can I ever explain it to my children? How do I begin?" Don't wait until you are in the emotional turmoil of a personal tragedy to learn about death. Discuss it with an informed member of your clergy when you can be objective. Then when a death occurs in the family, you'll be able to talk with your children with greater confidence.

In our society "dead" is treated as a pornographic word; parents' fear of the word creates fear in children. Use the correct words: "dead," "die," and "death." Don't camouflage them. Death should be discussed in the context of everyday events—when passing a cemetery, hearing about a death on the news, or having a funeral for a canary. Death is as real as life and should be treated as part of the normal life cycle. When parents flush the family goldfish down the toilet or throw it in the trash and then replace it with a new one before the child gets home, they deny the child the opportunity to grieve.

Sharing grief over a pet helps families prepare to deal with more painful grief later on (the death of a member of the family or the death of a friend). When a parent denies the death of a pet, a child sometimes gets the message that if he were to die, his parents might ignore his death and simply replace him with a new model, too.

The subject of death should be approached gently and tenderly. The conversation could be initiated by talking about flowers growing in the spring and summer, then followed by their fading away in the fall and winter seasons. This is the sequence of life. For all living things there is a time to grow, flourish, and then die. Explanations should be presented without lurid, gruesome, or terrifying descriptions. Adults should proceed slowly, step by step, in accord with their children's ability to understand. Fears will be lessened when the discussion is initially focused, not upon the member of the family who is dying, but on animals or plants.

Again, parents should not explain death with fictions and half-truths. Grandpa did *not* go on a long journey. He is *not* asleep. Loss is real; separation is painful. Death does indeed bring an end to life.

Sometimes children have misconceptions about specific words or terms. If they seem to be confused, say the same thing in a different way. For example, one little boy, when told that his mother died, asked when she was coming back. His father said, "She's not coming back. It's permanent." His son continued to ask questions that indicated that he was expecting to see his mother again. Finally, after much discussion, the father realized that his son equated the word "permanent" with what his mother used to get at the beauty parlor, and *that* only lasted three months.

Honesty and directness are also essential when explaining divorce to children. Parents should plan in advance for the inevitable questions that may be raised by their offspring: "Where will I live? With whom? When can I visit?" Even if details are not complete, children should know that they will be kept informed of the developments. Good mental health is not the denial of tragedy, but learning how to live with pain and loss.

One of the worst problems for children is the lack of understanding because of parental secrecy. When parents avoid talking about their divorce, children's fears become magnified. They replace reality with fantasy and psychological defenses. Parents hurt children by denying them the opportunity to cope productively with this painful reality of life. The worst actuality is often preferable to uncertainty. If a situation is mentionable, it is more manageable.

Difficult as it may be, the subject of divorce should be discussed with both parents present, if possible. This serves several purposes. It lessens the possibility of one partner making the other a culprit. Often one mate will place the complete blame upon the other: "Your father never cared for you." Or: "Your mother is selfish and only thinks about herself." When one parent holds the other totally responsible for the breakup, youngsters are forced into the painful position of having to take sides. There ensues the bitter contest for children's affection and parents' exoneration. Children are "used" in the conflict as a means of transmitting parental contempt and retribution. This only results in further insecurity on the part of youngsters. As one teen-ager said, "It's almost like Dad wants me to hate Mom, and Mom wants me to hate Dad. That leaves me with nothing."

With skillful preparation, parents can better plan for the welfare of their children. A carefully considered explanation indicates that both parents have a concerned, shared interest. When explaining divorce to children, parents should avoid minute detail. It is neither necessary nor wise to isolate a single issue. One mother tried to explain the reason for divorce by saying, "We can't agree on money. Your father is always complaining that I spend too much on clothes, food, everything!" Although financial difficulties may have been one of the causes for the division between husband and wife, the explanation only served to oversimplify the problem as evidenced by the child's response: "Mom, you can keep my allowance. Then you'll have enough money and we can stay together."

Simple events can seem trivial and surmountable. They are only symptoms of the overall and complex source of disharmony. Instead of citing a litany of problems, parents could simply say, "You've watched us for a long time. You've seen how unhappy we have been. There are so *many* reasons."

The parents could begin the discussion by asking the children questions: "You know Mommy and Daddy haven't been getting along, don't you? We've been sad for so long. Have you noticed this?" Let the youngsters talk. It is important to gain an understanding of *their* perception of the situation.

The following dialogue demonstrates a seven-year-old boy's confusion.

"Mom, are you going to get married again?"

"Why? Do you want me to?"

"Sure," the child said.

The mother's relief was cut short when the child added, ". . . to Daddy."

Language has different meanings for parents and children. Youngsters come to associate the terms "anger," "raising your voice," and "losing your temper," with painful separation. Let them know that it is only natural to occasionally have disagreements. A distinction should be made between playmates' squabbles about "who should play the monster and who should play the king" versus parents' *constant* intense disputes.

When explaining death or divorce, one of the most important parental responses is often nonverbal. If a parent holds his youngster's hand, the child will feel warmth and really know that he is not being abandoned.

One of the important rights parents can give their children is the right to feel. Parents should never turn away from children's thoughts or brand them as "insignificant" or "childish." Youngsters should not be made to feel that they must hide their genuine emotions for fear of parental scorn or condemnation. Children need to be given the opportunity to talk—to ask their questions, and state their fears and anxieties. Adults should try to listen not only to their children's words, but observe their nonverbal communication as well. While many children may say "I'm okay," they may transmit warning signals of having difficulty dealing with the crisis: their schoolwork may start to falter; they may have trouble going to sleep at night; they may begin to withdraw from family and friends; or they may have physical symptoms of distress.

What are normal reactions to a death? Grief is a natural expression of love and loss for people of all ages. A child's response to grief depends upon his concepts of death, his developmental level, and the way he related to the person who has died. Yet each child will grieve differently, as do adults.

Some children will not speak of the loved one who died. As a parent recalled, "My daughter never talked about my father after he died. I'd ask her to remember some of the nice things they did together, and that didn't work. Then I'd ask her to tell me about the times she had been angry, but she still wouldn't talk. She'd say that she didn't remember or she didn't want to talk about it. It hurt me to think that for six years she saw him at least once a week, and then all of a sudden he dies, and he's forgotten." In contrast, some children never seem to stop talking about the person who died. "After my mother died, I couldn't be in the room for more than two minutes with my sister without her mentioning 'Mommy this' or 'Mommy that.' It was crazy," complained an eleven-year-old brother.

Some children will cry hysterically when hearing about the death of a loved one; others will remain outwardly impassive and emotionless; while others may even laugh. Some will praise the loved one as the most wonderful person in the world; others will hate the individual for leaving them alone and abandoned. Some will blame themselves for the death; others will project their grief upon God, the doctor, the clergy, the funeral director, or members of the family. In short, reactions are varied and contradictory, and almost always unpredictable.

Children should not be deprived of the right to grieve in their own way. They should no more be excluded from sharing grief and sadness than they should be prevented from demonstrating joy and happiness. Each person should be given the opportunity to lament the end of life and family love in his own individual manner.

The first reaction to death or divorce is often tears—for crying is a natural emotion. A newborn enters life crying for more oxygen. In early life, tears are an infant's means of expressing needs, pains, and discomforts. Even after children are able to verbalize their wishes, they may continue to weep in order to release their inner painful emotion.

Crying helps to express that inevitable depth of despair that follows the slow realization that the death or divorce is not a bad dream. Unfortunately, however, if children cry when discussing their parents' impending divorce, adults often tell them, "Be brave. Show us how strong you are." Children should never be discouraged from crying! The admonition to "be brave" encourages children to bottle up their emotions and minimize their loss. Youngsters who stoically repress their grief many later find release in an explosion that could prove to be more dangerous than if it were expressed at the time of the crisis. Too often tears are reserved for one gender. Crying is mistakenly considered a female trait. This lesson is poignantly demonstrated when a little boy falls off a swing, bumps his head, and out of fright and hurt, begins to cry. The mother or father quickly runs to him, picks him up, and says, "Big boys don't cry."

All people should be permitted to cry, *fathers included,* because crying relieves tension. Some social scientists believe that the failure of men to outwardly express feelings is one reason why they may be more vulnerable to certain illnesses. Many also believe that the lower statistics of accomplished suicides for women, as well as their longevity of life, may be attributed in some degree to their greater "freedom" to cry out and let go of their feelings.

Parents should reassure children—both male and female—that crying can be caused by love and fear of losing this love. Youngsters are then allowed the opportunity of relieving tension and expressing their emotions about their loss. Adults, too, need to give vent to their feelings and should not feel that they have failed their children if they weep in front of them.

Parents and children who cry together and share the real meaning of pain and separation are usually drawn closer to one another. A high school student who was a member of a support group for children of divorced parents said: "Once I found out my parents were getting divorced, I didn't even want to look at them. They had always talked about my living up to their expectations. But what about *my* expectations? Now they had let *me* down. Mom and Dad tried giving me lots of pep talks, saying it was all for the best. Then one day they cried, and I started crying with them. Things changed. We were *all* sad. We were all in it together." Other members of the support group agreed that a turning point in their relationship with their parents occurred when they could express pain as a family.

While youngsters should not be denied the opportunity to weep, neither should they be urged to express unfelt feelings. They should not be subjected to emotional blackmail in which they are urged to cry or to react to a loss in a particular manner. Each child reacts differently. Some children need to cry freely. Others may not weep at all. A boy remembered when his father's sister died: "I felt bad, but mostly for my father. He looked so sad! But I wasn't sad for me. I never even knew my aunt. Maybe I had seen her five times, and that was it. When she died, everyone said it was okay to cry, but I couldn't."

Youngsters feel confused and hypocritical when told to express a sentiment they do not honestly experience. There are other outlets for emotions besides tears. Children should express only those feelings appropriate to their needs.

When learning about a death or a divorce, children may initially deny this reality. Denial is a natural reaction that takes many forms. In a state of shock, children may say, "Don't talk about it. It's not true." Secretly youngsters may think or pretend that their families will remain intact, or that their loved ones are really alive.

After being told that his parents were getting divorced, one boy casually said, "Oh." Then he asked, "Is it all right if I go play kickball?" The parents considered the child insensitive and asked each other, "Doesn't he love us? Doesn't he care?" They did not realize that the impact of a crisis is not always felt immediately or understood completely when the sad news is first relayed.

Children may look unaffected because they are trying to defend themselves against the loss by pretending that it has not really happened. The parents may even be relieved: "She's taking it so well." A lack of immediate response often signifies that children have found the situation too difficult to accept and fantasize that the death or divorce has not really occurred. Denial is not an abnormal reaction. Temporary forgetfulness often helps a person to put aside the upsetting reality by focusing on the other issues of living.

From denial—"No, not me"—children may turn in anger and say, "Why me?" Parents who are dealing with their own feelings of sadness and anger may have difficulty responding to their children's resentments. One child asked, "Mommy, why were you so mean to Daddy? If you were nicer, he wouldn't have left us." Parents should never react to a child's anger with threats of punishment. Children are suffering enough guilt and pain. Instead, children should be approached with patience and respect. Responses such as "How dare you speak to me that way after what I've been through," bring the discussion to a speedy conclusion. A parent may instead say, "I know it hurts you to hear this. I can understand how angry you must be. You've got good reason."

There is almost always some degree of guilt involved in almost every death and divorce both for parents and children. It is natural to blame oneself for past failures. After the Cocoanut Grove nightclub fire in Boston, one woman could not stop condemning herself for having quarreled with her boyfriend just before his death. Recrimination is an attempt to turn back the clock, undo the wrong events for which the survivor now feels guilty, and somehow magically to prevent the loss.

Guilt takes many forms. It can be directed outward with aggressiveness and hostility. "Mom, why didn't you call the ambulance sooner? If you did, Dad wouldn't be dead now." Or "Mom, if you didn't work so much, Dad would've been happier and then you wouldn't have had to get a divorce."

Guilt can also be turned inward, causing depression. Youngsters may lose their ability to concentrate on their schoolwork or on hobbies they had once loved. Others regress into bedwetting and thumb-sucking. Unresolved grief is found in withdrawal, delinquency, excessive excitability, self-pity, and defiance of authority.

More than adults, children are likely to feel guilt. In their experience, bad things happen when they are naughty. For example, when they hit a classmate or a sibling, they are punished. On the other hand, when they receive good grades in school, they are rewarded. The "desertion" of a loved one can therefore be perceived as a retribution for wrongdoing. They search in their memories for the "bad thing" for which they are being penalized. Adults experience the same process after a death. Every clergyperson has heard the question from the survivors: "Why am I being punished?"—and this from adults.

From a commonsense point of view, youngsters' guilt may seem unreasonable to the parents. One parent said in amazement, "My son is convinced that his mother and I are getting divorced because he couldn't figure out how to make his model airplane." Pangs of guilt are agonizing even when induced by a misconception of reality.

Parents inadvertently create guilt by unexplained or fictional interpretations. A college student reminisced about returning home from school when, as a first grader, he learned that his older sister "had gone away and would not come back." "Where did she go? What happened?" he asked. "Don't ask so many questions," was the only response from the parents. For years he suffered recriminations, convinced that he must have done something terrible to cause his sister's disappearance. His guilt was only relieved when he took a course on "dying, death, and bereavement" at the university and understood that all of these years he mistakenly believed that he was responsible for his sister's absence.

Children should understand that nothing they said, did, or thought had anything to do with what happened. Parents might say to the child whose sister died after a long bout with leukemia, "Perhaps you made her unhappy sometimes. But you also made her very happy. She loved you and always forgave you. She'd been getting so much attention during her long illness that you probably felt that you weren't getting your share. You may have even wished, sometimes, that she was dead and the family's suffering was over. She died because of her leukemia. You had nothing to do with her death."

In the case of divorce, parents should repeat again and again that they are only unhappy with each other, not with their children. Adults should assure their children that even though they will no longer live in the same house, they still have two parents. Divorce occurs between mother and father, not between parents and children.

Drastic changes in children's lives evoke feelings of panic. A family existence that once was taken for granted is no longer guaranteed. Some youngsters of divorced parents assume that because their father no longer lives at home, they will become poverty-stricken. In one case, when arrangements were made for a young girl to live with her father, the child asked, "How can I live? Daddy can't cook." She felt that her very survival was threatened by the breakup.

When someone dies, children are confronted with the reality that other loved ones will someday die, and that they themselves are now mortal. One girl witnessed her father die from a coronary. After his death, she began to sneak to her mother's room at night, standing close enough to her bed to hear whether or not her mother was breathing. One night her mother noticed her daughter standing over her. When the girl was asked what she was doing, she cried, "I lost Dad. I don't want to lose you, too." Whether or not these fears are rooted in reality, children's fears are very real to them. Adults should listen and attempt to discern the true anxieties.

In the case of a death, parents invariably ask: "Should the children attend the funeral?" "Would seeing the coffin only heighten children's fears?" "How would children feel being surrounded by weeping adults?"

The funeral is a rite of passage—an important occasion in the life of the family. The bad dream is real. The beloved will no longer be part of the familiar environment. Like other members of the household, children should have the privilege to express their love and devotion at the funeral.

Participation helps children to understand the finality of death. One twelve-year-old boy recalled attending the funeral of a classmate: "I knew Debra was really sick. For two years, she practically lived in the hospital, but it seemed like no matter how sick she got, she always pulled through. Then one morning my mother woke me up and said that Debra had died. I couldn't believe it—until I went to the funeral. When I saw the coffin, I thought, 'Oh, my God. Debra is in that box. She's really dead.' " When children are mature enough to comprehend in part what is taking place, they should be allowed to attend a ceremony to say "farewell" to a significant person in their lives.

Many children are discomfited by their unfamiliarity with the funeral rites and setting. Parents need to explain in advance approximately how the chapel will look and where they will be sitting. Children also need to understand the meaning of the religious rituals that they will be experiencing to reduce their fear and give meaning to the traditions they are sharing with the family. They should be aware that people may cry and that crying is okay—it is one way people have of expressing sadness that they won't be seeing their loved one again. If parents are unable to be close to the children at the service, a member of the family or a close friend should be asked to be with them and perhaps to hold their hand.

Though attending a funeral can be therapeutic, children should never be forced to attend. If apprehensive youngsters elect to remain at home, parents should not place any "shaming" pressures upon them or insinuate that they may not have loved the person who died. Instead, parents could gently suggest that together they could visit the cemetery at another time. Then the child could be given some role that will help him to feel important to the family—answering the phones, answering the door, or caring for younger children in the family.

The funeral does not end in the chapel but at the final burial place, the cemetery. Parents should not assume arbitrarily that the interment is too traumatic for children. Again, parents should explain in detail the procedure and consult them about their wishes and needs. Witnessing the burial may provide a realistic answer to the perennial question, "Where is my loved one now?" For children, like adults, the funeral helps in learning to accept the finality of death.

Children often focus on the physical aspects of death, wanting to know who will hold the dead person when he's lonely, how he will go to the bathroom, how he'll breathe, and whether he'll be afraid in the dark. One child was concerned that his mother would need her wheelchair in the casket.

In order to help children understand the meaning of death, they need to be told that there is no breath, no movement, no thinking, and no feeling. The body is still because life is gone. The child who is allowed to view and even touch a dead animal has a better understanding of the reality of death.

Parents also have difficulty helping children come to terms with divorce. They ask: "How do we help children cope?" "How do we answer their questions?" "What do they need to hear?"

- Children often employ bargaining power in an attempt to prevent their parents' divorce. One nine-year-old boy stated, "Okay, you can be divorced if I don't have to go to camp." Let the children know that just as they had nothing to do with causing their parents' divorce, there is nothing they can say or do that will reunite mother and father.

- In a desire to appease youngsters, some adults attempt to soften the blow by saying, "Don't take it so hard. Maybe we'll think it over again." Consequently, children may continue to believe that perhaps their parents will remain together. Once again, when the decision is irrevocable, honesty is the only formula. Parents should repeat that they will *not* live together again. The separation is unalterable.

- Children need to be continually reassured that they are loved and that the custodial parent will not leave them.

- If the other parent shows no interest in the children, this reality needs to be acknowledged. The custodial parent might explain that the non-custodial parent is preoccupied with his own life for the time being and that, though it is difficult to accept, he will not be calling or visiting for a long while; it's important to add, without bitterness, that they are very lovable, special children—that the absent parent will be missing out.

- Parents should not compensate for their guilt by giving their children everything they desire. Overindulgence deprives youngsters of attaining satisfaction by their own efforts.

- As stated, when one parent blames the other for the divorce, children are forced to take sides. Parents should make a conscious effort not to use the children to transmit their contempt and anger to their former partner.

- If parents remarry, they should avoid comparing their new partner with their previous one.

What are other guidelines for parents to help their children through either a death or a divorce?

- Parents need to contact the children's school and inform the teachers of the crisis. Otherwise, teachers might not react appropriately to any change in the youngster's grades or sudden sullenness or regressive behavior.

- Minimize changes in the child's life. Changes increase stress. If it is necessary to move to a new home or change a child's school, try to delay the change to give your child (and yourself) the opportunity to draw from your support systems in the community.

- A child should never be told that he is now the man or woman of the house, or a replacement for a dead sibling or a missing spouse. Forcing youngsters into being substitute adults or surrogate relatives only makes it more difficult for them to cope with the loss caused by a death or divorce.

When a child is told that he needs to take care of his mother, now that his father is no longer alive, his loss is compounded: he's robbed, not only of his father, but of his right to his childhood as well!

A fifteen-year-old girl said: "When Mom left I had to do everything. I washed the clothes. I cooked the meals. I cleaned the house. I looked after the kids. It was really hard. I didn't even have time to do my homework. My grades started to slip. But what could I do? I knew *I* was the only one who could do it because Mom was gone and Dad had to be at work. I was so afraid of letting everyone down. But sometimes I'd get mad, too. I'd think, 'All my friends are out having a good time, and look at me. It's lousy.' And then I'd start to hate myself for thinking that. . . ."

- Children should know that adults do not always have the final answers. The door should be kept ajar to youngsters' doubts, questions, and differences of opinion. Parents do not diminish themselves in their children's estimation when they say that they don't have all the answers. Rather, adults demonstrate their maturity when they state, "It's hard to understand why love doesn't last forever. Your father and I never wanted to hurt each other, but we did, and we didn't know how to stop." Or "Are you surprised that I don't know everything about death? Don't be. That's why we need to talk together. Let's help one another." Open, frank discussions encourage further mutual probings. A wise person once said, "I have some good answers. Do you understand the real questions?" Not all questions have final answers. Unanswered problems are part of life.

- Parents should not be afraid to express some of their own emotions of grief in front of their children. Children then receive permission to grieve from adults. To be able to show feelings openly without fear or embarrassment can help both children and parents to accept the reality of their loss.

- Parents should allow their children and themselves an opportunity to adjust at a realistic pace. If too much is expected, they will feel like failures and only create a more difficult environment for themselves and their children. One research study concluded that children mourn longer and more intermittently than adults. The statistics indicated that unlike adults, who were able to grieve intensely for a year or more, children are more likely to continue to mourn on and off for many years after the loss. When confronted with death or divorce, grieving does not stop when the funeral is concluded or when parents remove their wedding rings.

- Grieving can lead either to the edge of the abyss and threaten existence with feelings of meaninglessness and futility, or help one start to build the bridge that spans the chasm with those things of life that still count—memory, family, friendship, and love.

- Parents should consider some kind of counseling for their children if they deem it necessary. Certainly they would not be in a position to make this decision in the immediate period following the death or divorce. At this time, it is so difficult to separate the normal grieving pattern from the distorted. During the crisis, many people speak and act in ways that are not in keeping with their usual behavior. Grief and sorrow leave imprints upon the healthiest of personalities.

The difference between normal and distorted grief is not in the symptom but in its intensity. It is *continued* denial of reality even months after the funeral or the divorce; or *prolonged* bodily distress; or *persistent* frenzy; or *extended* guilt; or *unceasing* apathy; or *enduring* hostile reaction to others that requires help. In other words, each manifestation does not in itself indicate a distorted grief reaction; that can only be determined when such signs of grief are viewed in the total framework of behavior.

Even more important than *how* the child is acting, reacting, or overreacting, is for *how long?* After an initial period of mourning, children are often able to work themselves back to some degree of productive and near-normal living. Some danger signals might include delinquency, unwillingness to remain in school, problems in learning new material, unreasonable withdrawal, uncommunicativeness, excessive anger, or intense suspicion.

When parents are in doubt, they should not hesitate to seek advice from a therapist, psychiatrist, school psychologist, social worker, or child guidance clinic. Getting professional counseling is not an admission of a parent's inadequacy, but a demonstration of real love and concern for the child's welfare. It takes real strength for people of all ages to admit that they need help.

Parents must realize that by sorting out their own feelings they will be better able to understand their troubled children who come laden with questions and beset with fears. The real challenge for parents is not just how to explain death and divorce to children, but how to better make peace with it themselves.

By the Author

Explaining Death to Children. Boston: Beacon Press, 1967.

Suicide: Prevention, Intervention, Postvention. Boston: Beacon Press, 1971.

Concerning Death: A Practical Guide for the Living. Boston: Beacon Press, 1974.

Talking About Death: A Dialogue Between Parent and Child. Boston: Beacon Press, 1976.

Living—When a Loved One Has Died. Boston: Beacon Press, 1977.

(With Sharon Grollman) *Caring for Your Aged Parents.* Boston: Beacon Press, 1978.

When Your Loved One Is Dying. Boston: Beacon Press, 1980.

What Helped Me—When My Loved One Died. Boston: Beacon Press, 1981.

Talking About Divorce and Separation—A Dialogue Between Parents and Children. Boston: Beacon Press, 1982.

(With Gerri Sweder) *The Working Parents' Dilemma.* Boston: Beacon Press, 1986.

Time Remembered: A Journal for Survivors. Boston: Beacon Press, 1987.

In Sickness and in Health. Boston: Beacon Press, 1987.

BENJAMIN SPOCK
AND MARY MORGAN

Meet the Authors

DR. BENJAMIN SPOCK

Dr. Benjamin Spock was the sage to many of our grandparents as they turned to his advice to learn how to raise our parents. Yet his advice is as valued and current today, three generations later. His book Baby and Child Care *has sold well over thirty-three million copies and has been translated into thirty-nine languages. It is second in sales only to the Bible (which, appropriately, has been its nickname for decades).*

This tireless author, pediatrician, and political activist was born in 1903 in New Haven, Connecticut, the oldest of six children. He and his first wife had two children, Michael (who is married and has two children of his own and is Vice President of the Field Museum in Chicago, Illinois) and John (who is an architect in California).

Dr. Spock graduated from Phillips Academy, Andover, in 1921 and from Yale with a B.A. in 1925. He rowed on the Yale crew of 1924, which won gold medals at the Olympic Games in Paris that year. He attended Yale Medical School for two years, then transferred in 1927 to the College of Physicians and Surgeons at Columbia University, from which he received his M.D. in 1929.

Dr. Spock had an internship in medicine, a pediatric residency, and a psychiatric residency. He also took part-time training at the New York Psycho-analytic Institute. He served on the pediatric and psychiatric staffs of Cornell Medical College and New York Hospital. In 1947 Dr. Spock joined the staffs of the Mayo Clinic and the Rochester (Minnesota) Health Institute. From 1951 to 1955, he was professor of Child Development at the University of Pittsburgh Medical School and from 1955 to 1967 he was at Western Reserve University in Cleveland, Ohio. Since 1963 he has been writing columns for Redbook *magazine.*

Having joined the National Committee for a Sane Nuclear Policy in 1963 to protect children from the radiation of fallout, Dr. Spock became co-chairperson and spokesperson for the peace movement. He was the People's Party presidential candidate in 1972 and vice presidential candidate in 1976. He has spoken at over 800 universities at the invitation of the undergraduates.

MARY MORGAN

Mary Morgan, formerly program coordinator for Continuing Education in Psychiatry at the University of Arkansas Medical School, has been Dr. Spock's Program Coordinator for his lectures, press, and other speaking engagements since 1976. She has lectured on a wide variety of causes—the women's movement, the peace movement—and on aging, as well as on stepparenting. On October 1985, she and Dr. Spock were invited to speak at the National Stepfamily Association in Washington, D.C., where they are members of the board.

Mary Morgan is licensed by the U.S. Coast Guard as captain. She serves as co-captain along with Dr. Spock to their 35-foot sloop, Carapace, *which they live aboard in Tortola, British Virgin Islands.*

She organizes women's groups and workshops on women's issues in the Virgin Islands and in Arkansas. Her work has been published in Redbook *and* Parade *magazines.*

She is a marathon runner who also loves to snorkle, dive, sail, and windsurf. Mary's daughter, Ginger, age twenty-one, helped teach Dr. Spock and Mary the painful lessons of stepparenting.

9

TWO PERSPECTIVES ON STEPPARENTING

THE STEPPARENTING DILEMMA
BENJAMIN SPOCK, M.D., AND MARY MORGAN

A STEPPARENT'S VIEW—
by Dr. Benjamin Spock

I wrote an article for a magazine twenty-five years ago on how to be a stepparent, which I thought had a lot of wisdom. But ten years ago, when I became a stepfather to Ginger, my wife's eleven-year-old daughter, I found that I didn't know beans about being a stepparent. Or at least, I was unable, because of my miserable feelings, to carry out the suggestions in my own article of long ago. I had had no idea of how painful it would be to feel rejected by someone within my family or how hard it would be to react rationally.

I felt, though Ginger vehemently denies it, that for several years she largely ignored me. She rarely answered my greetings and questions, or did so only with minimal grunts. I remember, on one such occasion, asking angrily, "Ginger, why won't you ever reply when I say good morning?" and she answered, "I said hello, but it was so quiet you didn't hear it." It seemed to me she hardly ever spoke to me voluntarily and she wouldn't smile when I was in the same room. When I drove her to school because she had missed the bus, she wouldn't say "thank you" or "good-bye." To me there was no sign of apology or affection. Her resentment seemed relentless.

To try to overcome Ginger's feeling of being left out, my wife Mary and I invited Ginger and a friend to skip school for several weeks and sail with us in the Virgin Islands, but this made no difference in her behavior. In fact, she made me so angry on one occasion by saying something scornful about the treat we were providing that I became purple in the face and shouted at her furiously. That didn't faze her either. The contrast with how Ginger's friend (also age eleven) treated me was dramatic. She chatted with me amiably and always addressed me as "Benjy Boy," which I liked, especially under the circumstances.

We invited Ginger to spend her summer vacation with us, sailing in Maine, but she refused, saying that it sounded too cold and foggy and that she wouldn't know anyone. Instead she stayed with her father in accordance with our original visitation agreement, by which she could be with him when Mary and I were out of town. We'd settled in the same city to facilitate such shifts.

I tried to be understanding and patient, but I didn't succeed. I became more and more resentful of her seeming rudeness and expressed my frustration by becoming critical. I criticized Ginger's table manners, the mess in which she left her room each morning, the way she threw her wet towel and dripping wash cloth on top of her soiled clothes, her extravagance in shopping at the most expensive stores, the loudness of her radio, and her refusal to wear her tooth-straightening apparatus. I knew that all these efforts to correct and discipline her were mistaken, even counterproductive—all the books agreed on that—but I was obsessed with trying to make her behave.

I craved sympathy from my wife and wished she would crack down on Ginger's impoliteness. She listened to my complaints, but quite properly wanted to avoid appearing to turn against Ginger on the basis of my accusations. She could see, better than I, how Ginger was suffering. And she pointed out that my two adult sons had not summoned up much graciousness in welcoming her into our family, even though they were not going to live in the same house with us, or even in the same part of the country.

After a year of worsening relations, I went to a counselor who specializes in stepfamily problems. She wasn't able to offer me any magic solution—counselors never can. But she helped me a great deal by simply telling me that I had been living in a fool's paradise if I thought I would be accepted by a stepchild within a year or two. (Of course, some stepparents are a success from the start—and my admiration for them is boundless. It takes tact and patience.) To hear that what I was experiencing was to be expected did relieve a lot of my guilt and sense of failure. As a result, I became a bit more patient.

Recently, long after we had made a gradual peace, Ginger and I were asked to write companion pieces for *Redbook* magazine and also to appear on a television program. I urged her to write and speak frankly about how she had *felt* and how the relationship *seemed* to her at the time, not to try to judge who was at fault or who was right. I said I'd do the same. In describing her side of the relationship, Ginger emphasized how close she and her mother had been since her parents' divorce, what a shock it had been to find that her mother and a man whom she hardly knew seemed to be rapidly heading for marriage, how she feared losing her mother, and how abandoned she felt when her mother went sailing with this man in the Virgin Islands or in Maine for long periods of time.

When she came to describing how she felt about me, and how she treated me, it sounded like an utterly different relationship from the one I remembered. She denied any recollection of having given me the cold, hostile treatment that I recalled so painfully. She wrote, "I didn't hate him; I was just watching him." If she had felt any lack of cordiality at the time, she was sure it lasted only a few months, not years.

Her story made me wonder whether, in my misery, I had grossly exaggerated her hostility. But in any case, the point is that the intrusion of a stepparent can cause dismay and resentment so intense that it completely blots out reasonableness and politeness. (Could an adult be cordial when confronted with an armed robber in the bedroom?) The child's hostility will sooner or later get under the skin of the stepparent and cause anger, further convincing the child he is a mean, untrustworthy person.

When you look at the problem from the child's perspective, you can see why, in most cases, she feels deeply threatened. She has had her parent— usually the mother—to herself for several years in what is an unusually close relationship, since she hasn't had to share her with her father. When her mother falls in love, the child harbors an unconscious, irrational fear of losing her as, in a sense, she has lost her father.

The child feels no bond to this interloper; she is not the one who fell in love with him. Even if the prospective stepfather has unusually attractive qualities, it is hard for the child to see and appreciate these because he is, first, an outsider who is claiming a great deal of her mother's attention and affection.

The intensity of this hostility toward the intruder is similar to the jealousy of the older child, especially the first child, toward a new baby. I've seen a secure, happy, loving child of two years turn bitter, destructive, and cruel.

In retrospect it is clear to me that no matter how much I was suffering, Ginger was suffering more. But at the time I was so resentful of her attitude toward me that I didn't have room in my heart, as the expression goes, to feel much sympathy for her. I suspect that part of my resentment came from the fact that this was not an adult but just a little girl who seemed to feel fully entitled to make me miserable for years, and that I was utterly helpless to do anything to change the situation.

In the ten years that I have been in the family, Ginger's and my relationship has very gradually, but thoroughly, improved. My greatest triumph was when she recommended me as commencement speaker at her high school graduation, and I was able, by speaking scornfully about grades, to gain the favor of the class (at the expense of some faculty disapproval). Now we are good and affectionate friends. What brought about the change? I don't know for sure.

Most stepchildren will slowly become more accepting. They find that they have not been displaced in their mother's love, so their fears and resentments can subside. Besides, they are becoming more mature and realistic. As they mature, they learn that treating the stepfather better is in their best interest—it allows his better nature to come to the surface. So once the worst is past, the relationship can become a beneficial cycle, just as it was a vicious cycle at the start.

A PARENT'S PERSPECTIVE—by Mary Morgan

My firsthand experience with a steprelationship began in 1976, when I married Ben Spock and presented him with an eleven-year-old stepdaughter, Ginger.

Ginger was angry from day one. She had not invited this intruder into her life and she felt helpless and powerless against Ben's fame, money, and age. Ginger and I had lived together, just the two of us, for several years, and she liked having her mother all to herself. In addition to being mother and daughter, we had become close friends. When Ben came into the picture and "took her mother away," she rebelled by saying she wanted to live with her father, which she did for a short time. She felt abandoned by me and expressed her hurt feelings by briefly abandoning me in return.

Ginger also felt that any kindness toward Ben was a sign of disloyalty to her own father. I watched over the years as she struggled painfully with this issue of loyalty versus disloyalty, a struggle that kept her in a state of turmoil. Without being aware of it, I contributed to this turmoil by running down her father in front of her, forcing her to defend him.

I had to learn that while my marriage to Ginger's father was very much over, I was letting my anger toward him keep me emotionally involved in the relationship at Ginger's expense. When Ben pointed out that I was only adding fuel to her fire, I stopped doing it. And when Ginger no longer had to defend her father, her anxiety decreased considerably and the loyalty issue eventually resolved itself.

When Ginger would go to see her father, there was always a big fight about who would provide the transportation. We used the occasion to express our unresolved anger. She would feel torn between us, and it set the stage for uproar with each visitation.

Some ex-spouses use the late child support payment as blackmail for visitation. If the check doesn't arrive, then Daddy isn't allowed to come for the kids. The greatest losers are the kids. When Dad "doesn't care about them" enough to want to see them, they think their father has abandoned them once again. By allowing visitation regardless of the child support payments, the father *feels like more of a parent* and develops a greater sense of responsibility toward the child. Also it puts the burden of collection of the money back in the hands of the court instead of using the child as a pawn. I think there can be some real improvements in our collection system for alimony as well as child support, but that should be dealt with separate and apart from the issue of visitation.

If a mother has custody of the kids, which is usually the case, then she holds a lot of power. This power can be either used or abused at the time of visitation. She can abuse her power by playing games with visitation or she can make her power work for her by directing her energy toward helping her child enjoy visits with her other biological parent without guilt.

How the mother chooses to use her time away from her kids during visitation may make a big difference. Sometimes I would take the victim's role, reacting to their time together as though Ginger's father had won her over and they both were abandoning me. I allowed each visit to reopen the wounds of our divorce. I didn't want them to have fun together when I couldn't be a part of it. Each time she left me I felt helpless and unwanted.

My attitude was hurting her as well as myself. It had to change. As I reclaimed my power and gave up my role as victim, my resentment and jealousy over the time they spent together lessened. What particularly helped was finding new and interesting things to do during her visitations. Then I began looking forward to those times rather than resenting them.

At times Ginger would stir up my jealousy by coming home and describing a particularly fabulous meal her stepmother prepared for her. To me the implication was that she was getting better parenting from someone else. I could either resent this and play the victim role again or decline to play and respond to her with another wonderful meal of my own. I had to realize that what she was really telling me was that she needed more nurturing from me and that this was the only way she knew to ask for it. When I saw the situation in this light, I could respond to her needs more easily.

I wasn't the only one experiencing jealousy. Every day I felt torn as Ben and Ginger competed for my attention. I thought I had done a wonderful thing for my daughter by marrying the great Dr. Spock, but she didn't act as if she appreciated it at all. And Ben, who was supposed to be the leading expert in child rearing, had met his match in a relationship he had never experienced before—a teen-age stepdaughter, two generations removed.

I had assumed too much. I thought that since I loved both of them, they would automatically love each other. Wrong! A child doesn't love someone just because he has acquired her mother's love. On the contrary, Ginger was now confronted with competition for her mother's love, a situation which, being an only child, she had never experienced before. Ben kept buying her presents and wooing her affection. But when he bought her a bicycle, she promptly wrecked it—wonder why? She smashed every one of his advances with glee, as if to say, "Try that again and see what you get."

Ginger would also play "Let's You and Him Fight." Kids are experts in maneuvering their parents into playing this game anyway, but when there are stepparents to play out the scenario, there's far more energy and hostility to work with. The game usually began with Ginger saying something like "Ben said I could drive his car to town"—even though I had already said she could not. Now, on the surface it might appear that Ginger was raising the car issue because she wanted to go to town to be with her friends. But, though she might have been totally unaware of it, her deeper motive was to produce an explosion and a temporary "divorce" of her real parent and stepparent. She gained tremendous satisfaction in feeling that by dividing Ben and me, she would become closer to me.

One way to end the game was to decline the invitation at the very beginning. Ben and I learned to do this by discussing each issue together and setting limits *before* we dealt with Ginger.

Ginger also looked for ways to antagonize Ben. Once she found which buttons she could push, she pushed hard and often. Ben had never felt so pushed in his life! A prime example was Ginger's room. Ginger was living at home with us between the ages of eleven and sixteen before she went to boarding school. These were very traumatic years for Ginger, and I felt that the appearance of her room was a reflection of all the upheaval going on inside of her. The plates of rotten food which I often found under the wet towels under her bed represented her anger at her mother who was trying to control her by controlling her food. (The wet towels were just added "icing" on the cake.) I would constantly close the door in the hope of forgetting that that plate of garbage was really a symbol of what my child was feeling toward me. (Closing the door is called denial—and if you haven't tried it as a defense lately, let me recommend it as a way of giving your system a rest from stepfamily anxiety. Yes, I'll admit, it is temporary relief—but it is relief!)

Although I found comfort in closing her door and shutting off the pain, this kind of denial was not Ben's style. He would go into Ginger's room each morning after she left for school, hang up her wet towels, gather up the garbage, and expect that somehow this would *teach* her to do it herself. Not at all. It only taught her that if she left wet towels on the floor and food under the bed, Ben would clear them all away in the morning. She had him beautifully house-trained and she knew it. He knew better but he couldn't seem to stop. I saw him walk to the door that I had previously closed, step back, and try to stop himself, but just be unable to. The power this kid had in this one act must have compensated for all the powerlessness she had felt toward him. It was tremendously effective. I don't know anyone else who could get Dr. Spock to serve as her maid. But she paid a price. For although Ben would rescue her in the morning by cleaning her room, he would persecute her at night by denying her certain privileges, and she then would switch from persecutor to victim. As a victim, however, she would feel entitled to throw her wet towels back on the floor, inviting Ben to become persecutor again. This game lasted for about five years with many variations on the basic theme.

Letting go and staying out of this game was more than I could do at times. However much we bribed her, threatened her, pleaded with her, she would not give it up, because it was the one situation in which she felt a sense of her own power. In order to stop the game, Ginger had to develop her own separate sense of power and independence. And since this messy behavior had so much to do with her angry feelings toward me, I don't think she could really change until our relationship changed. She chose her bedroom for her battleground—the stage could have been any other setting. But since the room could turn Ben into a chambermaid, as well as express her anger at me, it served a dual purpose.

In any relationship, especially a steprelationship, it's very important to understand and deal with the anger. To the extent that this can be accomplished, the relationship can grow and survive and have benefits for all involved. Understanding where the anger is coming from, and avoiding taking this anger personally, is a real task.

I found in our stepfamily that the anger was often used as a mask, and that by looking beyond the anger I could see other, much harder to express, feelings. When Ginger and I examined her anger more closely, we could see that there was a tremendous amount of sadness and fear behind it. There was the sadness of realizing that her mother and father would never get back together, and the fear that she might be abandoned by me, as she felt she had been by her father, for this new man. These hidden feelings that she found so difficult to express led to stronger anger. Thus, when Ben and I would leave to go sailing or would travel on the lecture circuit, it was easier for Ginger just to refuse to see us by continuing to stay with her father when we returned rather than to admit how abandoned she had felt by our leaving.

I had a number of hidden fears also. Would I be jealous of Ginger if Ben found her attractive? And what would I do if this marriage didn't work? Would Ginger abandon me and go live with her father permanently? Would Ben leave me if he found my kid intolerable? And what would all of Ben's readers think if he failed as a stepfather—would parents stop buying *Baby and Child Care?* Would I ever have that closeness to Ginger that I had experienced before Ben came on the scene? Would I lose control if I couldn't make it all work? My sadness and guilt about the failure of my first marriage had given way to angry fights in court about Ginger's child support and custody. I didn't want to "fail" again.

Ginger used my behavior as an example of how to deal with her own feelings. As she watched me in court and saw my anger rather than my pain and sorrow about marital failure, she, too, let her anger mask her true feelings. Only when I would ask her what else besides anger was going on inside her, would she allow me to get close enough to see some of these other, more painful emotions. These sensitive discussions were far more productive than our usual angry bouts, which consisted of one furious power play after another.

If there is permission, and enough protection from the parent, the child will reveal the hurts, fears, and sadness more readily—and, as a result, will require less anger to cover them up. Kids also find it easier to express their painful feelings to parents and stepparents when the adults are willing to reveal their own guilt, sadness, and hurt feelings to their children.

Anger in a steprelationship is often displaced. I remember hearing about a stepson confessing to his stepmother with tears in his eyes that he had hated her for years. He was angry because she had never filled his expectation that he would finally have the perfect mother, one who would meet all the needs that his real mother had not met. In other words, all of the anger that this son had held on to for years was directed toward his stepmother because it was too terrifying to tell his own mother to "fuck off." It was as though his displaced anger was his way of trying to change his own mother and make her finally love him the way he had always wanted to be loved.

In such a situation the stepmother is in a dilemma because she really wants no part of this old history. She is not responsible for the relationship that these stepkids have with either of their parents; those relationships began long before she came on the scene; she is only responsible for her own relationship with them.

Many stepmothers tolerate abuse from their stepchildren because they think that if they let their true feelings out they may seriously jeopardize their marital relationship. They greet their stepchildren wearing a T-shirt that reads "I'm a door mat. Please abuse me at any time." Stepchildren sense this, along with the oozing guilt some women feel about having taken their fathers away from them. Don't be a victim to your stepchildren. None of you will benefit; it will only intensify your resentment and their disrespect. When the ball is passed your way, simply let it drop.

Whenever we tell people that Ben, Ginger, and I had to go for counseling because of our stepfamily problems, they are shocked! But we did—and it was beneficial for all of us. The counselor's words helped us develop more realistic expectations. I learned not to expect Ben and Ginger to love each other immediately. Their relationship needed time to develop. As I let go of my idealistic expectations, Ginger and Ben began to build their own relationship—separate and apart from me.

I had felt that their misery was because of me so I was determined to ease it, cure it, make everything okay. I had the grandiose idea that they needed me to make things work, but they really didn't. In fact, I was only deepening the wedge. I needed to step back and let the two of them make whatever relationship they wanted. And for a controlling person like me, it was very hard to step back. But letting go was the key to success. First I had to admit that the two of them might not want to have a positive relationship or, heaven forbid, they might have a successful one that I had no part in shaping. My first task was to become aware that I was trying to control the relationship and my second task was, out of this awareness, to consciously stop doing it. The first task was easy; the second was far more difficult. Even with awareness I would repeatedly catch myself trying to take charge of their interaction.

My real fears came from a lack of security about my own separate relationship with each of them. My relationship with Ginger, as she went through those early teen years, was in a real upheaval. (This would probably have been true, of course, with or without a stepfather on the scene.) And as she went through all of these changes, so did my relationship with her. I questioned my own role as a mother. What had I done, I wondered, to deserve this kind of abusive treatment from her? After I stopped trying to control the relationship between Ben and Ginger, I was able to put more energy into building a healthier relationship with her myself.

The same was true about the new relationship between Ben and myself. We "newlyweds" were madly in love, but our relationship certainly had many issues to resolve. Our conflict with Ginger masked the uncertainties I must have been feeling about Ben and myself at that time. Focusing my energy on Ben and Ginger's relationship served as a means of ignoring my own problems with Ben. It's always easier to see the faults in someone else's relationship rather than recognize your own.

The real growth in our stepfamily took place when I stopped trying to make Ben and Ginger love each other, and to demonstrate their love *when* and in the manner in which *I wanted them to,* in order to meet *my* needs. Ginger gradually responded more warmly to Ben as she felt she had more options in the relationship. Before, it had been shoved down her throat, and guess who had the biggest shovel?

Allowing Ginger to make the relationship suit her needs and not mine was an important breakthrough, which then led to an improved relationship with her stepfather. I'm not saying that every time a mother steps back and lets go, a good relationship will follow. Ginger might instead have decided to go her separate way and have nothing to do with Ben. What I *am* saying is that a happy ending is more likely if the two people involved work things out themselves. In order to do that, the biological parent must first be willing to accept the fact that these two people may just decline to have any relationship at all. They must have that option before they can feel free to move closer or further away. Without the choice of moving further away, there is no choice of moving closer.

Ben and I are focusing on the problems faced by stepfamilies in this chapter. Are there rewards in steprelationships? Sure there are. But you don't need help in dealing with those. We're describing the frustrations and conflicts we've worked through, painful as they have been, to help you learn to deal with your own. First, by offering you reassurance that you are not alone in your pain. Second, by making it clear that there is hope of survival. And third, by suggesting that you tell yourself that if Dr. Spock, the child-rearing expert, had so much trouble, then maybe you don't have to be so hard on yourself when your reality falls short of your expectations!

Ginger and Ben finally learned to appreciate each other after Ginger went away to boarding school at age sixteen. It's amazing how well separation can work when all else fails! The healing process had begun after years of war. At the end of three years, Ginger asked Ben to give the commencement address at her high school graduation. Ben was thrilled. Ginger's friends were impressed with Ben and told Ginger how lucky she was, which I'm sure helped boost Ben in Ginger's eyes.

Ginger, Ben, and I celebrated Ginger's twenty-first birthday on April 1, 1986, with a sense of deep family commitment and mutual caring. We have been through some difficult times. But with professional counseling, reading, and struggling, we survived it all. We have made it!

SUGGESTIONS TO STEPPARENTS—
by Dr. Benjamin Spock

Considering my poor record as a stepparent, you might wonder whether my advice has much to recommend it, but here goes, anyway. To simplify the discussion, I'll continue to assume that the parent is the mother and the stepparent is a man. First of all, be forewarned. When you know what is likely to happen, you'll feel less surprised, less hurt, less guilty, and less angry.

It's important for stepparents to realize that, to a child, the remarriage of a parent is the final severing of the original, intact family. As a result, even if you came along ten years after the death or divorce of her biological parent, irrationally, she probably sees you as standing in the way of her parents' being together.

You'll have to keep reminding yourself that your stepchild's antagonism and rudeness are not based on your failure, and are not personal attacks. They are her natural reaction to the intrusion of an outsider into the intimacy of the family. To the degree that a stepparent can recognize this, he will be less hurt and vengeful, and to that degree he will be able to keep from further antagonizing the stepchild. He can also be kept from trying to compete with

the stepchild's absent parent. And he is in a better position to show sympathy and affection toward the child, which will help her in overcoming her resentment. If you become defensive or try to compete with the original parent, you validate her feelings that you are out to take his place.

Unless things turn out better than expected, the stepparent would benefit from going to a counselor to sort out his feelings and to get the comfort of a sympathetic hearing, which the child's mother may not feel she can afford to give you, for fear of further alienating her child. A counselor can also make practical suggestions for reducing antagonisms and increasing good will.

It is wise for a potential stepparent (previous to the marriage) to delay moving in for several months, during which time the child can get used to this person as an individual, without having to accept him as a stepparent. (Of course, it's also sensible for *any* couple contemplating marriage to allow as much time as possible for getting to know each other well before making the final commitment.) During this waiting period the mother can, and should, be alert to any comments the child makes about the prospective stepfather, which can lead to discussions about him; or she can ask the child's opinion. This is not to give the child veto power over a possible marriage, but to give her the feeling of being consulted before the decision is made. If the child asks bluntly, "Are you going to get married?" the mother can answer, "We're thinking about it" or "He wants to, but we haven't decided yet."

It's a good idea for the prospective stepparent to take a stand-offish child out to occasional meals and sports events or on other excursions, without the parent, to try to overcome the child's feeling of being left out, and to give the child a chance to get to know the stepparent as a person instead of a rival. If there is any hobby they can participate in together, so much the better. For the younger child there is always reading aloud, if she will relent enough to accept it. If the child remains adamantly hostile, the mother has three choices: to wait longer, to give up the man (if she has doubts about him herself), or to marry anyway, knowing that it may take several years for the child to accept him. The more certain the mother is about her own love for the man, the more confident she should be about making the decision, on the assumption that time alone will probably ease the child's aversion.

Even when a child accepts a prospective stepfather from first acquaintance, it's well to remember that the child's feelings may change when he moves in and more clearly occupies at least half the mother's attention.

In most cases, a child continues for years to want both of her real parents to get together again, so she is likely to consider ardent physical affection between a prospective stepfather and her mother as a sign of unfaithfulness. This is a reason for the couple to go slowly in openly demonstrating the intensity of their feelings. On the average, boys are likely to show more hostility to stepfathers than to stepmothers because sexual jealousy is added to possessive jealousy. Similarly, girls are apt to be more hostile to stepmothers.

It is always helpful to some degree for a parent to recognize the child's jealousy, before or after the remarriage, and to talk about it sympathetically with the child for as long as it persists. You might say, "I know that sometimes you feel jealous and angry about Charles. You want to keep Mommy all for yourself. You wish that I'd never gotten to know (or marry) Charles." I wouldn't try to combine this sympathy with declarations of what a wonderful person he is, or with expressed hopes that the child will soon get to love him. Let the child hate and resent the stepfather, and know that her mother doesn't reject her because of this. Allowing her the right to own her feelings will help her, at least to a slight degree, to outgrow the jealousy.

Often it is a shock and one of the causes of the stepparent's painful feeling of isolation to find that his future wife who is so compatible, who seems so reasonable in every other area, has such different views when it comes to disciplining the children. These differences are inevitable in every marriage; but in the first marriage there is a long period in which the issues can be discussed and reconciled while the child grows from infancy. In the stepfamily, sharp differences begin coming to the surface abruptly and heatedly even before the wedding, at a time when neither partner is yet sure of the relationship. On the average, men tend to believe in a sterner, more authoritative kind of discipline than women. The only solution for such differences is frequent discussions in which the partners try to be open, but at the same time patient, tactful, and respectful. For to be critical or scornful of the other's opinions only leads to hardening of hearts and widening of positions.

In some cases a child's reluctance to show affection, or even polite acceptance, is based primarily on her loyalty to the absent parent. She has the instinctive feeling, of which she may not be conscious, that if she shows love or even friendliness to her stepfather, it will mean that she no longer loves or belongs to her own father (or reveres his memory), that she has let his place be taken by this comparative stranger. This fits in with our knowledge that most children of divorce go on hoping, year after year, that their own biological parents will someday, somehow, get back together again.

It may be helpful to explain that it is natural for a child to have this sense of loyalty, and this fear of disloyalty. The parent or stepparent can say, "Some children think that if they show that they like their stepfather, it means they don't love their real father anymore. But that isn't true. A girl can go on loving her own father just as much as ever and still care about her stepfather. Your stepfather has no wish to replace your father. He only wants to be friends; in fact, he knows that you will be happier in the long run, and that you and he will get along better if you can stay close to your own father and continue to be his child."

To help your stepchild learn to appreciate your humanness, share your honest feelings about your sense of newness and aloneness in her family. Remind her that she and her family share hundreds of fond memories that don't include you, and that you need help in getting to feel you really belong.

If a child insists on having photographs around the house that include her other parent, it's important to swallow your hurt feelings and understand the child's need to express her loyalty. She has a right to her memories, and pictures are one way to keep them alive. As she develops more sensitivity to you, she may later move those pictures into her own bedroom.

You demonstrate respect when you don't push a child. She should feel no pressure to call a stepfather "Daddy." Ask her what she wants to call you. She can call you by your first name or "uncle" or anything that suits you both. Don't use her choice as a barometer of your closeness. In fact, by not pressuring her to use a specific label you demonstrate respect for her judgment. And as a result, closeness is more likely to develop naturally.

When a stepchild comes to visit her father and stepmother on weekends and school vacations, there is a temptation for them to go overboard in entertaining her, to make doubly sure she has a good time, especially if there are no other children living in the household: lunch at McDonald's, movie or sports event on Saturday afternoon, perhaps again in the evening, and a special excursion on Sunday. This is more of a sacrifice of time and effort than most adults can cheerfully afford to make, so it often leads to strained feelings on their part, which get transmitted to the child. It is also apt to irritate the custodial mother, who often isn't able to afford such treats.

In the long run the child will feel more comfortable during visits if she is treated as a regular member of the family rather than as a special guest, sharing the responsibilities as well as companionship in your home. That helps her feel that the relationship is real, that she belongs. She doesn't have to test it. The adults can help her to make friends in the neighborhood by asking other girls to meals and serving "super" dishes (hamburgers and hot dogs). Children are sometimes bashful in approaching others in a strange neighborhood and need some encouragement to help them feel at home there. She should have some of her playthings at her father's place, even including a second bicycle if most of the kids in the neighborhood are using them. She should be expected to do her homework at your home and to have customary chores to perform, including helping with meals. Of course if the stepparent has other children who are living in the home, the visiting child should fit into the same family routines.

When there are children of both partners in a "blended" stepfamily, it is often difficult to decide how critical or lenient the two parents should be with their own and with each other's children. The human tendency, of course, is to favor your own child when there has been a conflict, which pleases her but causes resentment in the other parent and in your stepchild. On the other hand, a very conscientious stepparent sometimes leans over backward, giving the benefit of the doubt to the spouse's child and being stricter with her own. This gives her the feeling of being betrayed by the person who should be most loyal. At times a parent tries to make up for this sort of injustice by sneaking money or privileges to her own child. That breeds dishonesty and distrust. A spirit of family harmony can only develop in an environment of openness, honesty, and fairness.

Don't expect to feel the same way toward your own children and your spouse's. It's natural to have deeper feelings for your own, and there is no reason to feel guilty about that. The important thing is, try to be fair, try to see the other parent's and the other child's point of view, try not to lash out emotionally, and try to discuss the issues. In the long run the stepfamily can become genuinely friendly soonest when all members become convinced that the others are not really mean but are well-intentioned, if sometimes mistaken.

When each spouse has children who will be living together, even part of the time, there are a number of important issues to resolve before they move in together. Before the families merge, it would be well for the adults to bring out into the open the fact that there are bound to be conflicts, hurt feelings, resentments between the children, between children and stepparents, and between the adults. Everybody, including the adults, should be encouraged to air his feelings and gripes as a first step in resolving disputes. Discuss ahead of time how you will be sharing resources. Who has to share rooms and closets and bureaus? How will chores be reassigned? Whose TV programs take precedence? How will bathroom and telephone usage get decided? When possible, transitions are easier when you begin anew in a home that did not belong to either family, so territorial rights are not already established.

Most stepfamilies find that finances are tighter in the new relationship. Simply admit that reality and ask each family member for input as to how to make the best use of what's available. If there are religious differences, it's important to make a plan for how you will deal with the specifics—where, how, and with whose family you will celebrate each holiday—so compromises can be worked out ahead of time and holidays don't have to become battlegrounds for control.

A family meeting could be held once a week with the basic purpose of getting resentments aired, to have all members realize that they have a right to their feelings, and to show that honesty and fairness are worth striving for. One of the best ways to start is to simply admit, "This is new for all of us. We're not starting with each other at the beginning. We each have our own way of doing things (not necessarily good or bad, just different). It will take time and real effort to learn how to share our values, handle our responsibilities, and resolve our differences. Have patience with me and I'll try to have patience with you as we learn to become a family."

Parents need to keep communication open with each other about the children, too, even when it concerns negatives. When you stifle frustrations, they often poison the relationship. But remember that a parent doesn't appreciate hearing only the bad things about her child and the good things about yours. Try to be supportive and create an atmosphere of cooperation, not competition.

The children need to learn that they don't have to love each other, but they have to respect the other's right to be part of the blended family. For some children, peaceful coexistence is the most that can be expected. Creating areas of privacy, especially for older children, minimizes conflict.

In addition to family time, try to spend a little time with each of your children and each of your stepchildren and encourage your spouse to do the same. Each person in the family is entitled to a relationship with *every other member of the family* without having to be self-conscious about another's reactions.

All the professionals I've known in the counseling field and most stepparents agree that the stepparent should not try to be a disciplinarian in the sense of bossing, correcting, or punishing his stepchild, at least until he is thoroughly accepted. To the jealous child, this is the ultimate outrage—that

this uninvited, unwelcome invader is now issuing orders or punishments. The inevitable response of the child—spoken or unspoken—is "You're not my parent and I don't have to obey you."

But when I make the point that it's counterproductive and futile to try to correct or punish a stepchild until you are well accepted as a parent, I want to emphasize that you don't have to accept *abuse,* such as name calling, mistreatment of your possessions, or other forms of active rudeness. (Ginger dished out passive rudeness in ignoring me.) You can say immediately, seriously, and politely, "It makes me very unhappy to have you treat me this way. I wish you would be kind to me." Shouting at a child or slapping her gives her permission, to some degree, to be abusive to you again, for children follow their parents' example, if they dare. Your plea may or may not stop her on the next occasion; but you have made the point that you sincerely feel that you don't deserve abuse, won't accept it submissively, and are asking, respectfully, for a happier relationship. I wouldn't hesitate to repeat this speech on any future occasions when appropriate.

It should help resentful stepchildren to get into counseling or therapy, so that their fears of losing or half losing their true parent can be brought out into the open to be looked at more rationally; guilt about their evil wishes toward the stepparent can be relieved by their coming to see how natural and inevitable their feelings are; and they may admit to an outsider that there are appealing qualities to the stepparent.

The attempt at counseling should be made if the child demonstrates real unhappiness. However, many stepchildren will not grant their parent and stepparent the benefit of their cooperation. They may take the position, as Ginger did, that there is absolutely no problem with them, by which they mean that the trouble has all been caused by the inconsiderate parent and the unwanted stepparent.

In any case, it is valuable for all members of the merged family to talk things over fairly often—once a week, if possible. If the children at first can't speak frankly to, or in the presence of, their stepparent, they can confide their concerns to their own parent, who can help communicate their feelings.

In some cities there are stepfamily discussion groups that meet regularly; it's worthwhile for stepchildren, stepparents, and parents to compare notes, to find that others have the same problems and pains, perhaps even worse ones, and to hear other people's solutions. Inquire at your United Appeal office to find a group near you.

Being a parent is a tough enough job today. Being a stepparent is much more difficult. Stepparents have the frustrations and responsibilities, but not the authority and respect, of biological parents. It is calculated that by the middle of the 1990s there will be more stepfamilies than nonstepfamilies. Stepparents and stepchildren need all the support and understanding they can get.

By the Author

(With Reinhart and Miller) *A Baby's First Year.* New York: Duell, Sloan, and Pearce, 1954.

(With Lowenberg) *Feeding Your Baby and Child.* New York: Duell, Sloan, and Pearce, 1955.

(With Marion O. Lerrigo) *Caring for Your Disabled Child.* Boston: Macmillan, 1965.

(With Zimmerman) *Dr. Spock on Vietnam.* New York: Duell, Sloan, and Pearce, 1968.

Baby and Child Care, rev. ed. New York: Simon & Schuster, 1985.

Raising Children in a Difficult Time. New York: Pocket Books/Simon & Schuster, 1985.

Dr. Spock Talks with Mothers. Westport, Conn.: Greenwood, 1982.

The Problems of Parents. Westport, Conn.: Greenwood, 1978.

A Teenager's Guide to Life and Love. New York: Simon & Schuster, 1970.

SOL GORDON

Meet the Author

Dr. Sol Gordon is respected worldwide as one of the foremost writers, lecturers, and educators on responsible sexuality for youth. In recognition for his contributions to the field of sex education, he was awarded the American Association of Secondary Educators, Counselors, and Therapists (AASECT) Award in 1982.

The author is Professor Emeritus of Child and Family Studies and Director of the Institute of Family Research and Education at Syracuse University. He was responsible for developing and implementing the National Family Sexuality Education Month, which takes place annually in October. His class on Human Sexuality had an enrollment of over 400 students each semester.

Dr. Gordon received his B.A. and M.A. from the University of Illinois in 1947 and his Ph.D. from the University of London in 1953. He is actively sought after by popular television and radio shows including The Today Show, Donahue, 60 Minutes, *and* Good Morning America. *His humor and wisdom have intrigued audiences throughout the United States, Canada, England, New Zealand, Australia, Japan, Malaysia, Singapore, Israel, and Brazil.*

Dr. Gordon has been featured in a number of teen-age and women's magazines, and has served as a consultant for many films and audio cassettes.

Through his work, Dr. Gordon helps parents understand their valuable role as the primary sexuality educators of their children. He is committed to helping parents instill responsible sexual values in young people in an effort to reduce the incidence of venereal disease and unwanted pregnancies among teen-agers.

He and his wife, Judith, who has co-authored several of his books, have also been partners in raising their son.

His sources of inspiration are William James ("Wisdom is learning what to overlook"), Eleanor Roosevelt ("No one can make you feel inferior without your consent"), and the Talmud ("Expect miracles but don't count on them").

10

YOUR CHILD'S SEXUALITY

**INSTILLING POSITIVE SEXUAL ATTITUDES
FROM BIRTH
SOL GORDON, PH.D.**

Our children proudly announce that they are growing up in the "sexual revolution" as though that implies an exciting breakthrough! Each year there are more than a million pregnancies and half a million unwanted births among teen-agers. The Center for Disease Control estimates that ten to fifteen million Americans develop a sexually transmitted disease each year. (STD's are the most prevalent teen-age disease, second only to the common cold.) There are an estimated two million abortions annually. And half of all married couples suffer from some sort of sexual problem. This so-called revolution is hardly a cause for celebration.

Parents' Role

People are experiencing sexual freedom without awareness of the tremendous human cost. As parents, it is our responsibility to begin preparing children early on for the sexual decisions they will be making throughout their lives. We don't begin assuming that responsibility when our daughter has her first period or our son has his first "wet dream" (nocturnal emission), or when either is pressured to "have sex." Parents need to educate children from birth, welcoming their questions when they are two and three so that they will be comfortable asking questions when they are fourteen and seventeen.

I often ask children if they've received any sex education from their parents, and the usual answer is "no." Those who recall some discussion say "the big heavy talk" could be summed up with one word—"Don't!"

Parents are the sexuality educators of their children, whether they do it well or badly. Silence teaches no less eloquently than words. Studies consistently reveal that children do not acquire the information they need from parents. It is time for parents to reclaim this responsibility. They cannot, of course, be the exclusive educators of their children unless they are prepared to raise their families in virtual isolation—no books, newspapers, magazines, television, movies, public bathrooms, and most certainly no friends at all. However, parents can be the *primary* sex educators of their children, with schools, churches, synagogues, and community organizations as their partners in a lifelong process.

Society consistently underestimates the capabilities of parents and children. You can't tell a child too much. Ignorance, not knowledge, stimulates inappropriate or irresponsible behavior. If you tell children more than they can understand, they will simply turn you off.

Parents need to work at being "askable" and credible not only about sexuality but about everything—money, family relationships, school, friends, and drugs. This does not mean that the parents have to agree with whatever their children are saying. And it does not mean that the parents will always have an immediate answer (but how far, after all, is your local library?). If children know that they are always welcome to ask, parents are in the best position to educate as their own values direct them.

Most parents want to educate their children, but they are often uncomfortable and afraid that they don't know how. Obviously, parents who find it difficult to talk to their children about other important issues will not be ready to talk about sex. If you're uncomfortable in this role, just acknowledge it—most children will reassure *you*.

Many parents *are* ready, but want and need some support. Yet few educational institutions seem to be preparing parents for their important role as sex educators. Only recently have religious organizations and other groups taken this task seriously—and we have a long way to go. To become a competent sexuality educator for your children, read books by qualified authors, take parenting classes, and talk with other parents in nonthreatening group settings to increase your sexual awareness. If you have already made mistakes, correct them. Children are resilient—and they appreciate your honesty.

And when you talk to your children, don't tell them to keep the information confidential. Parents who give *misinformation* don't tell their children to keep it confidential, so children who are misinformed are becoming the sex educators in the neighborhood. It's about time informed children become sex educators, too.

Parents often think that they have to wait until a child asks before giving sex information. Children are constantly asking, if not with words, then by actions. Whenever a mother goes into the bathroom, a child of two or three may trail behind. When a father takes a shower, the same child wants to watch. The child also is sensitive to the way the parent responds to curiosity about his own body. This inquisitive behavior is an excellent opportunity to broaden the teachable moment. Parents who fail to take advantage of such events discourage the curiosity their children innately have.

Talking about the difference between "animal sex" and "making love" when taking a pet to the veterinarian to be spayed or discussing trust, responsibility, and respect when hearing a news report about a home for unwed mothers can be excellent learning opportunities.

When children are left to interpret events on their own, they make their own assumptions. That sometimes leads to misinformation. For example, one four-year-old boy insisted, "Daddies can nurse their babies." Fortunately the father did not laugh at his son or put him down. Instead, he asked his son how he came to that conclusion. Joshua explained that he had gone to the zoo with his baby-sitter a few weeks before, and together they watched a cow nurse its babies "with penises just like mine."

His baby-sitter missed the opportunity to teach him that mother cows nurse their calves with their udders (just as human mothers nurse their babies with their breasts). But because the father checked out his son's perception of what he was seeing, he was able to help him rethink his experience from a new, more accurate perspective.

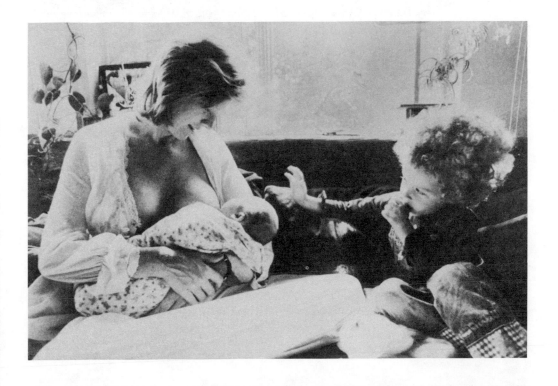

Questions Children Ask

Be prepared with answers to questions young children typically ask so you'll be able to express a comfortable, positive attitude toward their curiosity. Before answering, to find out what they are *really* asking, sometimes it's helpful to ask what they think the answer might be. The following are some of the most common sexual questions and events facing parents:

Q: Your three-year-old unzips his pants and rubs his penis while you are shopping.

A: *You whisper, "I know that rubbing your penis feels good, but that's something that is done in private. You need to zip up your pants now because we're in the store. Sometimes people get embarrassed when they see a boy touch his penis."*

Q: Your three-year-old daughter puts her arms around you, her father, and says, with a flirtatious grin, "Daddy, I want to marry you."

A: *"There's a love that daddies have for their daughters and a different kind that they have for their wives. You are a very special daughter and I love you very much. When you get older, I hope you marry someone you love in the way that Mommy and I love each other."*

Q: Your four-year-old asks, "What's the difference between boys and girls?"

A: *"A girl has a vagina and a boy has a penis. When girls grow up they can have babies. When boys grow up they can become daddies."*

Q: "When does a girl get a penis?"

A: *"She doesn't. She always has a vagina and a boy always has a penis."*

Q: While watching you bathe her infant brother, your four-year-old daughter notices his penis become erect. Pointing her finger, she yells, "Yuck! what's that?"

A: *"A boy's penis sometimes gets hard, or erect. It's quite natural and nothing to be concerned about."*

Q: Your five-year-old asks, "Where do babies come from?"

A: *"When a man and woman love each other they kiss and hug each other. When they do it for a while, their bodies sometimes become excited and the* man's penis becomes hard. If he puts his penis into her vagina, she may become pregnant. If she does, a baby will begin to grow in a special place in her body called the uterus."

Q: Your son then asks, "Do you ever do that when you *don't* want to have a baby?"

A: *"Yes, sometimes we do that to have a pleasurable experience. It's something people do when they are grown-up and love each other very much. When we don't want to make a baby we use birth control."*

Q: You are in your eighth month of pregnancy. Your five-year-old asks, "How will the baby get out?"

A: *"The baby will come out of my vagina, which is an opening between my legs. The vagina is made so it can stretch wide enough to allow the baby through. Then later it goes back to its regular size."*

Q: "Does that hurt?"

A: *"Yes, but it doesn't usually last very long. The doctors in the hospital will give me medicine if I need it. But it's sure worth it to give birth to someone like you."*

Q: Your five-year-old, waking in the middle of the night, hears you and your spouse making scary sounds and rushes into your bedroom. She calls out, "Mommy, Daddy, what's the matter? What's that noise?"

A: *"Mommy and I were making love. The sounds you heard are like the noise you make when you give me a big hug. I'll come into your room in just a minute and explain more about it if you'd like me to." After you've had a chance to regain your composure, sit with her on her bed and ask her to give you one big hug and then another. Afterward ask, "Did that sound like the noise you heard? See, those are not scary sounds. They're loving sounds."*

Q: Your six-year-old sees his newborn sister for the first time and asks you why she has a big ugly sore on her belly.

A: *"While Susan was inside Mommy, she got fed through a long cord that connected them together. The cord is called the umbilical cord. When Susan was born she didn't need that cord anymore because Mommy could nurse Susan, so the doctor cut the cord and made a cute little knot. That's called a belly button or a navel."*

Q: Your six-year-old opens a box of sanitary napkins that she's found in your closet and asks, "What's this?"

A: *"Those are called sanitary napkins. I use them when I menstruate. (Some people call it 'getting a period.') There's a place in every woman's body called a uterus. That's where babies grow. Every month, if she doesn't have a baby growing inside her, her uterus gives off a little blood that would have helped the baby grow. I use this pad under my clothes so they won't get stained."*

Q: Your daughter then asks, "When will that happen to me?"

A: *"Most girls begin to get their periods between the ages of twelve and fourteen. Some girls get them as early as nine and some don't get them until they're sixteen. It will happen after your breasts develop and some hair grows under your arms and between your legs."*

Q: Your six-year-old asks, "Why do you and Daddy sometimes lock the door when you go to sleep?"

A: *"Sometimes we want to make love and we want to do it in private."*

Q: While you are at a bowling alley, your six-year-old screams out, "Bastard!" ("screw," "fuck," or "bitch!"). Unfortunately children usually don't ask what these words mean in private. They just try one out in the midst of a huge crowd of people and wait for parents to react so they can determine just how powerful the word is.

A: *It's effective to explain the meaning of the word and ask if that's what the child meant to say. Then state that it is a word that is not appropriate to use in public.*

Q: Your seven-year-old asks, "When a daddy puts his penis inside the mommy, does he urinate inside her?"

A: "That is a good question. It seems like that should happen because the penis can do both things, but they can't both happen at the same time. When he is making love, no urine comes out—just semen."

Q: Your seven-year-old son calls from the back door, "Dad, Mom, come here quick!" You run out the door into the backyard, where you see Chuck, the neighbor's dog, mounted on your dog. Your son asks, "What is Chuck doing to Goldie?"

A: *"What they are doing is called copulating. That's how dogs have sexual intercourse—Chuck is putting his penis inside Goldie's vagina."*

Q: While at the movies with your eight-year-old son, the film shows a sheriff walking out of a woman's house saying, "They raped her!" Your son whispers, "Mom, what's rape?"

A: *"Rape means the woman had sex with a man because he forced her to. We'll talk about it when the movie's over."*

Q: You enter your bedroom to find your nine-year-old son sitting on the floor blowing up a condom that he found.

A: *"That's not a balloon, you know. It's a condom. (Some people call it a rubber.) We use it when we make love because we don't want to have a baby right now. A man puts it over his penis so when the sperm (or semen) come out, they won't make his wife pregnant."*

As children get older, parents often assume that they know answers to specific questions because they have already been given the answers once or twice before. Children understand concepts at a very primitive level when they are young and need more complex information as they get older. Also, because the desire to have intercourse is so far removed from the experience of most young children, they often ask to hear the same explanation over and over again so they can make sense of it all.

Q: Your ten-year-old asks, "Tell me again how a woman gets pregnant."

A: *"When a woman and man who love each other hug and kiss for a while, their bodies feel excited and tingly. When the man becomes excited, his penis gets hard. Sometimes he puts his penis inside the woman's vagina and sperm comes out through the tip of his penis. If a tiny sperm meets an egg inside a woman's body, a baby might be conceived. Then the baby will be born approximately nine months later."*

Q: "Mom, Dad, an eighth-grade girl got pregnant. Can you believe it?"

A: *"Yes, it is possible to get pregnant. But it's very difficult to be so young and have the responsibility of taking care of a baby all the time. It's not like just baby-sitting. I wonder what life will be like for the girl and for her baby. Think of how different that baby's life will be from the one that Aunt Ilene and Uncle Mark's baby will have."*

Q: "Isn't it old-fashioned to be a virgin today when you get married?"

A: *"There are some values that don't go out of style. There are many young people who are not having sex before marriage. They just don't talk about it because they are afraid they won't sound 'cool.' "*

When children walk in while a parent is dressing, nudity can help provide opportunities for questions. Dad can explain to his son that when the boy gets older his penis will grow larger like his father's. Mom can explain to her daughter that she wears a bra to support her breasts and that when her daughter is older, her breasts will grow so she can wear a bra, too. Don't carry nudity too far, though—when parents flaunt their naked bodies, children often become overstimulated and confused.

Most children will start you off asking questions, but if you have a five-year-old who hasn't asked yet, don't assume you're not "askable." About twenty-five percent of askable parents have shy children. These children might have an interest in their sexuality but are afraid to reveal their real feelings. In that case, use books like *Did the Sun Shine Before You Were Born?* to break the ice. Provide them with answers, whether they ask questions or not. You might also stimulate discussions by asking, "When I was your age I used to wonder about . . . do you?" helping them understand that their feelings are normal.

When talking about sexual parts of the body, use the correct names as you would for any other body part—use "penis," not "tinkler"—"vagina," not "that place down there." Ignoring specific body areas or using babyish terms can make them sound dirty or embarrassing.

Children are sexual human beings and remain so throughout their lives. The best way for parents to help their children develop healthy attitudes about sexuality is by example. If parents are honest and well-informed, children will learn the value of knowing the facts. If they're generous with affection for their children and loving toward each other, children will themselves learn to be loving partners and parents. In effect, if they are appreciative of their own sexuality, children will have an excellent opportunity to lead sexually healthy lives. And they will have learned how from the people who can teach them the best, and who care about them the most—their parents.

Sexual Assault Prevention

As a result of the recent publicity about sexual abuse, some parents are becoming uncomfortable about expressing affection toward their children. The appropriate response to this problem is not to withdraw signs of love from children. Children today need *more* hugging, kissing, and cuddling, not less. We also don't have to frighten children in order to safeguard them. Children who are loved, appreciated, listened to, believed, sexually educated, and prepared for the possibility of bad things happening have the best possible protection they can get.

When preparing them, tell your children that there is "right" and "wrong" touching rather than "good" and "bad" touching. (Sexual and seductive touching often feels good.) Teach them that they have private parts (penis, anus, vulva, breasts, and vagina) and public parts (the rest of their bodies). No one, except the children themselves, should be allowed to touch their private parts, and they should not touch anyone else's, even if they are asked to. If anyone tries to trick them into sexual activity, they should say "no" loudly and firmly and then get away quickly.

But let's not create the illusion that all a child has to do is say "no" and leave. An abuser, especially one who knows the child well (which is true in about seventy-five percent of the cases), can take advantage of a child whether the child wants him to or not. Help children prepare for the unthinkable by explaining to them, "If you are forced to do bad things, it's okay to lie and promise you won't tell. That kind of lie—when it's the only way to protect yourself from being hurt—is always okay. Then when you get away, tell me or some other adult you trust."

If your children do report sexual abuse to you, believe them and don't overreact. Many adults who were sexually abused when they were children reveal that when they told a parent of an incident involving sexual molestation they were either not believed or were punished. In many cases they report that the overreaction of their parents was worse than the abuse itself. Many parents respond with "Why did you let him do it?" "Why didn't you tell me before?" or "I can understand how it could happen once, but why did you let it happen again and again?" Judgmental statements like these cause the child to feel guilty. Adults who exploit children are the ones to blame, not young children (who are learning about right and wrong from adults). Children often feel confused when an adult they like and trust tells them it's okay to do something that seems wrong. And children feel powerless when threatened that if they tell anyone what happened, they, or members of their family, will be hurt.

If your child is molested, express your trust and your acceptance. You can communicate both with a warm, comforting hug, the reassurance that you are glad the child told you, and the message that you love and will help the child through the ordeal.

No, you don't have to worry that if children are warned about sexual touching they will grow up sexually dysfunctional. Children can learn the difference between sexual exploitation and cuddling.

We've had enough hysteria about letting children visit with grandparents or be hugged by teachers or camp counselors. Common sense, combined with extra precaution about choosing and being able to visit a day-care center or camp at any time, is sufficient. Children need to be aware of strangers, but children can still be friendly to *anyone* when accompanied by parents. And children should be encouraged to respond appropriately to teachers in a school. The risks of children being hurt are not so great that we must deprive them of the experience of being with relatives, teachers, counselors, or friends.

Satisfying Curiosity

Dealing with the issue of sexual exploitation is very different from responding to expressions of curiosity among young children. Children play "doctor" to compare themselves with children of the same sex and to learn what children of the opposite sex look like beneath their clothes. They learn the same way they experience the rest of their world—by looking and touching.

If you open your bathroom door and find your four-year-old son and his friend exploring each other's genitals, don't overreact by threatening, punishing, or shaming them. Instead, suggest that they get dressed and divert them

to another activity. Later explain to your child, "It isn't a good idea to play with or touch the sexual parts of anyone else's body or allow anyone to touch yours." You might add that you are aware that he has some questions and that you have some pictures that you can show him to help him satisfy his curiosity. But don't make him feel guilty for being inquisitive—curiosity is normal.

Concerns About Homosexuality

Homosexuality refers to an adult who finds himself or herself irresistibly attracted to members of the same sex and pursues sexual relations with that person. According to our research, about five percent of the population is exclusively homosexual, and we don't have control over that. People are not gay because of one form of parenting or another. They don't choose to be— they just are, for reasons we don't as yet understand.

Many parents are concerned about homosexuality and believe they can prevent it by encouraging their male children to engage in male-oriented play (sports and war games) and their female children in female-oriented activities (play house and put on makeup). A boy who enjoys playing with dolls or reading poetry is no less masculine than one who enjoys roughhousing, just as a girl who is into sports is no less feminine than one who enjoys domestic activities.

Channeling children into sex-role stereotyped activities or behaviors does not ensure heterosexuality. If that were the case, there would be no homosexual professional football players and lesbian ballerinas. When parents criticize children's behavior with judgmental statements like "Only sissies cry" or "Girls don't fight," they damage their children's self-image. Children who are allowed to enjoy a wide range of activities, and express emotions freely and spontaneously, have healthier sexual attitudes.

What we do know is that it is normal for children to have some homosexual thoughts and impulses. And some even have homosexual experiences during childhood, especially during preadolescence. When they recognize that those feelings are normal, they won't be as likely to label themselves and make premature decisions about their sexual preference.

Single Parenting

According to the latest census data, there are approximately ten million single-parent families—one of every seven children in this country lives in a one-parent household. Single parents, relax—there is no reason to suppose you can't be a perfectly good sexuality educator of your children of either sex. What is most important is creating a stable atmosphere for your children, and this can be done as well in one-parent as in two-parent families.

Single parents have some personal decisions that offer unique challenges, though. One of the most pressing is whether to allow a date to stay overnight.

The main issue is how well you communicate with your children. (This goes for children of all ages.) First, regardless of the circumstances, your children need to be well informed about sexuality and the fact that, as a single parent, you are dating and attempting to develop relationships. Once having established that, my view tends to be on the traditional side. In the process of establishing a relationship, single parents may be relating to many people. It would not, then, be a good idea for a series of people to remain overnight, regardless of whether sex is involved. This can confuse the child and create tension and disappointment in having to relate to a number of strangers.

Should a relationship become more permanent, however, and you are confident that it will remain this way for a long period of time, then you may want to discuss your intentions with your children, encouraging them to express their emotions. In this way, you would get a really good sense about how they feel about another person (as opposed to their biological parent) coming into the picture. When children are given the chance to share their feelings without being put down, they not only feel a part of the family but also learn to respect the views of others, even though they may disagree. This does not mean, however, that you allow your children to make your decisions for you.

There are many single parents who feel strongly about "waiting" until after they are married. These parents *should* wait and should not be intimidated or talked into another kind of arrangement.

Parenting the Handicapped Child

Parents of children who have handicaps—your responsibilities to educate your children are the same. Your children are just as sexual as other children. Their inability to hear, see, and think as well as their peers, or walk or move their arms, doesn't negate their physical and emotional need for intimacy. They need the same information, approval, and sense of values as "normal" children. They also need to learn that it's important not to exploit others or allow themselves to be exploited sexually. However, they require more understanding, as they generally have greater fears about failure and rejection. Parents can suggest creative ways to get their needs met in spite of their handicaps. (Remember, sexuality doesn't have to involve sexual inter-course to be meaningful.)

Have I Missed the Boat?

Parents, those of you who didn't talk to your children until their preadolescent body changes frightened them—it's not too late. But don't start by asking them about *their* sexual thoughts and behaviors. Raise issues by talking about other people's attitudes or actions (i.e., "What did you think about Ann Landers's response to the thirteen-year-old girl who wanted to have sex with her seventeen-year-old boyfriend whom she deeply loved?"). Or put an appropriate book on the coffee table and playfully warn your child, "Don't read this book!" Most children will get the point, provided that there is some explicit understanding that you will respect their privacy if it's requested.

Parents often assume that it is the mother's responsibility to teach her daughters and the father's responsibility to teach his sons. Children can be taught by a parent of either sex. When there are two parents in the family, each can offer a unique perspective to their children, whether they are girls or boys.

Parental Understandings

The following are a few brief messages that need *parental* understandings in order to PREPARE TODAY'S YOUTH FOR TOMORROW'S *mature* and responsible family:

1. Of the ten most important aspects of a good adult relationship, sex is number nine. Love and caring are number one. Number two is a sense of humor. Number ten is sharing household tasks together.

2. Sex is never a test or a proof of love. "If you really loved me, you'd have sex with me" is always a line.

3. If you consider yourself to be in love, you are. But there are two kinds: mature and immature. Mature love is energizing, strengthening—imma-ture love not only feels like a burden, it is also exhausting. Immature love happens quickly but the excitement diminishes with time—mature love deepens over time. Immature love rarely occurs when life is going smoothly. Mature love proves itself when life throws us a curve (i.e., illness, or financial difficulties). It often requires hard work. Immature

love often leads to feelings of vulnerability and dependency. It causes people to hide their true feelings because they're afraid of hurting the relationship. Mature love feels strong and respectful. People share their feelings to resolve problems and strengthen the relationship.

4. Masturbation is a normal, healthy expression of sexuality at any age. It doesn't "use up" sperm (reducing fertility), cause blindness, or make hair grow on the palms of one's hands. In fact, it can help young people become comfortable with their own bodies and learn what turns them on, so later they can express their needs to their partners.

   How much is too much? Once is too much if you don't like it. Any behavior can become compulsive. People eat too much, not because they are hungry, but because they have high levels of anxiety. People drink too much alcohol, not because they are thirsty, but because they are anxiety-ridden. People sometimes masturbate too much, not because they are horny, but because they are nervous, tense, and upset. But if you absolutely *must* have a compulsion, choose masturbation. No one has ever died from overmasturbating, but hundreds of thousands of people die every year in the United States alone from disorders related to overeating and overdrinking.

5. "Wet dreams," the release of sperm while dreaming, are normal and healthy. Virtually all boys experience them. They only become a problem when boys don't understand what they are and begin to worry about them. Or when a parent, sibling, or camp counselor notices spots on the sheets and teases or punishes him.

6. There's nothing wrong with sexual thoughts, either. There's a difference between *thinking* about something and actually *doing* it.

7. Children mature at different times. Some develop earlier than others.

8. The size or shape of a girl's breasts has little to do with her sexuality. Some males prefer large-breasted women and some prefer small. A boy who chooses a girlfriend on the basis of the size of her breasts or some other bodily characteristic will have no more than a sex object. What's more important is how she feels about herself and how she projects those feelings. Many small-breasted girls are concerned that they won't have the capacity to nurse a baby. After a baby is born, the mother's breasts fill with milk, whether they started off small or pendulous—breast size is irrelevant.

9. A boy's penis size is also of little importance. Boys often compare theirs with their friends' in the locker room to determine their relative masculinity. While in the flaccid state, there is wide variance in penis sizes; when erect, most penises are approximately the same size. As far as being able to satisfy a woman, penis size makes little difference anyway. A

woman's vagina contracts to fit the size of the penis and receives friction and pleasure, no matter how large the penis. Nearly all of the female's sensory organs are in the clitoris and the outer third of her vagina, anyway, where they are reachable by a penis of any size. Penis size is only an issue when it becomes a source of anxiety for its owner.

10. A girl *can* get pregnant the first time she has intercourse, no matter how noble her intentions. And, though her chances of pregnancy are lower when she has her period or the two to three days before or afterward, there is *no* time when she is not vulnerable unless she abstains from sex or she (and he) are both using reliable forms of birth control.

11. Babies are precious: they deserve to be wanted. They shouldn't be the consequence of irresponsibility.

12. Sex should communicate caring and intimacy between people who are mature and able to handle the consequences—it shouldn't exploit! When young people become physically intimate too early, they risk serious emotional as well as physical vulnerability. A key point to remember is that people who feel good about themselves are not available for exploitation and don't exploit others. Our *responsibility* as parents and educators is to promote self-esteem. The message we need to project is "We are not complete without you!"

Young people have a strong need for autonomy; this includes having respect for differences of opinion. It is crucial to teach children to respect each other and themselves. Often their first experiences of love and relationships set the tone for future feelings and perceptions of the opposite sex, as well as for themselves. That's why it is especially important to help teen-agers learn to wait until they, and their relationships, are responsible enough to handle the risks of intercourse.

An Appropriate Double Message

"No!" may be the best oral contraceptive, but by itself it is not an effective means of communicating to children. The single message is not working. "No," "Don't," "Stop"—it's not effective with alcohol and drug abuse or smoking and surely not with sex. Also not working are silence or ignorance.

What *is* working is the message: "Look, honey, I don't want you to drink, but if you go to a party and you drink anyway, I don't want you to drive. Call me and we'll arrange alternate transportation. I won't give you a hard time." Or "Look, sweetie—you know my position about sex . . . I think you are too young. Sex changes things between people and you are not ready." (There has to be some disadvantage in being young.) It's even okay to say "I think you should wait until marriage"—despite the fact that these days less than 10 percent of couples are both virgins on their wedding night. Then add, "But I want you to know about birth control, and if you ever find yourself in a position where you are not accepting my values, at least protect yourself with contraception."

A double message? Yes, of course. Does it imply hypocrisy, or does it encourage young people to have sex? No, and in fact, parents who talk with their children openly about their sexual values find that there is a tendency for their children to delay their initiation of sexual intercourse. And those who do engage in sex are much more apt to take responsibility for themselves by using birth control. As a result, they are less likely to have unwanted babies.

The Old Double Standard Is Still Alive and Well

While in today's "liberated" society sometimes the female is the one who is pushing her boyfriend to "prove his manhood" by having sex with her, most often the male is still the one who is out for conquest. He rehearses his lines well to get the greatest benefit from the smoothest talk. When the female is caught unaware, she can become his unwitting victim. Since a girl doesn't generally call her parents first and ask for permission to have sex, it's important to help her develop skills ahead of time to resist the pressure. Some light conversation about how to respond to possible come-ons is often very effective in helping girls respond assertively. That's an excellent form of contraception!

Suggest some male "lines," asking her to think up some possible retorts. For example, you might ask your daughter, "If he says, 'If you really loved me, you'd want to give yourself to me,' what would you say?"

If she draws a blank, you might suggest, "If *you* really loved me, you wouldn't ask me to prove my love for you!"

Try the following suggestions and add some of your own:

HE: "Don't you want to make me happy?"
SHE: "Don't you want to keep me safe?"

HE: "It'll give me an opportunity to get to know you better."

SHE: "I'm afraid that I'm learning all I need to know about you right now!"

HE: "When a guy starts, it's too painful to stop."

SHE: "Well, then, go on without me. I can wait until you're done."

HE: "Do you want me to break up with you?"

SHE: "Not really, I'll do it for you."

HE: "I'll pull out in time."

SHE: "I'll pull out of this relationship first."

HE: "Are you frigid?"

SHE: "No, just smart."

HE: "Don't you trust me to be there for you if anything happens?"

SHE: "Can I trust you not to pressure me to do something that could risk my future?"

HE: [In the car] "Honey, would you like to get in the back seat?"

SHE: "No, that's okay, I'd rather sit up front with you."

HE: "I want to prove to you that I'm a real man!"

SHE: "You can do that by showing me respect and treating me like a real woman."

Preparation for sexual decision-making needs to begin well before puberty. By building their self-esteem, you help your children cope later on with the double standard, which makes life so difficult for teen-agers. Many young girls think that they won't amount to anything unless some boy wants and loves them. Many, if not most, boys assume that there is something wrong with them if they don't have sex before the age of eighteen. A study conducted by Planned Parenthood in Chicago surveyed a thousand young men. They were asked if it was okay to lie to a girl and say that they were in love with her in order to have sex. Seventy percent said "Yes." Many girls who have sex for the first time don't think they're having sex at all. They think they're "making love." They look at themselves as spontaneous and romantic, and if one is spontaneous and romantic, one doesn't plan ahead for sex. Girls are brainwashed, sometimes by their own parents, not to look upon themselves as sexual human beings and succumb to having sexual experiences without any consideration of birth control.

It appears to them that thinking about birth control is wrong, since it would suggest premeditated sex, which they have been taught is bad. They give no thought to the possible consequences of their actions, hoping instead that fate will be kind to them.

Ironically, few boys ever have sex spontaneously. They are planning, organizing, and thinking about this for some time. I'm not saying that it is bad to be sexual. People who know that they are sexual and who want to have sex eventually can better control their impulses than people who think it is wrong to be sexual and who think that there is something wrong with their desires. Those who know that strong sexual drives are normal and natural tend to be more responsible in all areas of sexuality.

Offering an Alternative

It is difficult to prepare children for the strong sexual drives that exist during the adolescent years. Calls for repression and self-control are not sufficient, especially when they are not accompanied by information. When lecturing in schools, a student will often ask me, "What you say is all well and good, but what do you do at the peak of passion?" Almost no adult seems to be able to respond to a child's "peak of passion" plea. When adults are present, you can see the color drain from their faces.

The youngster's question must be countered with: "What are you going to do when you're pregnant?" or "What are you going to do when you get someone pregnant?" If you're at the peak of passion, why not masturbate? It's satisfying, a lot of fun, and doesn't create any babies.

But when I have directly confronted parents and asked whether they would prefer their children to have sexual intercourse or to masturbate, their response frequently is that this is an unfair question. Why isn't it a fair question? No significant reduction of irresponsible teen-age sexual behavior is imaginable unless young people feel free to masturbate. People are sexual. And young people are single longer because they're marrying later. When they say they're horny, they mean it. They feel sexual tension. They want relief. In my judgment, the best relief for sexual excitement and tension for teen-agers is masturbation.

The Maturity Factor

Sometimes parents have been accused of giving contradictory messages. For instance, sex educators state very clearly that sexual intercourse is good; yet we don't want teen-agers to engage in it. (This does not refer to other forms of sexual expression such as kissing, necking, and mutual masturbation.) I propose waiting to engage in sexual intercourse *at least* until after one's eighteenth birthday, going to college, or working or living on one's own. There is a difference between being nineteen or twenty and twelve or thirteen years of age. Children in their later teen years know more, are, we hope, more mature and better able to deal with the consequences of even irresponsible behaviors. There is no contradiction here. One must reach a certain age to vote, to drive a car, or to sign a contract. In my opinion, there is no reason why there shouldn't be an *age* for initiating sexual intercourse. (At least if you are not going to wait until marriage.)

Sexuality as Part of a Larger Picture

I do not mean to imply that we should restrict all sexual behavior. There can be more sexual excitement in holding hands, looking into each other's eyes, kissing, caressing, or massaging than in the actual sexual act. In fact, much of what constitutes sexual intercourse is not even pleasurable for many young people, because they don't have enough understanding of how to enjoy each other and to appreciate its deeper meaning. Often the motivation to have sexual relations is not for pleasure or for intimacy but out of a false notion of self-affirmation: for boys sex often means proving masculinity—for girls, femininity.

There is a great deal of pressure put on young people to engage in sexual behavior. Yet some of the most bored, alienated, and unhappy young, and indeed older, people move from one sexual partner to another. Sex without intimacy is not generally a satisfying experience. People make mistakes, experiment, and have brief encounters, however, and from this reservoir of experiences forge their basic attitudes about sexuality.

Parent-Child Relationships

The nature of the relationship between parent and child is critical. Parents who have a warm, positive relationship with their children find that their children tend to incorporate more of the parents' values than those who have distant or antagonistic relationships. Parents need the confidence that their children will work out their own particular values and life-styles. Even those parents who have good relationships with their offspring often reach an impasse when it comes to speaking openly and freely about sexuality. It must be made clear that youth are entitled to privacy. They should not be expected to tell the parents everything. This can be painful to caring parents who think their children should reveal the intimacies and intricacies of their lives. Sometimes children kid around to mask what really happens or tell their parents what the parents want to hear. Professionals who are counseling or working with such parents can help them understand their children's goals and learn alternate modes of communicating.

Sometimes parents who genuinely mean well lose their children's confidence just by the way in which they express themselves. The following is a list of phrases guaranteed to turn off young people:

1. "I want to have a serious talk with you."
2. "We trust you, but . . ."
3. "When I was your age . . ."
4. "Because we say so."
5. "As long as I don't know about it."
6. "Act your age."
7. "It's about time you (got good grades, straightened your room . . .)."
8. "Just a minute!"
9. "After all we've done for you!"
10. "Are you telling me the truth?"
11. "That's not your idea, is it?"
12. "Don't you dare talk to me that way."
13. "Get off your high horse."
14. "Wipe that smile off your face!"
15. "What will the neighbors say?"

Instead, consider the impact of the following phrases:

1. "It's difficult to understand sometimes."
2. "I hear what you're saying."
3. "Want to talk?"
4. "I'm with you."
5. "I can finish this later."
6. "I want to be able to concentrate on what you have to say."
7. "You sound concerned."
8. "Whenever you're ready to talk, let me know."

Adults need to be especially careful when a youngster says that he is in love. The initial reaction might be to respond in one of the following ways: "You'll get over it," "When you get older, you'll laugh about it," or "It's puppy love." Never slight a child experiencing being in love. Instead, help the child make distinctions between mature and immature love.

Parents are justifiably concerned about the "liberated" society their children are facing. Some parents react by trying to scare their children out of taking risks, but that often backfires when the children learn that the parents' claims were exaggerated or untrue. Be informed yourself and share information about the realities of pregnancy and sexually transmitted disease honestly with your children. Knowledge leads to responsibility and tends to lessen promiscuity. I can't imagine anyone becoming *more* interested in sexual activity as a result of learning about the likelihood of pregnancy or the possible consequences of sexually transmitted diseases.

Providing information is not the only point of being an askable parent. It is also important to be able to identify with children and their feelings. As they approach adolescence, those feelings can become intense. Think ahead about the problems your child will encounter during the teen years: "I don't feel good about myself and only would if I had a boyfriend (girlfriend)." "Everyone is having sex and I'm the only one who isn't." We often forget that we need to support young people who don't want to have sex. More than one half of the teen-age female population will not have sex during the high school years, and the same is true for forty percent of the boys. Few today brag about their virginity, though, so children basically hear from the actively sexual population.

Try not to be known by your child as having a standard response to almost all crisis situations. I asked my college students to recall a single sentence that most characterized what they considered an inappropriate parental response to a serious problem that they had. A surprisingly large percentage of students, even those who claimed that they got along reasonably well with their parents, recalled sentences like:

FROM MOTHERS	FROM FATHERS
"Life is tough all over."	"Life isn't fair."
"Count your blessings."	"Moderation, moderation."
"Where did I go wrong?"	"For crying out loud!"
"Go ask your father."	"Go ask your mother."
"There are kids starving in Ethiopia."	"Life is too short to be miserable."

"And you ask me why I'm so   "Be careful."
  nervous?"

"Definitely not!"   "You'll fall for anything."

And please—in response to a child's concern—don't tell him not to worry. When is the last time someone told you not to worry and, because of that, you stopped?

If you happen to have a child who does a lot of things wrong (for example, he doesn't clean his room, doesn't take his homework seriously, or watches too much television) try to make a point of dealing with one thing at a time. Concentrate on only one or two issues and, temporarily, let everything else go. This is usually successful if, at the same time, you try to improve the quality of the relationship by being involved in experiences together. Most children appreciate that their parents mean well. In fact, getting along with parents is one of the best indications of good adjustment we have.

> Telling children all the *not to's*—
>   don't
>   smoke, drink, get high, have sex, stay out late—
> doesn't help much
>   unless we are able to help them discover just how to feel
>   good about themselves.

Sometimes parents forget that children need models more than critics and that they want their parents to respect their integrity, privacy, and ability to be involved in family matters. Above all, perhaps, they want love, so they can return it, and information so that it can lead to self-acquired wisdom.

> If your child shuts you out
> anyway
>   Knock gently on his (her) door
> and say gently
>   Honey, I love you. I want to
> talk!
>   Persist even if the child says "Go away."

Don't wait for a crisis to tell your child you love him. Kids need occasional hugs and kisses without any special reason (even if at first they seem not to like it).

Allow your children to express unhappiness, disappointments, and sadness without making them feel unworthy, guilty, or your lack of empathy or understanding. Mention every once in a while—"Listen, if anything happens,

---

you make a mistake—no matter how dreadful—I'd like to know about it. If there is ever a crisis in your life, I'll never reject you. I'll help you, and if I don't respond appropriately, let me know."

Above all, never, never, break off communication with your children no matter what they do. It is your job to instill responsible sexual values, but if your child doesn't accept them, don't withdraw the closeness that they need more than ever. Whether or not they share your values, they need your love.

By the Author

for children

(With Judith Gordon) *Did the Sun Shine Before You Were Born?*, rev. ed. Fayetteville, N.Y.: Ed-U Press, 1985. A sex education primer for children, ages 3–7.

Girls Are Girls and Boys Are Boys—So What's the Difference?, rev. ed. Fayetteville, N.Y.: Ed-U Press, 1986. A nonsexist liberating sex education book for children, ages 6–10.

(With Judith Gordon) *A Better Safe Than Sorry Book.* Fayetteville, N.Y.: Ed-U Press, 1985. A family guide for sexual assault prevention.

for teen-agers

Facts About Sex for Today's Youth. Fayetteville, N.Y.: Ed-U Press, 1983.

Facts About STD. Fayetteville, N.Y.: Ed-U Press, 1983.

Protect Yourself from Becoming an Unwanted Parent. Fayetteville, N.Y.: Ed-U Press, 1983.

Ten Heavy Facts About Sex. Fayetteville, N.Y.: Ed-U Press, 1983. Comic book.

(With Kathleen Everly) *How Can You Tell If You're Really in Love?* Fayetteville, N.Y.: Ed-U Press, 1983. Comic book.

When Living Hurts. New York: Union of American Hebrew Congregations, 1985.

The Teenage Survival Book, 4th ed. New York: Times Books, Random House, 1986. Cited as one of the best young-adult books in 1976 by the American Library Association.

for parents

(With Judith Gordon) *Raising a Child Conservatively in a Sexually Permissive World.* New York: Simon & Schuster, 1983 (hardback); Fireside, 1986 (paperback).

textbooks

Psychology for You, rev. ed. New York: Sadlier—Oxford, 1983.

(With Mina Wollin) *Parenting—A Guide for Young People,* rev. ed. New York: Sadlier—Oxford, 1983.

(With Craig W. Snyder) *Personal Issues in Human Sexuality.* Boston: Allyn & Bacon, 1986. College text.

video

"How Can I Tell If I'm Really in Love?" A fifty-minute Paramount Home Video developed for teen-agers.

list of recommended books

For a listing of books and audiovisual materials in the area of human sexuality, write to Ed-U Press, P.O. Box 583, Fayetteville, New York 13066.

EILEEN SHIFF

Meet the Author

Eileen Shiff is the director of the Child and Family Studies program at Glendale Community College, where she teaches parent education, marriage and family, and family crisis management courses. Before teaching full-time she was a marriage and family counselor and a consultant for businesses, schools, government, and social service agencies. She is one of the founding members of the Arizona State Board of Directors of Parents Anonymous, where she has served for six years.

Eileen has a B.A. in Child Study–Education at Jackson College, Tufts University, and an M.S. in Family Studies at Arizona State University. She is a certified Reality Therapist, having trained with William Glasser, M.D., Mary Ann Wall, and Ed Ford.

She and her teen-age daughters, Karen and Allison, have written a mother–daughter advice column for Impact Parenting Magazine *since its inception. Her daughters have served as youth consultants for her work. Most important, they've taught her the real meaning of parenting.*

Eileen, her husband, Arthur, and daughters live in Phoenix, Arizona.

11

TEACHING YOUR CHILD TO MAKE EFFECTIVE CHOICES

PREPARING FOR THE CHALLENGE OF ADOLESCENCE
EILEEN SHIFF, M.S.

From the moment of a child's birth, we reach out to protect and care for him, cuddling his body, stimulating his mind, socializing his personality, and attempting to shield him from others' germs and his own groping fingers. But sometime between his arrival in the world as a helpless, dependent newborn and his departure from our home as a (hopefully) responsible, resilient adult, we need to stop trimming his nails, choosing his friends, and anticipating his needs.

If we "protect" him by solving his problems and saving him from the consequences of his mistakes, we leave him weak, vulnerable, and dependent. Real protection means strengthening him—teaching him to make effective decisions for himself so he can cope resourcefully with the challenges that will inevitably confront him.

Life is full of choices, whether our children make them deliberately or choose by default. The more effective their choices, the more control they have over their lives. Even more important than his innate ability, a child's life choices can determine whether he becomes a winner or loser.

"Winners" view problems as challenges, anticipating and working out constructive detours when they see obstacles ahead. Their positive, resourceful attitude helps them get more of what they want out of life because they do what they can to resolve problems, rather than dwell on issues that are out of their control.

"Losers" aren't aware that they have the power to make choices. They look at their strengths and weaknesses as gifts and character flaws, as though their behavior were determined by heredity and fate. They see problems as roadblocks—excusing themselves, projecting blame on others, and giving up at the first sign of difficulty. As a result they are perennial victims, always vulnerable to life's stresses.

Our Choices as Parents

As an adult, how do you approach your own problem-solving when confronted with difficulties? This is an important question for it is your attitude that largely determines how your child will approach his life choices. Does your attitude communicate:

> *"I can't help it, I am what I am. Don't expect me to change, that's just my nature."*

People who are not willing to use new information and life experience to improve the quality of their lives and relationships are not allowing themselves to mature. They perceive change as the destruction of comfortable, familiar behavior patterns, and they resist risking new ones, labeling them as "wrong" or "phony." As a result, problems build until they become overwhelming. If things aren't going well, these people focus on how *others* should do things differently, rather than take responsibility for their own actions. They aren't aware of what they risk by *not* changing.

Instead, consider the power in the attitude:

> *"What I tried didn't work, so I will explore other possibilities."*
>
> *"I couldn't fix the problem as a whole—I'll break it down into small, manageable steps and then tackle the first one right away."*

When we take responsibility for our behavior, setting goals and making concrete plans to achieve them, we teach our children to take control over theirs.

In making decisions, it's important to learn what you *can* and *cannot* control in order to focus your energy efficiently. You can't change your past. That's finished. You can anguish over things you regret having said or done, or over opportunities you wish you had taken, but no amount of guilt or depression can alter what has already occurred. You also have no control over other people, the weather, and many life events. But you can control what you think and do in the present to deal with situations, and you can plan for your future. Recrimination about the past and worry about the future not only waste energy, they often prevent us from functioning success-fully in the present.

Control Versus Influence

As parents, it's important to understand the difference between control and influence. We cannot control our children, but we can control what *we* think and do to anticipate and deal with their behavior, influencing them to act responsibly.

As an example, if you are standing in line at a bank and your two-year-old child begins to cry, determine the reason for the crying to decide how to handle her behavior. If she's overtired and overstimulated, she needs some help calming herself down. If she's purposely acting up to manipulate you to do something for her, it's important not to reward her for her tantrum.

If she is crying from exhaustion, instead of yelling at her for being baby-ish and bad (that will only make her more upset), help her identify what she's feeling: "You've had a long day and it's hard for you to have to wait with me in this long bank line. Would you like me to hold your hand? Or would a big hug help?" Rather than intensifying her feelings of helplessness, you're help-ing her think of some productive things to do about her frustration. With experience, she'll eventually learn to communicate her needs to you. Her tears are likely to subside as you reach out to soothe her.

If, on the other hand, she increases her decibel level as she rolls on the floor, screaming for you to take her for some ice cream, she's having a full-blown temper tantrum. Unfortunately you cannot *make* her stop her irra-tional behavior. In fact, the more you scream, hit, or humiliate her to try to *force* her to be quiet, the more agitated she becomes.

If you retaliate with a tantrum of your own, you may release your anger temporarily, but you lose your parenting effectiveness because you are model-ing the behavior you are trying to get her to stop. On the other hand, giving in to her tantrum by taking her for ice cream teaches her that temper tan-trums (especially when performed before an audience) lead you to a quick surrender. Both empower her out-of-control behavior.

With the help of our experts, you now have a wide range of strategies from which to choose. As a result, you can decide not to allow your child's behavior to control yours. You can ignore her (as long as she isn't being destructive). You can carry her out of the bank and give her a supervised Time-Out. You can remove yourself from the commotion. Or you can do the unexpected: lower your voice to a whisper (she'll have to stop screaming to be able to hear your secret). If tantrums are a recurrent problem, tape-record one and play it back after she has calmed down to demonstrate the powerlessness of yelling. Help your child learn that while positive behavior doesn't necessarily mean she'll get what she wants, she has a better chance of getting it if she asks for it civilly than if she throws a temper tantrum.

Making the choice not to let your child's behavior control yours gives your child a model of rational behavior that will stand her in good stead as she is growing up and coping with her own frustrations. By maintaining your own "center," you teach your child that you recognize your responsibility for your behavior.

Furthermore, the better you are at identifying and choosing among alternative behaviors, the more competent you are as a parent. You don't have to sink to your child's level. When he makes surly faces, you don't have to make faces back at him; when he hits you, you don't have to hit him back; and when he screams, "I hate you," you don't have to scream, "I hate you, too." Your child learns how to express his anger primarily from observing you. Rather than punish him, teach him more constructive ways to express his emotions.

Mealtimes are especially ripe for conflict between parents and children in their fight for control over *what* and *how much* the child should eat. Parents want children to eat "good" (nutritious) food, while children find it hard to believe that there could be anything "good" about certain foods (like spinach or liver). And parents have their own preconceived ideas about how much children should eat, while children want to eat when they are hungry and stop when they are not.

Children have their own means of defending themselves when adults try to control their eating. When infants and toddlers are forcibly fed, they usually lock their gums shut or spit the food back in their parents' faces. Toddlers and preschoolers might be pressured to put food they don't like in their mouths and even to chew, but they can refuse to swallow. Older children might eat the food and then vomit. Attempts to control what children eat set the stage for dangerous eating disorders. Instead, create a positive attitude toward food:

1. Keep an interesting assortment of healthful foods in the house and model positive eating behavior yourself.

2. Have discussions with your children about nutrition, emphasizing the value in eating from the four food groups.

3. Be flexible about what foods you prepare and how they are served. For example, children generally prefer snacking on raw vegetables during the day to eating cooked vegetables during meals.

4. Involve children in the planning, shopping, and food preparation. They are likely to eat zucchini if they have the opportunity to shred, mix, and help bake it into bread.

5. Provide attractive, child-sized utensils and plates and allow children to serve themselves.

6. Above all, provide a relaxed, comfortable environment during mealtimes.

Since control not only doesn't work but creates its own problems, it's far more productive to *influence* children to develop good eating habits.

Putting Behavior in Perspective

It is easier to evaluate the alternatives you have in dealing with your child's behavior when you are able to put the behavior in context. Do you remember the first time you watched a frightening horror movie? You probably felt your hands perspire, your heart pound, your breathing quicken, and your muscles tighten as you gripped the arms of your chair. You were experiencing the terror as though you were living it. If you saw the same movie a second time, you'd be better prepared for the crazed behavior and surprise endings. This time you could appreciate the special effects with more detachment because you'd know what to expect. In the same way, when you understand your child's needs and goals, you can anticipate behaviors that are typical of his stage. As you learn to look at his behavior more objectively, you'll increase your tolerance and reduce your tension, enabling yourself to discipline him more rationally.

Our choices of how to deal with our children's behavior are based on the contrast between what we think a child "should" be doing and our perception of his actual behavior. The mother of the six-year-old who uses a four-letter word in public is likely to respond with disgust and outrage. Yet his father might encourage the same behavior because he sees the raw language as a sign that his son is "all boy."

Check out your expectations and perceptions to understand the role they play in your responses. The following exercise will help you develop a more constructive perspective of your child. (Caution: Reading ahead without actually doing the exercise yourself would be like watching an aerobics program and expecting your heart and muscles to benefit!)

List ten adjectives that describe your child. Then put a checkmark beside the ones that are positive. How aware is he that you value him for those qualities? Get into the habit of reinforcing him for at least two of these each day. In addition to increasing his feelings of self-worth, you are feeding yourself more positive thoughts about him.

Next, circle the negative adjectives. What do you tell yourself about him when you concentrate on that list? As Dorothy Briggs described in her chapter, if you are focusing on his negative qualities, he can't help but pick up negative "vibes." You don't have to say the words to communicate disappointment—children are perceptive. They can read your emotion in the expression of your eyes, the tone of your voice, and the tightness of your jaw. In order to truly communicate positive feelings, it's important to internalize them first. To reinterpret his behaviors in a more positive light, examine them within the context of his developmental stage (using the Developmental Checklist in Resources for Parents). Then relabel each behavior to reflect the purpose it serves. The negative list below could easily describe a two-year-old:

NEGATIVE LIST   REVISED LIST

manipulative ------------> creative

negative ----------------> independent thinker,
                            developing autonomy

wild -------------------> testing his limits

defiant -----------------> practicing separation

selfish -----------------> not yet able to appreciate the
                            needs of others

The revised list is not an excuse for negative behavior. It is a tool to help you develop some objectivity so you can discipline your child more effectively. If you see his behavior as designed to hurt you, you'll perceive him as "bad" and look for ways to punish him. On the other hand, if you see his actions as fulfilling some of his developmental goals, you'll be able to tell yourself, "He's learning to become a separate person who thinks for himself. He needs some guidance to discover how to do it appropriately. Some of his negativity is a sign of growth, even if I see it as obnoxious."

It is natural and healthy for our goals to clash with our children's at times. A child's goal is to explore and test his world, learn to make decisions, and become less dependent on parents. Ours is to guide and protect him. He is focused on short-term fun, while we are concerned with the long-term consequences of his behavior (trying to prevent him from closing doors to his future). It helps to recognize that his frustrating behavior is not directed at *us* personally. He is pushing us because of what we represent—his barriers to fun, freedom, and independence.

When parents say, "Ray's crying at nursery school makes me feel guilty," "The way Evan dresses makes me so ashamed," or "Suzanne's whining makes me scream!" we indicate that we believe our children's behavior has the power to determine our own.

It's not the crying, poor taste, or whining that sets us off. It's our interpretation of the behavior. In fact, we have some days when we see a behavior as "cute" and others where we see the same behavior as "repulsive."

We can change the way we deal with our children by changing what we tell ourselves about their actions. For instance, imagine that you ask your ten-year-old daughter, Sharon, to clear the kitchen table and put the dishes into the dishwasher while you leave for the airport to pick up your mother-in-law. Your daughter assures you that she will get to the kitchen in "five minutes" and that it will look fantastic by the time you and Granny come home. Her final words are "Trust me!"

While driving home from the airport with your newly arrived house guest, listening to her stories about your immaculate sisters-in-law, their beautiful homes, and their perfectly behaved children, you pray that your daughter's interpretation of "fantastic" matches your own.

But as you enter the house, you are horrified to find your kitchen as much of a wreck as it was when you left, and Sharon in the family room listening to records with three friends. Consider the effect each of the following would have in either escalating your emotions until they control your response, or defusing your anger so you could rationally discipline your child.

ESCALATOR: "How could Sharon do this to me? I'd *never* have let my mother down like that because I loved her too much." Or: "I *always* followed through on important commitments to my mother because I respected her."

DEFUSER: "Neglecting the kitchen doesn't mean she doesn't love or respect me. When her friends came over, she probably forgot about her promise. Even though I was a devoted daughter, my mother might remember an incident or two where I was less than perfect myself."

ESCALATOR: "That kid ruined everything! Now I can't face my mother-in-law."

DEFUSER: "This is very embarrassing, but I won't make it into a crisis. I don't have to let it destroy the visit. I've handled more significant problems and I'll get through this one."

ESCALATOR: "Sharon's pushing my button. She knows how to get to me!"

DEFUSER: "If I don't overreact, she won't get any payoff for pushing."

When you tell yourself, "She's self-centered and spiteful," you assume an "I'll show her . . ." kind of attitude. It's far more productive to tell yourself, "I am very embarrassed that the kitchen looks disgusting, and I'm upset that my daughter didn't keep her commitment to me. But Sharon didn't neglect the kitchen to humiliate me. She most likely got involved with her friends and forgot about her promise. She needs to experience some appropriate consequences to help her remember to follow through on her commitments next time." While it is only human to be upset, you can choose to keep the situation in perspective.

When you have difficulty stopping your emotions from escalating—they seem to be racing out of control—take some time out, away from your child, to release some of your stress productively (through exercise, a phone call to a supportive friend, a shower, meditation, slow deep breathing, or whatever works best for you). Then decide how you will teach her to behave more responsibly next time. In choosing your strategy, keep in mind that the goal of effective parenting is not to get back at your child, but to resolve the specific situation constructively and to help her learn skills to deal with future issues.

To create some emotional detachment from the situation, you might ask yourself how you'd advise a parent who described a similar incident to you. (It's much easier for most of us to be rational when dealing with other people's problems than we are with our own.)

It is also helpful to develop a wider perspective of your child's behavior, seeing it as part of a pattern over time. We tend to magnify the significance of a problem when we look at it in isolation, using it as proof that we've failed our child as parents and that she's failed us as a child. Instead, look at the larger picture. If she has followed through on your requests six times out of eight during the past week, as opposed to only two times out of forty the past month, that's not failure—that's progress!

Building Inner Strength

Dr. William Glasser, renowned psychotherapist and teacher, sees people as having four basic psychological needs for personal fulfillment:

1. Belonging and Love
2. Power/Competition
3. Fun
4. Freedom

When we help children strengthen themselves in these areas, they learn to meet their needs productively and, as a result, they make more effective choices. And parents who learn to meet their own needs constructively are positive role models for their children and are less dependent on their off-spring to fulfill their needs for them.

Belonging and Love

One of the most basic needs children have is to belong—to immediate families, extended families, peer groups, and the community. Unfortunately, the contemporary child's need for belonging is often frustrated by changes in social structure and family priorities. With school boundaries shifting, schools closing, nuclear families moving away from their extended families and long-term friendships, and family units splintering and restructuring, children today lack a sense of community, continuity, and connectedness.

Many young people spend a great deal of time unsupervised, in empty houses, in front of televisions, being shuttled to lessons in large carpools, and just "hanging around." Even when the family is home together, family members are likely to be watching TV (in separate rooms), talking on the telephone, hooked up to stereo earphones, or just "doing their own thing" with little interpersonal involvement.

It's not enough just to love your child or even to tell him you love him. He needs to *feel* loved. When your child perceives you as caring, he tends to be more sensitive to you and is more likely to value what you have to say. Your accessibility makes it easier for him to bring up those sensitive questions that seem to require casual, comfortable interaction before they emerge. And as you are interacting, you are depositing memories in his memory bank, building a foundation for a positive relationship with him during his adolescent years.

To demonstrate your caring, become involved as a family unit and on a one-to-one basis. Jogging, walking, cooking, hiking, camping, cleaning the car, carpentry, and tennis offer excellent opportunities to develop closeness and warmth between parent and child. These are activities that require energy, effort, and awareness of each other, as opposed to passively watching movies or television. A daily investment of quality time with each child is likely to net rewarding dividends.

To paraphrase Dr. Alfred Adler, the Austrian psychiatrist who founded the school of individual psychology, we act according to our own individual perceptions of life. By becoming involved with a child, we better understand his world through his perception, helping us to better understand *him*.

It takes more patience and special understanding to seek out the company of the difficult child because he often appears to purposely create distance. Yet the difficult child has an even greater need to interact positively with his parents. Sharing an activity that you both enjoy often stimulates positive feelings that can develop into a mutually caring relationship.

Power/Competition

The need for *power* is very different from the *power goal of misbehavior* described earlier by Dr. Dinkmeyer. The need for power refers to the positive need to control oneself, not the goal of controlling others. In fact, the child who meets his own needs productively has no desire to misbehave by manipulating others.

Children develop a healthy sense of power through the respect and appreciation of parents and peers and the realization that they are important, that they are valued, that they make a difference. This sense of power may be heightened through their involvement in constructive groups (4-H clubs, scouting, or religious or service organizations) where they can experience the power of contributing to the well-being of others.

Power also comes from the confidence in knowing they are capable of making good choices. Having good decision-making skills strengthens children to face the increasing pressures that they will cope with as they near adolescence—the pressures to cut classes, experiment with drugs and sex, and "rip off" society.

According to Victor Frankl, the Viennese author and psychiatrist, while people face a number of life events over which they have little or no control, they have the power to decide *how* they will cope with each situation. Though there are many decisions that we as parents need to make for our children, especially when they are young, it's important to give them a voice in *how* they will face each experience.

When taking a child to a potentially frightening experience—his first day of school or a visit to the dentist, the doctor, or the hospital—choices can offer a sense of power. For instance, after the child is told he will be having a tooth pulled (with a description of what the experience will be like for him), ask, "Nickie, would you like me to hold your hand or would you rather bring in 'Muttie' to cuddle?" The decision to have the procedure has been made *for* him, but giving him a say in *how* he will experience it gives him a feeling of personal control. After the ordeal, asking "What did you do to help yourself get through it?" reinforces his power to cope with temporary pain and fear.

When you offer a choice, be sure it is an honest one. When it's time for dinner, don't ask your three-year-old daughter, "Would you like to eat now?" and then become furious with her if she responds with a "no." Instead, give her notice ahead of time so that she can finish whatever she is doing. Then simply announce, "It's time for dinner." If the intent is to use decision-making to avoid a confrontation, a more productive choice would be "Are your arms strong enough to carry the salad or the potatoes to the table?" Offer choices that make use of her strengths rather than create a power struggle.

When a child learns to value herself and gets recognition from others for her positive qualities, she does not need to compete for power through dysfunctional behavior.

Fun

You teach your child the value of fun when you demonstrate a positive attitude toward life. You enjoy the present. Parents who view life through negative filters can be real "downers." They see something going well and say, "It'll never last." When something is going poorly, they moan, "What do you expect?" It's not surprising that these parents often have whiny, negative children.

In past generations, children learned to create fun using their personal resources—imagination and energy. They played games for pleasure, not simply to win. Today's child is generally programmed with a fully scheduled week of lessons and highly competitive adult-managed sports. He often fills unscheduled time, passively watching television or playing with automated toys, leaving little opportunity to develop creativity and initiative.

Children who learn early to take responsibility for providing their own entertainment are less likely in the future to depend on artificial stimulants to "turn themselves on."

Help your child develop a sense of humor about life as you work on developing your own—you'll both need it for adolescence!

Freedom

Freedom is the need for self-determination—your child's freedom to express his thoughts and feelings and to explore and enjoy his world. It is the freedom to choose his own friends, hairstyles, toys, clothing, and goals without being held back by sex-role stereotypes or parental preferences.

Freedom of privacy is very important to young people, as it is to adults. They appreciate parents knocking before entering their rooms, leaving diaries unread, letters unopened, and secrets respected. Often the specific issue is not as important as the youngster's freedom to share or protect what belongs to him.

Parents often inadvertently block their children's freedom to fully experience life by tying all behaviors to lofty goals. When you tell a child, "If something is worth doing, it's worth doing well," he may back away from trying anything new because he is afraid of "failure." As a result your child misses out on many of life's pleasures. Like photographers who shoot a number of photographs to increase their choices before enlarging the ones with the greatest promise, it's important for children to have the opportunity to spend their early years sampling a wide range of activities before specializing. As your child gets older, teach him to set priorities: to work hard in specific areas like academics; and to just enjoy some activities without any need to compete or succeed.

In forming their identities, our children need the freedom to test themselves, their relationships, and their environments. It's important to allow them the freedom to test when the possible consequences are harmless, while we set firm limits on behaviors that could be damaging to themselves or to others.

The needs of power and freedom are interrelated. Children who are trusted to make appropriate decisions for themselves have more freedom. That freedom, in itself, results in power and a healthy sense of self-worth.

Conflict of Needs

Sometimes a child has conflicting needs. For example, one nine-year-old's need for academic achievement was strong, but his need to fit in with his classmates was even stronger, so he gave in to the requests of his "friends" and purposely marked some of the answers wrong in his math workbook to lower the class curve. He needed help in evaluating the consequences of specific behaviors in order to learn to make more productive choices for himself in the future.

More often, though, the conflict exists between the needs of the child and those of his parents. When conflict becomes excessive between you and your child, find out if any of his needs, or yours, are not being adequately met. Your child may be having a difficult time with friends or school, and be venting his frustration on the family. Or *you* might be having a problem with your spouse, job, or friends that you are taking out on him.

Also consider the possibility that you could be having difficulty with a particular child because you have unrealistic expectations of him or because of what he represents to you. Perhaps he was born at a time that interfered with your life plans. He might remind you of a competitive sibling of yours, or even remind you too much of yourself. Sometimes a parent's most effective choice is recognizing the importance of enlisting the help of outside resources. An objective, well-trained counselor can help you define the problem and explore viable options. Then you can choose to resolve the problem productively.

Fulfilling Our Needs

We learn how to satisfy our needs by recalling "pictures" of specific things, events, or activities that have been satisfying to us in the past. Although all people have the same basic needs, each person's picture of how to fulfill those needs is uniquely his own. The following are pictures that children I've worked with have described as satisfying specific needs in each of the four areas:

BELONGING:
"sharing a secret with my friend"
"getting invited to a party"
"eating dinner together with my family"

POWER/COMPETITION:
"being accepted as part of the 'in' crowd"
"doing something that gets Grandma to smile"
"saying something important enough that my friend says, 'Hey, I never thought of that!' "

FUN:
"cleaning the windows with my dad"
"splashing in a puddle"
"doing magic tricks"

FREEDOM:
"choosing the wallpaper in my room"
"spending my allowance on whatever I want"
"crossing the street by myself"

When the picture of what a child wants matches with what he has, he functions well and is satisfied. For instance, Robbie wants you to drive him to a friend's house. You say, "Sure." As a result, he is happy.

But when what he wants is different from his reality, he experiences frustration. When Robbie asks you for a ride, if you respond instead with "I can't drive you now—I have the flu," he would become frustrated. The further away the picture of what he wants is from his reality, the greater his frustration. If he wants to go to Phillip's house now but another time would do almost as well, that frustration would be mild. However, if Phillip is having a birthday party that starts in ten minutes, Robbie's frustration would be intense. It is important to teach him how to channel that frustration in a way that best meets his needs without interfering with the needs of others, helping him explore other means of getting to the party.

Frustration is a warning signal that his reality doesn't match his expectations and that it would be in his best interest to do something different, just as the generator light on the dashboard is a valuable warning that it's time to check under the hood. When you try to talk your child out of his frustration or rescue him from it, you teach him to bypass his personal warning signals, reducing his personal effectiveness and leaving him vulnerable.

When children aren't aware of the constructive choices available to them, they sometimes use dysfunctional behavior to deal with frustration— whining, crying, getting depressed, lying, giving up, or dumping their anger on a convenient scapegoat. If they internalize their stress, they might let the stress eat at them, resulting in psychosomatic illnesses.

As they get older, some youngsters add more "sophisticated" choices: drinking, taking illicit drugs, or binge eating to deal with frustration. Any of these might release frustration temporarily, but in the long run, the results are generally destructive to young people and to their relationships. Children learn some of their options from watching the behavior of their parents and other significant people in their lives. They learn others from experience. They remember the behavior and try it the next time they become frustrated. After a number of times it becomes part of their behavioral pattern, even though it may no longer be satisfying a need.

Many times parents want to protect a child from the consequences of his decisions and then punish him for their own frustration or embarrassment over the incident. For example, a mother of a seven-year-old became furious with her son's principal for keeping Matthew after school because he was late four mornings in a row. Matt's mother complained that staying after school meant that he had to get on the late bus with the older children and he couldn't go home with his friends.

She explained to our parenting class, "Mrs. Simpson should have told me that Matt was late again, and then I'd have given him a good spanking!" It sounded almost as though she thought the principal had denied her the privilege of punishing him herself. What did her son learn from the consequences of being late to school? He lost the privilege of riding home on the bus with his peers. His inconvenience helped him remember to be at school on time the next day. It was less annoying to get up a half hour earlier in the morning than to have to go home on the "big kids' " bus. What would Matt have learned from being hit by his mother? That his mother was "being mean." His energy would have been focused on getting back at her rather than on getting himself to class on time. She would have denied him the opportunity to learn from the consequences of his actions.

Reality Therapy

Reality Therapy is a method developed by Dr. Glasser to help people learn how to get what they want out of life. By teaching your child the following steps, you can help him learn to use his frustration to motivate himself to set realistic goals and then explore constructive ways to achieve them.

1. DEMONSTRATE CARING: As you do things together, get into his world and share yours with him. At the same time model responsible behavior and reinforce him when he demonstrates positive decision-making skills.

2. FIND OUT WHAT HE WANTS, what's important to him, and then help him evaluate his goal to decide if it's realistic.

   "Do you want to pass your math test tomorrow?"

   "Do you want to get along better with your teacher?"

   "Do you want me to be able to trust you?"

3. ASK HIM, noncritically, WHAT HE IS DOING, thus helping him learn to take responsibility for his behavior.

   "What are you doing to get a passing grade on your math exam?"

   "What did the teacher say you were doing during English class?"

   "What time did you come in for dinner?"

(Don't ask *why* he's doing what he's doing—that leads to defensiveness and excuses.)

4. GET HIM TO EVALUATE HIS BEHAVIOR BY HELPING HIM SEE THE CONNECTION BETWEEN WHAT HE WANTS AND WHAT HE'S DOING.

> *"Is worrying helping you pass your math test?"*
>
> *"Is chewing gum in class against the rules? How does breaking the class rules help you get along better with your teacher?"*
>
> *"Is coming in later than we agreed on helping me develop trust in you?"*

If he states that what he is doing is not helping, teach him to use his frustration to change his behavior.

> *"Would you like things to be better?"* or
>
> *"What is the price you're paying for doing that?"*

(Don't let him sidetrack you with a discussion of what *other* people are doing or why a rule is not fair. If he tries to shift the responsibility or change the subject, get him to refocus on *his* behavior.)

If your child complains that the teacher was being mean for giving him detention when he was "just nibbling on his lunch because he was starving," say:

> *"I can see that you think that the penalties for eating food during class are unfair. Since you don't have the power to change the rule, what can you do to help yourself remember not to snack during school hours anymore?"*

5. HELP HIM MAKE A PLAN to improve his behavior, creatively exploring alternative solutions. At first you will have to design most of the plan for him. With more experience in plan making, he will learn to do it himself.

Build in success by making the plan simple and small in terms of behavior and the time allotted to do it in:

> *"Do . . . for two days and then we'll talk about it."*

Keep focused on what he will *do,* not what he will *stop doing:*

"I'll hit my punching bag when I get cranky."

not

"I won't hit my brother next time I'm mad."

Make the plan specific and dependent on *your child's* behavior, not on anyone else's:

"I'll spend thirty minutes, without any distractions, working hard on my English paper. After that I'll make corrections and then do a final draft."

rather than

"I'll get an A on my English paper tomorrow."

Begin the plan as soon as possible. The earlier he begins, the more likely he is to follow through.

6. HELP HIM EVALUATE HIS PLAN.

"Do you think this is a good plan?"

"Is it reasonable?"

If not, work with him to redesign it.

Help him anticipate the behaviors that usually sabotage his good intentions:

"What kinds of things could get in the way of your carrying out your plan?" (procrastination, laziness, etc.)

"What will you tell yourself when you think about putting things off for 'just one more day'?"

If he uses excuses to avoid taking responsibility, either when asked to evaluate his behavior or when making a plan, ask him to reevaluate:

"Is passing your math exam important enough to work on it, even if it means you'll have to miss tennis practice?"

Ask him to summarize the plan to be sure he understands it. Be certain he's aware of the possible consequences of not following through:

"What did we decide would happen if you decided not to follow through?"

7. GET HIS COMMITMENT TO THE PLAN so he will take responsibility for carrying it out:

"Can I count on you to keep your commitment?"

The child's inner confidence and the strength of your relationship with him are important. If he sees that you are interested and caring, and that you believe that he is capable of being successful, he's more likely to believe in himself. To reinforce his commitment, have him sign the agreement or shake hands on it.

8. ALLOW HIM TO EXPERIENCE REASONABLE CONSEQUENCES so he will learn from the experience. Don't distract him from what he is learning by criticizing, punishing, putting him down, or interfering with the consequence. (Otherwise, he'll focus on his frustration with *you* rather than on what he will do differently next time.)

9. HELP HIM EVALUATE HIS FOLLOW-THROUGH:

"What did (or didn't) work for you?"

"What would you do differently next time?"

"What did you learn from the experience?"

If your child's plan dealt with his misbehavior—and he continues to misbehave—state, after allowing the consequence to occur, "I can see this plan is not working. Please go to your room to make a plan that *will* work."

Then, after he has developed a new plan and you have contributed your input, ask, "What do you think should happen if you don't stick with the new plan? Can I count on your following through this time?"

If your child continues his negative behavior, it might be wise to seek help from a qualified counselor. Some parents see the need for assistance as a sign of incompetence. They don't recognize the value of an impartial, skilled, helping professional. Counselors, social workers, psychologists, and psychiatrists take their own children to other professionals when they need another perspective. Seeking counseling is not a sign of weakness, it is an indication that you care enough about your child to work at your relationship.

Most importantly, don't give up. If you perceive your child as hopeless, he'll stop believing in himself.

Reality Therapy in Action

Max used Reality Therapy to help his four-year-old daughter develop some social skills. According to the preschool teacher, Mara was the class loner. She went to school in the morning with a pout, her head down, and her feet shuffling "like a Raggedy Ann doll." The few times she interacted with her classmates, she behaved the way she did with her older brother—teasing the other children to get noticed.

What Mara needed was help in looking at her goal (friendship) and what she was doing to get it (acting uninterested or being annoying), to determine whether her behavior was helping her make friends. Since it wasn't, her father helped her develop a concrete, specific, realistic plan to *be* a friend. The following is a re-creation of their dialogue.

FATHER: "Would you like to have a friend?"

MARA: "Yuh, but they're mean to me."

FATHER: "What are you doing to show someone in the class that you'd like to be her friend?"

MARA: "No one likes me!"

FATHER: Warmly, "What did *you* do today with Erika?" (A girl Mara particularly liked.)

MARA: (Grinning mischievously) "I was teasing Erika. I pulled out a block and her bridge fell down."

FATHER: "What do you think she tells herself about you when you tease her like that?"

MARA: (Sighing) "She gets mad. She calls me a baby."

FATHER: "Is that the way you want her to think about you?"

MARA: (Shakes her head from side to side.)

FATHER: "How would you like her to see you?"

MARA: "Like a friend."

FATHER: "What could you do to show her you want to be her friend?"

MARA: "I don't know."

Her father helped her recognize the signals she was sending off to her classmates, using a mirror to help teach her friend-making skills.

EILEEN SHIFF, M.S.   285

FATHER: "Who, in your class, has friends?"

MARA: "Ronnye."

FATHER: "What does Ronnye do that other children seem to like?"

MARA: (Shrugs)

FATHER: "How does Ronnye's face look when she walks into the class?"

MARA: (Smiles)

When Mara smiled, Max responded in kind, explaining that when he looked at her happy face *he* felt happy. He told her that when he saw her smile, he thought, "Mara looks sweet and friendly. I like being with her." (They both checked out their broad smiles in the mirror.) He then asked her to demonstrate how a shy child looks when she enters the classroom, being very specific about facial expression and body language. Role playing in front of the mirror helped Mara understand, in concrete terms, how others respond to direct eye-to-eye contact, a warm smile, and friendly body language.

Finally, Max asked Mara which child in the class seemed to want a friend. (It's easier for a shy child to try new behaviors if she focuses on another child's needs rather than dwell on her own fears of rejection.) Mara mentioned Lindsay, a quiet, sensitive child who had recently moved to the area from another state.

Mara's father worked out a plan with Mara to walk over to Lindsay, look directly at her, flash her a friendly smile, and say "Hi" first. Then she'd invite Lindsay to play in the housekeeping corner. While generally there is a greater chance of success (especially with young children) when focusing on modifying one behavior at a time, Mara was able to coordinate several behaviors at once.

Max was careful to point out that there was no guarantee Lindsay would be friendly to her in return—that all Mara could control was what *she* would do.

FATHER: "What's the worst thing that could happen if you follow through with your plan?"

MARA: "She'll say 'no.' "

FATHER: "What's the best thing that could happen?"

MARA: "She'll play with me."

FATHER: "Is it important enough to you to play with Lindsay that you'll follow your plan?"

MARA: (Nods)

Together they reviewed the plan and Max helped her practice her new skills. When they finished, they shook hands on the agreement and then Max gave her an encouraging hug.

The next morning, Mara followed through with her plan. She looked directly at Lindsay and said "Hi" first, smiling tentatively. Lindsay smiled back. Mara then asked Lindsay to play in the housekeeping corner. Lindsay joined her for about twenty minutes but then left with another child to play on the playground.

If Mara's plan had been to make a "best friend," she would have experienced failure because she would have been vulnerable to Lindsay's reactions. Because the plan focused only on what *Mara* would do, she achieved success. Mara's father reinforced her for carrying out her plan effectively and for the opportunity to have fun with Lindsay. The next plan would continue to build on that success.

One of the most influential ways to teach a child that she is not controlled by the behavior of others is by showing her, through your own modeling, that you recognize your own choices. For example, if you are on a shopping trip with your daughter and you encounter a rude salesman, demonstrate that you don't have to be thrown by his behavior—you can respond assertively, ignore him, or report him. You don't have to get irrational yourself or waste time with him, giving him the power to ruin your day or make you late. (You also teach your daughter to accept delays, rudeness, and incompetence as a part of life—an inconvenience, not a catastrophe.)

Of course it's easier to remain cool with people we aren't involved with personally than it is with family members. With our children, emotions (both positive and negative) are far more intense because of the depth of our feelings.

Anger can be particularly strong when our needs and those of our children conflict, as demonstrated by the following example. Phyllis, a divorced mother, was exasperated with her nine-year-old daughter because Debra "wouldn't let" her spend time alone with a new male friend. Phyllis needed some *freedom* to enjoy her new relationship while her daughter had a need to *belong* to her original family. Debra held on to the fantasy that if she kept her mother from dating, her father might move back home again. When Phyllis went out with her friend Michael, Debra often called her mother to come home immediately, complaining about severe stomach cramps. This led to angry fights because Michael was tired of Phyllis's "spoiling" her daughter at his expense.

Debra's psychosomatic illness was successful in preventing her mother from enjoying time alone with her new friend. Phyllis was sympathetic to Debra's needs at the time because she knew her daughter's pain was real. But during the week she would criticize, nag, or be sarcastic to her daughter, exploding in anger over seemingly insignificant events. Phyllis was angry because she assumed that Debra was purposely trying to ruin her fun, as though she were punishing her for the divorce. But instead of confronting the issue and resolving the problem, Phyllis was getting even with her daughter for interfering with her new relationship.

With the increased stress in her home, Debra felt progressively less secure when her mother went out with Michael. As the weeks went on, the problem intensified.

After taking Debra to the doctor to rule out physical illness, Phyllis worked with our class to learn how to teach Debra to meet her own needs more appropriately.

First, Phyllis told Debra that she would never be remarrying Debra's father—that they no longer loved each other—but that each loved Debra very much. She added that just as Debra had nothing to do with the breakup of their marriage, she also couldn't put it back together. Phyllis said, "I understand how difficult it must be for you to watch me go out with someone other than your dad, but since our marriage is over, would you prefer that I allow myself to have some pleasant Saturday evenings with friends or spend each weekend crying about your dad?"

After Debra responded that she understood, but still didn't like what was happening, Phyllis explained, "I wish things could be the way they used to be, too." She then asked what Debra could do to make the next Saturday night pleasant for herself. Debra decided that she'd invite a friend for a sleepover so she would enjoy herself, too, rather than make herself sick thinking about all the "could-have-beens."

Because of Debra's need to belong to her original family, she had been unconsciously using her psychosomatic pain to control her mother. It was only after she understood that her parents' marriage had truly ended, and realized that her need for belonging could be met through her close relationship with her mother and father individually, that her stomachaches stopped.

Her mother also encouraged her to express her concerns so they could be dealt with openly and honestly, rather than letting her frustration eat at her. Debra learned that she could take control over her life as long as she didn't deny other people the opportunity to take control over theirs. She did not have the power to get her parents back together, but she did have a choice as to how to cope with the divorce. She could decide to be either miserable or okay, but her mother wasn't going to leave in the midst of a date anymore.

Conflicts in any relationship are inevitable because of the differences in people's perceptions and expectations. Conflicts are inherent in the parent-child relationship because personal needs, goals, and perceptions of parents and children are often at odds with each other. Rather than approach conflicts as crises, use them as opportunities to teach your child to solve problems.

Strengthening Values

It would be wonderful to be able to teach a child solutions to the personal and relationship conflicts he'll be facing throughout his life. But because his complex world is changing so fast, we can't anticipate all the issues that will confront him. Even if we could, our answers might not fit for him. It's far more productive to strengthen a child's values in order to help him develop a solid foundation on which to base his own decisions.

Many parents are hesitant to discuss values because they haven't defined their own or they don't want to sound "uncool." They claim, "I have no right to impose my values on my children." To paraphrase Dr. Thomas Lickona, researcher and author on moral development, while we don't have a right to impose our values on our children, as parents we have the responsibility to share ours with them.

When we don't talk about values, we give our children the message that we don't consider our values to be of much worth. Our silence gives them license to do whatever they think is in their own best interest. Sometimes it's important for youngsters to think beyond themselves, to consider the needs of *other* people and society in general as well as their own.

We have the strongest influence on our children, especially when they are young and most impressionable. But we have competition. Peer groups, teachers, rock music, television, movies, and magazines all make their impact, too. If we don't lobby for our own beliefs, we are allowing louder and stronger influences to fill the void.

Television has a particularly strong influence on children's values because of the incredible number of hours children watch (approximately thirty hours per week) and *what* they are watching (soap operas, crime shows, and violent cartoons). Children get a sensationalized view of violence, sex, and substance abuse from television (especially cable) before they've developed the values they need to process what they're seeing.

Parents would be wise to set some standards with children on television use in terms of viewing hours and program content. If your child does watch a show that promotes negative values, you might watch the program with him and use events on the screen to discuss consequences of specific actions. When viewing a movie that encourages the viewers to root for the robber who got away, for example, you might ask, "Do you think it is right for a person to take things, even if there is no chance of getting caught?" . . . "When people steal things from your Aunt Bettie's boutique, how do you think that affects her store manager when inventory time comes up? . . . Do you think it is fair for your aunt to have to pay for merchandise that people steal from her?"

In the same way, you can use life experiences as they occur to help your child develop critical thinking skills. For example, picture your ten-year-old daughter asking to go to the toy store with two girls who have previously bragged about having stolen small items from stores. Your daughter tells you to relax—she won't take anything without paying for it, no matter what the others do.

You'd like to forbid her to go, but although you can keep her home that day, she'll simply learn not to tell you the truth next time. You cannot control her choice of friends, since you aren't with her all the time.

It's more productive to influence her to make good decisions out of her own conviction, not merely out of fear that you will find out. You might ask (warmly, not "shot-gun style"), "What will happen if you go shopping together and the other girls steal things and then get caught? Are you aware that you might be taken to the police station because you will be considered part of the group?" . . . "Is their friendship worth risking a police record?" . . . "Do you think people who put you in such a compromising position are really friends?" Focus realistically on the possible consequences, helping your child picture what it would be like for her to have to endure them. By asking her to question her values (rather than simply lecturing her) you challenge her thinking instead of turning her off.

Too often parents wait until children are sexually active, using drugs, or have dropped out of school before discussing values. At that point young people have already made life-shaping decisions. Discuss your values with your children when they are young; and then continue to discuss them in greater depth as your children mature. That means coming to terms with your own values, demonstrating their importance to you by your life choices. It is in sharing our values that our children begin to shape theirs. We have little control over whether they will accept or challenge ours, but it is our responsibility to express them.

Peer Pressure and Drugs

Strengthening values is particularly important in helping children counter peer pressure. When we teach children to make good decisions, we generally get a sense of where they stand and to what extent they can be trusted. When children are with friends, though, they often do things together that they would never do alone.

Peer pressure is especially powerful when it comes to experimentation with drugs—this is where your child's sense of self and his ability to make

choices are put to the test. The job of teaching children to resist drugs is no longer one of teaching them not to talk to, or accept anything from, strangers. Today the "pusher" is likely to be a close friend the child values and trusts. Examples of enticement range from the subtle pressure of knowing that some popular kids are "doing drugs" to the overt pressure of being handed a joint at a party by someone saying, "Come on, grow up . . . it won't hurt you." When we prepare children during their early years to stand by their decisions in the face of outside pressure, we develop greater trust in them and they, in turn, develop more confidence in themselves.

Don't wait for adolescence to begin helping your child become drug resistant. Begin at birth, building his sense of self-worth and instilling in him a respect for the health and well-being of his mind and body. Help your youngster learn to make appropriate decisions and stand by them, even when those decisions aren't popular. Also be aware of the messages your own behavior conveys. Parents who use cigarettes, alcohol, or tranquilizers to calm their nerves or get a "quick fix" are, in effect, encouraging children to use drugs as stress reducers and problem solvers.

When we don't prepare our children ahead of time by giving them information about the short-term and long-term effects of drugs on the mind and body, they become more vulnerable to the influences around them that seem to condone drug use: the nonchalance of many teachers and administrators, the powerless attitude of many parents, and the reticence of police to confiscate drugs at youth events where young people are openly drinking liquor and smoking marijuana. Without information and values to base their decisions on, children often assume that drugs could not be so bad if authority figures aren't enforcing the penalties for their use.

Begin early to develop a family prevention plan:

1. Let your children know, from infancy on, that they can speak with you freely on any subject. As Dr. Sol Gordon emphasized in his chapter on sexuality, be "askable." If your children know you won't be judgmental when they ask questions, they'll be more likely to share their concerns with you and, as a result, you'll have the opportunity to give your input.

2. Educate your children about the long-term and short-term effects of drugs on young people. That means reading the latest research and being familiar with street terms so you will be a credible resource. Be prepared for them to play devil's advocate. Sometimes they will challenge you in order to get you to argue the other side so they will have ammunition to back up their own position. Some of the typical arguments children offer for using alcohol and marijuana, the first drugs of choice for young experimenters, are the following:

   "Marijuana has been around since before your generation. It's no big deal."

   (Provide them with pamphlets or books describing current research on the effects of the drug on the system.) Then add, "The research we have today on the long-term effects of marijuana is on the pot that was used in the '70s. Today, marijuana is four times as strong as it was back then."

   "I don't do drugs. I just drink."

   "Alcohol is a drug, the one that is most abused today by children and teen-agers."

   "Josh has been using pot for years and he's one of the smartest kids in the school. It couldn't be so bad."

   "Marijuana consists of more than 421 chemicals. They interact differently in each person's body. And some of the effects don't show up until years later."

"You and Dad go to cocktail parties, what's wrong if someday I go to parties where people use marijuana?"

"Alcohol is also a mind-altering drug, but there are differences. First of all, marijuana is an illicit drug. There are legal consequences of being caught with it in your possession. Second, unlike drinking, just by being in the room where people are smoking marijuana you're absorbing the chemicals as you breathe. Finally, unlike alcohol that is sold in legitimate stores, there isn't any agency supervising the processing and distribution of marijuana. At times it has been laced with PCP and other very dangerous substances."

In addition, arrange for a competent leader to work with your children within a group of peers—in school, a club, scouts, or a religious organization. Children are more apt to internalize positive values when they are reinforced in a productive setting with other youngsters they like and respect. (That's making use of positive peer influence.)

3. Discuss why those who use drugs push others to use them. (It's not because they are interested in their welfare. How many youngsters take such a personal interest in whether or not their friends study, eat healthy foods, or exercise?) It is because regular users are just as concerned about peer acceptance as nonusers. When drug users can get others to join them, they perceive that as approval.

4. Help children become sophisticated about specific manipulative tactics friends might use to pressure them. Television commercials and advertising billboards are an excellent source of teaching material.

5. Help them weigh the pros and cons of drug use.

PROS: "Why are drugs so appealing to some children?" (By finding out what they are thinking, you'll be in a better position to offer them information and express your values.)

- reduce tension
- gain group acceptance
- feel more grownup
- try a new experience
- get a "high"

Ask if there are other, risk-free ways to do the same things. Don't be afraid to help them question their thinking. For example, if your daughter says,

"That's what you need to be accepted," you might ask, "Do you really think that you will lose Andrew's friendship if you won't use drugs with him?" or "Is someone who accepts you only if you use drugs a real friend?"

CONS: "What would you risk by taking drugs?" (Be specific, helping your child imagine herself experiencing the consequences.

- diminished motivation, lack of goals
- inability to think clearly and make competent decisions
- difficulty remembering, learning, and concentrating
- lack of energy
- drop in grades
- health problems
- reduced fertility
- loss of trust, respect, and privileges

6. When children face peer pressure, they need to be able to respond quickly and decisively or the pressure will intensify. By anticipating problems ahead of time, you're preparing your child to confront pressures head-on rather than be victimized by them. When pressure is mild, your child can simply say "No thanks" or "I don't want to." As it escalates, the response needs to become stronger as well:

"Don't you want to be in the 'in' group?"

"Do I have to stop thinking for myself to be accepted?"

"You'll feel great!"

"I already feel good about myself."

"Let's enjoy today. You don't know about tomorrow."

"It's been coming on time up until now. I don't want to ruin the quality of the days I have left."

"You haven't convinced me it's so bad."

"I don't need to. I respect your right to make decisions for yourself. I'd appreciate the same from you."

"You don't know what you're missing unless you try."

"There are plenty of things I'd prefer to learn without having to experiment on myself."

"If you were a real friend, you'd trust me."

"A real friend wouldn't be pushing me to do something I don't think is right for me."

"Are you afraid to do it?"

"I don't want to do it."

If the pressure gets too intense, your child can communicate decisively with his body language—by leaving!

7. Join together with parents in your community to set some common goals and standards to help children resist drugs. If you reduce the drug problem within your child's peer group, you'll be reducing potential conflict for him.

8. Be alert to *possible* symptoms of drug use in your child so you can reach him before it becomes a serious problem. (The following list includes behaviors that could have any number of causes. Drug use is only one possibility.)

- uninterest in life ("vegging out")
- abrupt change of peer group
- detachment—spends much of his time alone in his room
- lethargy or hyperactivity, mood swings
- poor impulse control (tantrums frequently)
- time confusion
- lack of conscience, few inhibitions
- unusual hunger (especially for sweets)
- recent learning problems (difficulty with concentration)
- lack of interest in dress or hygiene
- irritability, restlessness
- money problems
- difficulty sleeping
- dilated or pinpoint pupils, bloodshot, glazed, runny eyes (excessive use of eye drops)
- breathing problems, hacking cough
- evidence of drug paraphernalia—tweezers (roach clips), plastic bags with herbs that look like oregano
- efforts to camouflage odor on breath, on clothes, and in room (compulsive use of mouthwash and incense)

If you suspect drug use, don't overreact. A majority of children experiment with drugs. Be grateful that you are aware of potential problems in time to do something about them.

To be helpful to your child, keep your concern focused on him. ("I'm concerned about you," not "What will people think of me?") He needs your support more than ever at this point.

Drugs and competent decision-making are incompatible. At a time when young people need accurate information on which to base their relationship, educational, and personal decisions, drugs distort their perceptions. In addition, children who learn to deal with problems by blocking them with drugs don't develop the skills necessary to anticipate and deal with conflicts. While they often assume a facade of pseudosophistication, children who cloud their minds with drugs during their youth stunt their emotional growth.

In Conclusion

Developing the tools to make effective decisions is more important today than ever before because of the dimension of choices that have become available over the last decade. Our children are growing up in a world that is not bound by traditional role expectations. As a result, they are freer to explore personally satisfying options.

It's no longer enough for us to help a daughter "package" herself attractively so that a strong man will want to marry her, support her financially, and make important decisions for her "forever after." Young girls who don't develop skills to be independent leave themselves vulnerable if they decide to work in the future, whether for personal fulfillment or out of financial need. The only jobs available to them will be unsatisfying and low-paying.

It's also not enough to educate a son so that he can have a good career, expecting his wife alone to care for the domestic and emotional needs of the family. Today he is likely to be sharing the child-care responsibilities and pleasures. It's important for him to develop some nurturing skills of his own. (If the marriage dissolves or his wife becomes ill, he could have partial or full responsibility for the children.)

People often focus on what they'll leave their children financially to provide them with security. Security comes not from the size of their bank accounts, but from our children's ability to take control of their lives by making effective decisions at each stage of the life cycle. Help them:

- learn productive ways to feel good about themselves
- develop strong values to live by

- develop the ability to communicate their concerns and to resolve conflicts constructively
- set goals that are realistic yet full of dreams
- evaluate what they are doing to achieve their goals
- seek out alternative paths when what they're doing is not working for them
- analyze the risks involved in each choice, weighing the outcomes in terms of the possible dangers and benefits of each
- determine which risks are worth taking
- create and follow through with a plan of action
- take responsibility for their choices, learning to substitute "I decided to" for "He made me" or "I had to"
- reinforce themselves for worthwhile choices

With the reduced supervision and greater personal freedoms children are "enjoying" today, there come an incredible number of choices (some with serious consequences), powerful peer influence, and decreased traditional support. When our children learn that they are capable of making effective decisions, no matter how intense the peer pressure, they develop personal power for today and for the future.

Epilogue

LOVE them just because they are who they are, unique individuals, unlike anyone else—

LIMIT them in areas that might cause them or others harm (with love and caring, not with humiliation)—

And then, help them learn to make good decisions so that when they reach the end of their teen-age years, you'll have the confidence to . . .

LET THEM GO.

References

Dreikurs, Rudolf, and Grey, Loren. *A Parents' Guide to Child Discipline.* New York: Hawthorn/Dutton, 1970.

Ellis, Albert. *How to Raise an Emotionally Happy Child.* California: Wilshire, 1966.

Elkind, David. *The Hurried Child: Growing Up Too Fast Too Soon.* Reading, Mass.: Addison–Wesley, 1981.

Frankl, Viktor E. *Man's Search for Meaning: An Introduction to Logotherapy,* rev. ed. New York: Simon & Schuster/Pocket Books, 1963.

Gesell, Arnold, Ilg, Frances, and Ames, Louise Bates. *The Child from Five to Ten,* rev. ed. New York: Harper & Row, 1977.

Ginott, Haim. *Between Parent and Child.* New York: Avon, 1969.

Glasser, Naomi, ed. *What Are You Doing?* New York: Harper & Row, 1980.

Glasser, William. *Take Effective Control of Your Life.* New York: Harper & Row, 1984.

Glasser, William. *Reality Therapy.* New York: Harper & Row, 1972.

LeShan, Eda. *When Your Child Drives You Crazy.* New York: St. Martin's Press, 1985.

Lickona, Thomas. *Raising Good Children.* New York: Bantam Books, 1985.

Peck, M. Scott. *The Road Less Traveled: A New Psychology of Love, Traditional Values, and Spiritual Growth.* New York: Simon & Schuster, 1978.

Satir, Virginia. *Peoplemaking.* Palo Alto: Science and Behavior Books, 1972.

Simon, Sidney B., and Wendkos, Sally Olds. *Helping Your Child Learn Right from Wrong: A Guide to Values Clarification.* New York: McGraw-Hill, 1976.

Turiecki, Stanley, and Tonner, Leslie. *The Difficult Child.* New York: Bantam, 1985.

Watzlawick, Paul, Weakland, John H., and Fisch, Richard. *Change.* New York: Norton, 1974.

MYRA CATES

Meet the Author

Over the past eighteen years Myra Cates has taught students from preschool through junior college. Currently she is the staff coordinator for a preschool that has received accreditation from the National Academy of Early Childhood Programs. She also facilitates parent–toddler interaction classes, working to build a mutual admiration during what can be considered a "tumultuous" time for both parent and child. She is committed to the belief that the confidence and self-esteem of a parent determines competent nurturing.

She received her B.S. at State University College at Cortland in New York and a master's degree in Education from Boston University.

Married for seventeen years, she and her husband, Jeffrey, thirteen-year-old son, Matthew, and nine-year-old daughter, Lindsay, live in Phoenix, Arizona.

12

RESOURCES FOR PARENTS

DEVELOPMENTAL CHECKLIST
BOOKS FOR FAMILIES WITH SPECIAL NEEDS
CHOOSING A QUALITY PRESCHOOL OR DAY-
    CARE CENTER
MYRA CATES, M.ED.

DEVELOPMENTAL CHECKLIST

The following chart describes behaviors that are considered typical for children at specific ages from birth through ten years. Your child will not fit this checklist precisely—each child has his own rhythm and pace for growth—but it *can* help you to understand the sequence of your child's development. Use the checklist to put your youngster's social, cognitive, and physical development into perspective rather than as a means for judging your child against "the norm." Because development is uneven, with sudden spurts and setbacks, your child will not develop and mature at exactly the same rate as the ages on the chart. There's a great deal of variety in the timing of every child's personal development. Value his uniqueness.

To a large extent, your child's personality determines how he moves through these developmental milestones. The individual nature of the growing child that makes one shy and timid, for instance, or another assertive and assured, is intrinsic to the child's very being from birth. Therefore, no two children will ever behave the same way at any given stage of growth or development. Nor will one parent–child interaction be like any other parent–child interaction.

The unique nature of your child is yours to discover. You'll find many subtleties to his complex temperament; some behaviors will be what you expect from a child his age, others will not. There will be highs and lows along the way. Sometimes you will feel euphoric, thinking, "This kid can do no wrong." And then again there will be times when you feel despair and disappointment, wondering, "How can my child behave this way?" Most parents go through this turmoil. It is crucial to keep in mind that your child's innate temperament renders you powerless to mold him into your ideal. Rather than attempt that, think of his individuality as something to treasure and appreciate.

Concentrating on your child's performance and emphasizing the age at which a particular behavior "should" be reached is unproductive and can be detrimental to your child and to your relationship. With his timetable, he may be ahead of or behind the chronological age given for a particular behavior and still be in the normal range of development. These variances are not significant in the long run.

Fast walkers and talkers are not offered any more guarantees in life than slow walkers and talkers; they are no more privileged. It's more important for

you to look at the behaviors that will be coming next. Having such a vantage point, you may be able to anticipate your child's needs at each age and set reasonable expectations for his behavior and growth. Ultimately, your job of helping him adjust to life's challenges may be managed more smoothly. Always remember that one of the keys to effective parenting lies in your talent for interpreting and appreciating your child's individuality.

For the following information I especially give thanks to the pioneers in child research, Drs. Gesell, Ilg, and Ames, who have provided a basis for the understanding of children at each stage of development.

First Year of Life (Birth to Twelve Months)

Social Development

months

3	—smiles
7–11	—shows distrust of strangers; may cry when mother leaves
7–11	—imitates actions ("pat-a-cake," "so big," "bye-bye")
11	—gives affection: hugs, kisses to familiar adults
11–14	—mimics actions of others
12	—uses mother as a helper
11–14	—plays independently while occupying the same play area with other children (parallel play)

Language Development

3–4	—coos
5–6	—babbles
8–12	—"talks" with gestures (shakes head "no")
8–12	—calls significant people by name ("Mama," "Dada")
10–14	—follows simple directions ("sit down," "come here")
11–15	—expresses needs verbally
11–15	—mimics voice intonation and body language of others
12–14	—enjoys using nonsense words
12–16	—says two or more words in addition to "Mama" and "Dada"

Cognitive Development

3	—discovers hands, exploring them with his eyes and mouth
3	—begins to anticipate feedings (makes sucking motions at the sight of breast, bottle, or food)
4–10	—behaves more purposefully
4–10	—repeats rewarding activities
4–10	—demonstrates very active curiosity
4–10	—increases manipulation of objects
6	—begins taking hold of objects he touches
10–12	—uncovers hidden objects
10–12	—intensifies imitation

Physical Development

3–4	—rolls over
4–5	—sits briefly with support
6–9	—appearance of first baby tooth
7	—sits unsupported for a few seconds
7–9	—pulls to standing position
8–9	—balances in a sitting position for a minute
8–10	—stands with support
8–10	—claps hands
8–10	—fills and empties containers with several objects
8–10	—turns pages of a book, a few at a time
9–12	—begins using thumb and index finger to grasp object
10	—creeps forward on hands and knees
10–11	—begins to let go of objects voluntarily
12–14	—walks alone

One-Year-Old (from Twelve Months to Twenty-four Months)

Social Development

—is strongly attached to parent or consistent caregiver

—expresses affection and hostility toward adults

—begins strong negative stage at approximately eighteen months

—imitates housework, helping with simple routines

—begins simple make-believe at approximately eighteen to twenty-four months (talking on telephone, feeding baby)

—treats other toddlers as inanimate objects (poking, pushing)

—enjoys dressing up in adult clothes

—alternately clings to and resists familiar adults

—begins to be proud of personal achievements

—refuses to share possessions

—enjoys interactive games like ring-around-the-rosy

Language Development

—enjoys picture books, nursery rhymes, and repetitive songs

—asks for "more"

—says "all gone"

—points to familiar objects when named

—"speaks" with words and gestures

—gives appropriate sound to match animal's name

—has vocabulary of fifty words by twenty-four months

—develops greater interest in language

—raises voice at end of word(s) to suggest question

—uses the same word to represent many things

—says "good-bye"

—makes simple phrases using two or three words ("Daddy, home")

—listens to and enjoys simple stories

Cognitive Development

—manipulates objects, discovering color, texture, shape, and size by exploring with his senses

—watches people and their activities intently

—finds objects that are the same

—points to objects when named

—builds towers with objects that are graduated in size

—learns through trial and error

—creates mental pictures at approximately eighteen months

—imitates actions

—points to parts of his body

—finds objects that have been moved from one hiding place to another

Physical Development

—walks unassisted by thirteen to fourteen months

—climbs up stairs

—rolls ball

—stacks three blocks, making tower

—fills and dumps containers

—draws with crayon or pencil

—draws circular shapes in imitation

—turns pages of a book one at a time

—walks with push and pull toys and wagons

—walks up stairs with assistance, lifting same foot first each time

—climbs up steps and slides down small slide

—enjoys being pushed on swings

—enjoys rolling balls and spinning toy wheels

Suggestions for Parents
of Infants and Toddlers

Understand and respond to your baby's unique signals, comforting him before fussiness builds, whenever possible. (Expect that, at times, he will be inconsolable, no matter how competent a parent you are.)

Offer your infant opportunities to safely manipulate objects with his hands, mouth, and feet.

Select appropriate finger food for the older baby to feed himself.

Use routines such as diapering and feeding to communicate playfully.

Plan developmentally appropriate activities.

Expect your toddler's social skills in sharing and taking turns to be minimal.

Provide a safe area for rolling, sitting, creeping, and walking.

While interacting with your baby, use words to label his environment, speaking slowly. Encourage him to respond in his own way.

Suggested Activities

With your infant:
— face-to-face cooing, smiling, touching, gentle tickling, rocking, bouncing, and singing.
With your older baby:
— "pat-a-cake," "so big," "bye-bye," "peek-a-boo," and imitation games.
With your toddler:
— "What's missing?" games, action songs, dancing, and movement games.

Two-Year-Old (from Twenty-four Months to Thirty-six Months)

Social Development

— complies with parental request only fifty percent of time
— listens to music or stories for five-to-ten-minute periods

—imitates use of the words "please" and "thank you"

—helps adult with chores (places napkins on dinner table)

—enjoys pretend play in "dress-up" clothes

—responds to other children as inanimate objects

—tantrums easily

—exhibits intense emotions

—begins dramatic play

Language Development

—has vocabulary of approximately 250 words

—speaks in two-word phrases: "Where doggie?" "Daddy gone."

—uses specific words for bathroom use

—says "no" frequently

—names familiar sounds (bell, clock, truck, animals)

—points to described object

—tells age by holding up fingers

—describes himself as a "boy" or "girl"

—follows directions for two successive commands

—points to objects, asking "What's this?"

—describes items as being "open" or "closed"

—locates familiar objects on request

Cognitive Development

—works three-piece puzzle

—identifies four everyday items in pictures

—draws vertical and horizontal lines

—copies a circle

—identifies big and little objects by pointing

—puts things "in," "on," and "under" upon request

—fits four-part nesting toy together

—describes activities portrayed in pictures

—matches shapes

—places five or more rings on peg sequentially

Physical Development

—manipulates doorknobs and handles successfully

—stacks five to six blocks to make a tower

—turns pages of a book one at a time

—plays with pull-apart toys

—unscrews nesting toys

—rolls clay balls

—grasps pencil between thumb and forefinger

—pounds pegs

—walks up and down stairs holding rail, approaching each new step with the same foot

—jumps in place

—tosses ball to an adult a few feet away

—kicks large ball

—somersaults forward, with help

Suggestions for Parents of Two-Year-Olds

Children at this age need careful supervision.

Keep any group activity to minimum duration (5–10 minutes).

Encourage your child to verbalize his feelings.

Set clear limits (i.e., "Sand belongs in the sandbox"), but recognize that your child is likely to test them.

Model consideration and responsibility.

Help your child learn to take turns by encouraging cooperation. (Don't expect the skill to be developed until age three.)

Provide:

A climate of safety, security, and acceptance.

Freedom to initiate his own activities.

Opportunities to demonstrate independence and responsibility (pour his own juice, wipe the table, etc.)

Diversions and substitutes when behavior breaks down.

Opportunities to work with manipulative and constructive materials.

Equipment to climb on, crawl through, jump on, slide down.

Dolls for experiences with mother/father–baby relationships.

Raw materials (sand, mud, water, clay, paint) to discover and experiment with.

Realistic creative play props (kitchen set, telephone) to enhance pretend play.

Language experiences with songs, finger plays and nursery rhymes.

Three-Year-Old (from Three to Four Years)

Social Development

—dances and sings accompanied by music

—imitates behavior of other children

—spontaneously greets familiar adults

—is learning to play cooperatively with others, taking turns

—remembers to say "please" and "thank you" at times

—demonstrates love and concern for younger siblings

—enjoys playing with several children, selecting a favorite friend

Cognitive Development

—understands concept of "big" and "little"

—finds ten body parts when asked

—uses descriptive words "heavy" or "light"

—puts together two-piece objects

—enjoys finger plays

—matches one-to-one with three or more objects (e.g., one dog goes in one doghouse)

—finds long and short objects

—tells what things belong together

—groups objects by category

—imitates counting to ten

—duplicates simple patterns with beads or blocks

—works six-piece puzzle

—uses "same" and "different" to describe objects

—identifies three colors

—knows three shapes: square, triangle, circle

—describes drawings

—shows some understanding of past and present

—enjoys dramatic play

—works with materials provided rather than creating a new activity

—attention span broadens

—follows two unrelated directions

—gives first and last name when asked

—answers simple "how to" questions

—talks about experiences happening around him

—talks about common objects and discusses how they are used

Physical Development

—completes three-piece puzzle

—snips with scissors

—paints and draws with a variety of strokes—vertical, horizontal, and circular

—traces simple forms

—jumps from eight-inch step

—kicks big moving ball

—rides tricycle short distances (approximately five feet)

—swings without pumping motion

—climbs and descends four-to-six-foot slide

—does forward somersaults

—walks up stairs, using alternate feet on each step

—marches to music

—catches bounced ball with both hands

—balances for two to five seconds on one foot

—can walk heel-to-toe for five feet

Suggestions for Parents
of Three-Year-Olds

Use language to describe objects and the actions your child is performing with them.

Offer opportunities to work with classification activities: matching, grouping, and sorting.

Capitalize on your child's cooperative, helpful nature by providing opportunities for independent jobs.

Reinforce your child's developing capacity to share.

Provide:

A warm, nurturing setting, free of judgment and evaluation.

Many first-hand sensory experiences.

Music and movement experiences to imitate.

Simple short stories to help your child understand himself and his world.

Large picture books with repetition.

Experience with language games, nursery rhymes, and finger plays.

Time and a variety of materials for dramatic, imaginative play.

Guidance to help your child understand cause and effect.

A positive model for handling conflicts and fears.

Opportunities for language activities that are directly related to your child's experiences.

Four-Year-Old (from Four to Five Years)

Social Development

—selects friends

—demonstrates sensitivity to others

—comforts playmates when they are upset

—enjoys interacting with four to five children without continual supervision

—has difficulty distinguishing between fantasy and reality

—thinks about ideas and designs own projects and dramatic play

—explores a variety of roles through creative play

—dramatizes sections of stories

—cooperates in group games, following rules

—adds to adult conversation

—works independently for twenty to thirty minutes

—takes turns with groups of other children

—enjoys competition in play

—behaves erratically

—makes surly faces and talks back when denied something he wants

—prefers to play in groups

—becomes overbearing and negative at times

—enjoys showing off

—is physically and verbally aggressive

—attacks with name calling

—is careless and destructive with toys

—enjoys telling "tall tales"

Cognitive Development

—identifies first, middle, and last position

—counts by rote from one to twenty

—names a part of a picture that is missing, is inappropriate, or that doesn't belong

—matches one-to-one when manipulating ten items

—understands "behind," "beside," "next to"

—understands "long" and "short"

—stacks ten blocks in imitation of a pyramid

—draws a man with a head, a trunk, and four limbs

—identifies color of a given object

—matches letters and numbers

—knows eight colors

—names the missing object when it is removed from a group of three

—describes objects as "heavy" or "light"

—enjoys rhyming words and repeats familiar rhymes

—tells when, during the day, certain activities occur

—remembers four objects seen in a picture

—reproduces a triangle

—names five textures

—sorts objects

—follows a series of three directions

—pairs objects together

—employs compound sentences

—identifies top and bottom of objects

—uses contractions

—is interested in outside world, beyond home and school

—enjoys questioning

—uses imagination creatively

—describes opposites, using analogies

—relates familiar story without picture clues

Physical Development

—dresses independently

—cuts two-inch circles

—draws representational pictures (house, man, tree)

—pastes and cuts simple shapes

—cuts along a curved line

—copies a cross and a square

—prints name in capital letters

—swings independently, pumping by himself

—balances on one foot four to eight seconds

—changes direction while running

—walks across balance beam

—hops backwards with both feet

—plays bounce and catch with a big ball

—walks down stairs, using alternate feet

—maneuvers tricycle around corners

—can hop on one foot five successive times

Suggestions for Parents of Four-Year-Olds

Help your child explore his world outside of the home.

Offer a variety of props for dramatic play.

Help your child appreciate differences between real and imaginary. Allow him to tell "tall tales" without labeling him a "liar."

Focus on realistic behavior goals, taking into account your child's need to experiment and test.

Provide:

Language experiences rich with rhymes, fantasy, humor, and exaggeration.

Opportunities to understand the concepts of numbers, size, weight, texture, distance, position, and time.

Outlets for expression of your child's high energy level and tension buildup (punching bag, bean bag, balls, sandbox, waterplay, swings, slides, and tricycles).

Creative materials to practice his increased control in drawing, cutting, and pasting skills.

Discipline with consistency and patience, offering choices whenever possible.

Opportunities for cooperative family projects (washing the car, painting the fence, etc.).

Five-Year-Old (from Five Years to Six Years)

Social Development

—becomes more socially aware, responding more sensitively to others

—enjoys interacting with four to five children cooperatively

—enjoys pretend play, imitating adult roles

—tattles

—assumes rules are to be obeyed

—dramatizes stories

MYRA CATES, M.ED.   319

—plays boisterously

—is centered on family life at home

Cognitive Development

—counts twenty items

—names ten numerals

—describes "left" and "right" by demonstrating on his own body

—recites alphabet

—prints first name

—arranges objects in a series by width and length

—names upper and lower case letters

—arranges numerals from one to ten in order

—matches upper and lower case letters

—reproduces diamond shape

—finishes a simple maze

—tells days of week in order

—adds and subtracts with numerals up to the number three

—knows day and month of birth

—recognizes up to ten printed words

—tells what happens next

—counts by rote to one hundred

—labels objects "half" and "whole"

—understands concepts: "some," "many," "several"

—knows address and telephone number

—tells simple jokes

—recounts daily experiences

—uses prepositions "through," "away," "toward," "over"

—tells a simple story in sequence

—understands the concept of "opposite"

—uses "yesterday" and "tomorrow" appropriately

—asks meaning of new words

Physical Development

—prints first name, using capitals

—writes numbers from one to five. (They might appear to be unusually large, or small—or reversed.)

—pictures what he will draw before actually drawing it

—draws simple representational pictures (house, man, tree)

—reproduces a triangle

—colors within the lines a majority of the time

—cuts pictures from magazines

—balances walking forward, backward, or sideways on a balance beam

—skips

—enjoys swinging independently

—climbs a ten-foot-high slide

—hammers nails

—balances on one foot with eyes closed for eight to ten seconds

—hangs independently from horizontal bar

—jumps from height of twelve inches, landing securely on feet

—rides a bicycle

—bats a ball gently thrown from a short distance

—demonstrates left- or right-hand dominance

Suggestions for Parents
of Five-Year-Olds

Encourage your child's sense of curiosity by supporting his independent exploration.

Present fascinating materials that are relevant to his interests, helping him understand the effects of his actions on the environment.

Model curiosity and wonder.

Ask questions about cause and effect, encouraging your child to predict and hypothesize.

Use hands-on experience to teach new concepts.

Encourage him to use toys, equipment, and art supplies to express his thoughts and record his experiences.

Stress the value of cooperation and compromise rather than competition and winning.

Provide:

Experiences with numerals and letters, involving recognition and writing, opportunities to use the calendar.

A climate where individuals' rights are respected and rules apply to all.

Books which show men, women, girls, and boys in a variety of roles.

Experiences to help your child understand others' views.

Out-of-home experiences to excite your child's imagination and understanding of people's roles.

Opportunities to involve him in rule making.

Experiences in problem solving.

Cooperative projects that involve working together (gardening, cleaning, cooking, etc.).

General Overview of Development from Six to Ten Years

Social Development

—Peer influence increases with age but family still maintains significant influence.

—Six-to-seven-year-olds begin to assert their individuality and separateness. The need for independence increases with age.

—Six-to-seven-year-olds follow strict adherence to rules.

—Personal privacy becomes a significant issue.

—Relationships are more cooperative and are becoming more stable and important. However, prosocial behavior may decline slightly at the end of the middle years (up to age twelve) owing to competitive drive.

—Youngsters develop sensitivity to others' feelings.

—Children begin to question adult authority. Parents are no longer considered all-knowing.

—Seven-to-ten-year-olds seek out friends with similar interests and personalities—loyalty begins.

Cognitive Development

—Six-to-seven-year-olds begin to develop skills in classifying and working with numerals.

—Girls are more advanced in verbal skills; boys are more advanced in math and spatial relations.

—Vocabulary increases far ahead of comprehension.

—Children develop an understanding of conservation—that amount, weight, volume, and area remain the same despite change in appearance (i.e., water poured from a glass into a bowl does not increase or decrease in volume because of the shape of its container).

—Six-year-olds begin to learn to tell time.

—Six-to-seven-year-olds determine a person's guilt according to the amount of damage his behavior has caused, rather than by his intent.

—Six-to-seven-year-olds understand that dreams occur because of their own thoughts.

—Eight-to-nine-year-olds determine the degree of guilt according to a person's intentions, rather than by the resulting damage.

—Interest in competition grows.

—New skills increase feelings of accomplishment.

—Same sex peer groups are established, encouraging conformity.

—Clubs and gangs become popular.

—Boys choose active physical activities; girls choose less active, more imaginative play.

—Boys are more aggressive and argumentative than girls.

—Fears of this age center on school failure and being avoided by peers.

Physical Development

—Growth is usually slow until the onset of puberty.

—Concept of left and right is well established by seven to eight years of age.

—Growth spurt may start by nine years in girls and eleven years in boys.

—Boys are taller than girls from ages six to eight; at nine, girls begin growing taller.

—Brain increases in weight.

—Motor skills improve with maturation—strength, speed, balance, eye–hand coordination, and flexibility.

Six-Year-Old Traits

—short attention span and high energy make conformity to long hours of structured activities in grade school stressful

—appears cocky and aggressive, demanding to be first and wanting to be best

—sensitivity, competitiveness, and bossiness create instability in friendships

—has greater difficulty getting along with friends and younger siblings

—frustration often results in outbursts of temper tantrums

—dual loyalties toward home and school, parents and teachers, create ambivalence ("Mommy, that's not how to do it. Teacher says to do it this way.")

—exuberance results in silliness and out-of-bounds behavior

—demonstrates sex role differences in whom he plays with and what activities he enjoys

—appetite is large, but is particular about what he eats; table manners are poor

—is often indecisive and inconsistent

—may appear destructive—enjoys taking apart toys and mechanical devices to see how things work

—complains about physical aches and pains

Seven-Year-Old Traits

—less boisterous, more introspective—may appear to be shy and withdrawn

—pensive, serious, and self-absorbed

—perfectionistic—goals are often set too high

—wants approval from adults—enjoys being trusted with household responsibilities

—short attention span and restlessness—is easily distracted

—listens more than he talks

—takes pride in building collections

—resists taking responsibility for his own actions—excuses himself, blames others, or makes up stories to cover up the truth

—is sensitive to what others say and do, often expressing frustration with tears

—tattles and whines

—is becoming more reasonable—makes positive contributions to family discussions

—resents parental nagging

—negative and moody

—is jealous of siblings—often considers himself to be the least favored child—"poor me" attitude

—great interest in food (boys have larger appetites than girls)

—dawdles when eating and dressing

Eight-Year-Old Traits

—open to new experiences, more outgoing, and willing to take chances than at seven; activity level increases

—more socially aware of peer groups, wants to belong

—unable to attend to one activity for too long

—less cooperative about doing household tasks than at seven

—enjoys one-to-one activities with parents (e.g., baking, simple cooking, and carpentry)

—is curious about people, places, and things

—enjoys playing with his collections

—chooses his own clothes, though his judgment is often poor—is careless about putting them away

—soaks up praise

—loves riddles and magic

—thinks beyond himself, beyond today, and beyond his family

—has huge appetite

—is judgmental, especially about parents' behavior, yet is sensitive to personal criticism

—is charmed by, yet hostile to, opposite sex

—more self-assured

—relationships begin to have new significance; friends are very important

—eager, enthusiastic, and careless

—prone to accidents

—participates in group activities and organized sports

—more dependent on and demanding of mother

Nine-Year-Old Traits

—learns to take responsibility for his own actions

—high energy, often playing to the point of fatigue

—responsible, inner directed, independent worker

—able to plan and organize

—outspoken and critical of adults

—inconsistent appetite and sleep patterns

—poor posture

—less interested in fantasy, more involved in the real world

—appreciates being trusted

—overly concerned with performance, wants to please

—boys enjoy staying unkempt; girls are very concerned about their appearance

—peer conformity in dressing is important

—sets high standards and gets down on himself when he doesn't achieve them

—is easily upset

—begins hero worship of older member of the same sex

—lots of physical habitual movements: fingers in hair, slouching, picking at nails

—disdain for opposite sex intensifies

—enjoys repetitive activities—bouncing balls and skipping rope

—is concerned about right and wrong, being fair

Ten-Year-Old Traits

—generally well-adjusted, more relaxed

—girls are beginning to advance ahead of boys in sexual development and social skills

—enjoys mystery and adventure

—clumsy and awkward owing to rapid, uneven growth

—strong allegiance to peer groups rather than to parents, which may cause conflicts

—distinct interests and talents

—restless

—self-conscious about physical changes; differences in physical maturity among peers widens

—may be outspoken and critical of adults

—boys physically demonstrate their friendship by wrestling and pushing; girls hold hands, giggle, and share secrets

—gang loyalty is stronger in boys than in girls

—teasing between boy and girl groups

—general positive self-concept

—enjoys family times together, though beginning to value time alone with peers

—often rebels against parents' rules

Suggestions for Parents
of Children Ages Six to Ten

Provide opportunities for your child to develop skills in sports and music.

Encourage your child to join quality clubs and teams to feel part of a productive group.

Support and facilitate your child's attempts to produce a finished product.

Provide suitable choices, allowing your child to initiate his own plans and activities.

Provide appropriate outlets for your child to challenge his individual performance—using stop watches and timers.

Express nonsexist attitude toward activities.

Use reasoning rather than threatening or using physical force.

Avoid head-on power struggles through compromise.

Model consideration, generosity, and sensitivity to others.

Invite your child to participate in the decision-making process, especially when it comes to household jobs. Relieve boredom by suggesting changing jobs periodically.

When helpful suggestions are important, give them privately. Children are sensitive to humiliation before others.

Use an allowance as an opportunity to learn self-reliance.

Peer teasing is often a problem during the middle years. Help your child understand that if he doesn't react, there is no payoff for the teaser.

Help your child learn to release his emotions without hurting others.

Mealtimes are an opportunity for positive family interaction, not criticism.

Children become "parent-deaf" when parents nag. Allow notes, alarm clocks, and buzzers to do the reminding instead. Reinforce your child for following through on commitments with a thank you, either verbal or written.

Create an environment that is supportive, focusing on progress and accomplishment, not on mistakes.

Catch your child's attention before you make a request of him.

Support and encourage your child's problem-solving skills.

Provide a climate where individuals' rights are respected and fair rules apply to all.

Allow your child a sense of privacy by providing space for his belongings.

References

Caplan, Theresa and Frank. *The Early Childhood Years.* New York: Putnam, 1983.

Cataldo, Christine Z. *Infant and Toddler Programs.* Reading, Mass.: Addison–Wesley, 1983.

Cooperative Educational Service Agency: *Portage Guide to Early Education,* 1976.

Dodson, Fitzhugh. *How To Parent.* New York: Signet, 1971.

Elkind, David, and Weiner, Irving. *Development of the Child.* New York: Wiley, 1978.

Elkind, David. *A Sympathetic Understanding of the Child: Birth to Sixteen.* Boston: Allyn and Bacon, 1974.

Gesell, Arnold, Ilg, Frances, and Ames, Louise Bates. *Infant and Child in the Culture of Today.* New York: Harper & Row, 1974.

Gesell, Arnold, Ilg, Frances, and Ames, Louise Bates. *The First Five Years of Life.* New York: Harper, 1940.

Gesell, Arnold, Ilg, Frances, and Ames, Louise Bates. *The Child from Five to Ten.* New York: Harper & Row, 1974.

Hendrick, Joanne. *Total Learning for the Whole Child.* St. Louis: Mosby, 1980.

Hess, Robert. *Teachers of Young Children.* Boston: Houghton Mifflin, 1975.

Hildebrand, Verna. *Introduction to Early Childhood Education.* New York: Macmillan, 1981.

Leach, Penelope. *Your Baby and Child from Birth to Age Five.* New York: Knopf, 1985.

Maxim, George. *The Very Young Child.* California: Wadsworth, 1980.

Morrison, George. *Early Childhood Education Today.* Toronto: Merrill, 1980.

Read, Katherine, and Patterson, June. *The Nursery School and Kindergarten.* New York: Holt, Rinehart and Winston, 1980.

Weissbourd, Bernice, and Musick, Judith, eds. *Infants: Their Social Environments.* Washington: NAEYC, 1981.

White, Burton. *The First Three Years of Life.* Englewood Cliffs, N.J.: Prentice-Hall, 1975.

BOOKS FOR FAMILIES
WITH SPECIAL NEEDS

A universal concern of parents is the social well-being of their children, since the quality of a child's life is strongly affected by how well he is accepted and how well he gets along in the world. Parents of children with special needs are particularly concerned about their youngsters' ability to accept themselves and to be accepted by their peers. To strengthen the self-image and social skills of all children, I am including a list of books about young people who have unique needs with the hope that it will deepen children's awareness and understanding of themselves and each other. Ultimately, these stories can free youngsters' minds to look beyond labels to appreciate the individuals inside. I am also including a book list for parents to offer information and insight on each of the topics that follow.

Learning Disabilities and Behavior Problems— Books for Children

He's My Brother by Joe Lasker. Chicago: Whitman, 1974. A sensitive boy talks warmly about his younger brother, Jamie, who has a learning disability. This honest, positive portrayal demonstrates the differences between learning disabilities and mental retardation. (ages 4–8)

Keep Stompin Till the Music Stops by Stella Pevsner. New York: Seabury Press, 1977. This book describes twelve-year-old Richard and his frustrating dyslexia. While his perceptual difficulties are described realistically, the author emphasizes his admirable personal qualities. (ages 9–12)

Kelly's Creek by Doris B. Smith. New York: Harper & Row, 1975. Nine-year-old Kelly's reactions to his perceptual and motor problems are discussed empathically. The book specifically describes teaching techniques that are used to help him. Children will enjoy reading about how he gains self-confidence and the respect of his peers in sharing his unique interests. (ages 9–12)

Square Head and Me by Henry Louis Haynes. Philadelphia: Westminster Press, 1980. The friendship between two youngsters, one learning-disabled, unfolds as they spend time together on a farm. This book explores their relationship with sensitivity. (ages 8–12)

Staying Back by Janice Hale Hobby with Gabrielle Rubin and Daniel Rubin. Gainesville, Florida: Triad, 1982. Eight children talk openly about the reasons for their repeating a grade in school. Included are questions for discussion between parent and child to help the reader come to a greater understanding of the realities in school retention. (ages 5–12)

Learning Disabilities and Behavior Problems— Books for Parents

Accept Me as I Am by Joan Friedberg. New York: Bowker, 1985.

Allergies and the Hyperactive Child by Doris J. Rapp. New York: Cornerstone Library, 1979.

Better Learning: How to Help Students of All Ages Overcome Learning Problems and Learning Disabilities by Judith Bakssin. Englewood Cliffs, N.J.: Prentice-Hall, 1982.

The Hyperactive Child (a handbook for parents) by Paul H. Wender, M.D. New York: Crown, 1973.

Hyperactive Children: Diagnosis and Management by Daniel J. Safer, M.D., and Richard P. Allen, Ph.D. Baltimore: University Park Press, 1976.

No Easy Answers: The Learning Disabled Child at Home and at School by Sally Smith. New York: Bantam, 1981 (paperback).

No One to Play With: The Social Side of Learning Disabilities by Betty Osman. New York: Random House, 1982.

Raising a Hyperactive Child by Mark A. Stewart and Sally Wendkos Olds. New York: Harper & Row, 1973.

Your Child Can Win: Strategies, Activities, and Games for Parents of Children with Learning Disabilities by Joan and Norma Macneill. New York: Morrow, 1983.

The Gifted Child— Books for Children

A Different Kind of Boy by Barbara Hise. Phoenix: Resources for the Gifted, 1980. A beautifully illustrated, thoughtful book looking at the problems of being unique through the experiences of a young boy. This story helps young people with special gifts learn to accept and appreciate being different. (ages 5–9)

The Gifted Kid's Survival Guide: For Ages 10 and Under by Judy Galbraith. Minneapolis, MN: Free Spirit Publishing. This realistic approach to giftedness explains what the term means, helping children understand their creative, questioning minds. Children explore the common characteristics of gifted children, the teasing of other children, perfectionism, restlessness, and intensity—and how to deal with these problems. (ages 6–10)

The Gifted Child— Books for Parents

Getting Kids Ready to Take on the World by Eileen Hoard. Phoenix: Kolbe Concepts, 1983.

Gifted Children: A Guide for Parents and Teachers by Virginia Z. Ehrlich. Englewood Cliffs, N.J.: Prentice-Hall, 1982.

How to Help Your Gifted Child: A Handbook for Parents and Teachers by Gina Ginsberg and Charles H. Harrison. White Plains, N.Y.: Monarch Press, 1977.

Parenting the Gifted: A Manual by Sheila C. and Joseph Perino. New York: Bowker, 1981.

Families with Working Parents— Books for Children

By Yourself by Sara Gilbert. New York: Lothrop, 1983. This book helps children in dual career families get in touch with feelings about being on their own—their anger, sadness, loneliness, or pride. Through specific suggestions for using their time alone wisely, children are helped to derive a sense of confidence from the importance of their role in caring for themselves. (ages 10 and up)

Sonya's Mommy Works by Arlene Alda. New York: Julian Messner/Simon & Schuster, 1982. The author tells the story of six-year-old Sonya coping with the changes in her life now that her mother has gone back to work full-time. Sonya shares her feelings of regret, loneliness, and longing for the mommy that used to be home all the time. With the continued understanding, patience, and love from her devoted parents, Sonya adjusts to her two-career family. (ages 4–8)

Working Parents—
Books for Parents

2001 Hints for Working Mothers by Gloria Gilbert Mayer. New York: Morrow, 1983.

Working and Caring by T. Berry Brazelton. Reading, Mass.: Addison–Wesley, 1985.

The Working Parents' Dilemma by Earl Grollman and Gerri Sweder. Boston: Beacon Press, 1986.

The Working Parents' Survival Guide by Sally Wendkos Olds. New York: Bantam, 1978.

Separation, Divorce, Single Parenting,
and the Restructured Family—
Books for Children

Daddy's New Baby by Judith Vigna. Chicago: Whitman, 1982. A young girl is insecure about her father's remarriage. Her worries intensify when she learns that he will be having a baby with his new wife. In time, though, she learns to adapt to her new reality. (ages 5–8)

Do I Have a Daddy? A Story About a Single-Parent Child by Jeanne Warren Lindsay. Buena, CA: Morning Glory Press, 1982. This is a lovely, gentle story about a young boy who wonders why he never sees his father. There is an additional section at the back of the book written for single parents to help them understand their children's concerns and needs. (ages 6 and 7)

How It Feels When Parents Divorce by Jill Krementz. New York: Knopf, 1984. This is a moving record of the impressions of nineteen children who have endured their parents' divorces. Through interviews and black-and-white photographs, this book helps the child who has experienced divorce in the family recognize his own emotions as he hears the anger, shock, pain, defiance, and final acceptance that the children express. (ages 8–19)

Talking About Divorce and Separation: A Dialogue Between Parent and Child by Earl Grollman. Boston: Beacon Press, 1975. With the goal of encouraging communication between children and their parents, Dr. Grollman helps children understand what divorce means for them. He is especially sensitive to children's sense of failure and guilt. He explains that the divorce is taking place because the parents don't want to be married anymore, not because of anything the child might have said or done. (ages 5–9)

What's Going to Happen to Me? When Parents Separate or Divorce by Eda LeShan. Bristol, Florida: Four Winds, 1978. In her warm, empathic style, Eda LeShan speaks with youngsters about the realities involved in the breakup of a marriage, emphasizing the fact that the child is not to blame. She demonstrates sensitivity to children's need for love when parents are preoccupied with their feelings of anger and sadness. (ages 9–13)

Separation, Divorce, Single Parenting, and the Restructured Family— Books for Parents

Helping Your Child with Divorce: A Compassionate Guide for Parents by Edward Teyber, Ph.D. New York: Pocket Books, 1985.

How to Win as a Stepfamily by Emily B. and John S. Fisher. New York: Dembner, 1982.

Making It as a Stepparent: New Roles, New Rules by Claire Berman. New York: Perennial Library/Harper & Row, 1986.

The Parents Without Partners Sourcebook by Stephen L. Atlas. Philadelphia: Running Press, 1984.

What About the Children: A Divorced Parent's Handbook by Francine S. Spilke. New York: Crown, 1979.

New Baby— Books for Children

How to Be an Older Brother or Sister: What to Expect When It Happens to You by Mike Venezia. Chicago: Children's Press, 1986. This is a light, humorous approach to helping a child adjust to the arrival of a new baby. The comical pictures and delightful text help the older child develop an awareness of what to expect—both positive and negative—from his new role. (ages 3–9)

The New Baby by Fred Rogers. New York: Putnam, 1985. Colorful photographs and Fred Rogers's gentle style help the firstborn accept the challenge of accepting a new sibling. The story reassures the first child that his place will remain his alone and encourages him to share his feelings with his parents so they can respond to his needs. (ages 3–6)

The New Baby at Your House by Joanna Cole. New York: Morrow, 1985. Supportive narrative and more than fifty moving photographs capture children's reactions to their new siblings. The emotions range from pride to jealousy as children learn to gain an appreciation for their baby brothers and sisters. The author has also included a practical guide for parents to help them minimize sibling rivalry. (ages 3–10)

Peter's Chair by Ezra Jack Keats. New York: Harper & Row, 1967. Peter has a difficult time dealing with the idea of giving up his personal things to a new baby brother or sister. But in time he learns that while he'll be giving away some of his belongings to the baby, he will be getting new toys and furniture that are more appropriate for a big brother. (ages 3–6)

New Baby—
Books for Parents

Billy and Our New Baby by Helene S. Arnstein. New York: Behavioral Publications, 1973.
That New Baby by Sara Bonnet Stein. New York: Walker, 1974.

Adoption and Foster Care—
Books for Children

The Adopted One: An Open Family Book for Parents and Children Together by Sara Bonnet Stein (open family series). New York: Walker, 1979. This story realistically explores the relationship between the adopted child and his new family. An informative text for parents is included. (ages 3–9)

How It Feels to Be Adopted by Jill Krementz. New York: Knopf, 1983. Children open their hearts to share their concerns, hopes, and fears in explaining what it means to be adopted. The descriptive black-and-white photographs make their stories come alive. (ages 8–18)

I Am Adopted by Susan Lapsley. London: Bodley Head, 1974. Charles relates what adoption represents to him and to his adopted sister Sophie with his statement "Adoption means belonging." This is a charming book that helps children understand their adoptive parents' desire to love and care for them. (ages 3–6)

My Little Foster Sister by Muriel Stanek. Chicago: Whitman, 1981. An only child at first finds it difficult to accept her new little foster sister, but later learns to love and appreciate her. The challenges of making a commitment to a temporary sibling are explored. (ages 5–8)

Why Was I Adopted? by Carole Livingstone. New York: Lyle Stuart, 1978. Through humorous pictures and text, the author presents a delightfully refreshing approach to adoption as a very natural, welcome, exciting event. Her explanation is honest and direct while reinforcing the child's sense of self-worth. The author covers most questions that children are likely to ask. (ages 5–12)

Adoption and Foster Care— Books for Parents

Adoption: The Grafted Tree by Laurie and William Wishard. New York: Avon, 1979.

The Adoption Resource Book: A Comprehensive Guide to All the Things You Need to Know and Ought to Know About Creating an Adoptive Family by Lois Gilan. New York: Harper & Row, 1984.

Dear Birthmother: Thank You for Our Baby—The Book About Open Adoption by Kathleen Silber and Phylis Speedlin. San Antonio: Corona, 1983.

Foster Parenting Young Children: Guidelines from a Foster Parent by Evelyn H. Felker. New York: Child Welfare League, 1974.

A Guide for Foster Parents by Irwin Sarason. New York: Human Sciences Press, 1976.

Blind/Visually Impaired— Books for Children

Apartment Three by Ezra Jack Keats. New York: Macmillan, 1971. Two brothers first approach a blind man with fear and then with interest and friendship, as he helps them understand how he experiences his sightless world. The boys marvel at what the man can learn through his other senses. (ages 5–8)

Katie's Magic Glasses by Jane Goodsell. Boston: Houghton Mifflin, 1965. Five-year-old Katie looks forward to clearing up her fuzzy world with new glasses until she peers through her father's glasses and reacts with concern. Her apprehension gives way to delight, though, when she receives her own glasses, which work just the way the doctor promised they would. (ages 5–8)

My Mother Is Blind by Mark Reuter. Chicago: Children's Press, 1979. An eight-year-old boy's life undergoes many changes when his mother becomes blind. Readers will be especially fascinated by the description of how his mother does routine tasks like shopping and cooking. (ages 5–8)

The New Boy Is Blind by William E. Thomas. New York: Messner, 1980. A child in Ricky's classroom (who later becomes his best friend) relates how Ricky and his very protective classmates and mother help him adjust to coping on his own. Children will identify with both his fears and his growing satisfaction as he develops greater personal independence. (ages 6–10)

Seeing in the Dark by Elizabeth Rider Montgomery. Champaign, Ill.: Garrard, 1979. Eight years old and blind, Kary is determined to function with normal children. Her courage earns her classmates' acceptance as she faces the challenges of being mainstreamed into a normal classroom. (ages 5–7)

Through Grandpa's Eyes by Patricia MacLachlan. New York: Harper & Row, 1979. A young boy shares a very warm relationship with his blind grandfather. This gentleman teaches him that he "sees" with his heart, his fingers, and his ears. (ages 5–8)

Blind/Visually Impaired— Books for Parents

The Blind Child in the Regular Kindergarten by Josephine Stratton. New York: Charles Thomas, 1977.

Blindness: What It Is, What It Does and How to Live with It by Thomas J. Carrol. Boston: Little, Brown, 1961.

Practical Guidance for Parents of the Visually Handicapped Preschooler by Patricia L. Maloney. New York: Charles C. Thomas, 1981.

Raising the Young Blind Child by Shulamith Kastein et al. New York: Human Sciences Press, 1980.

MYRA CATES, M.ED.   337

Hearing Impaired—
Books for Children

A Button in Her Ear by Ada B. Litchfield. Niles, Illinois: Concept Books/ Albert Whitman Co., 1976. After Angela's hearing problem is diagnosed, she enjoys the wonderful benefits she gains from wearing a hearing aid. Normal children will develop not only a sensitivity to the problems of the deaf but an appreciation for the gift of hearing. (ages 4–9)

Claire and Emma by Diana Peter. New York: John Day, 1976. The moving story of two- and four-year-old sisters, who were deaf since birth, is told by their mother. She recounts their experiences with hearing aids and speech lessons as they learn to lip-read and speak. (ages 5–9)

Handtalk: An ABC of Finger Spelling and Sign Language by Remy Charlip and Mary Beth Miller. New York: Parents' Magazine Press, 1974. This handbook uses enchanting photographs of actors shaping letters with their bodies. Normal children as well as hearing-impaired youngsters will delight in learning finger spelling and sign language. (ages 6–9)

I Have a Sister: My Sister Is Deaf by Jeanne W. Peterson. New York: Harper & Row, 1977. A girl affectionately describes her younger sister, who is deaf. She explains what her sister can and cannot do, focusing on her strengths. The reader will particularly enjoy experiencing the quality of the girls' relationship. (ages 5–8)

Lisa and Her Soundless World by Edna Levine. New York: Human Sciences Press, 1974. Eight-year-old Lisa's problems and triumphs are illustrated as she faces the challenges of growing up in a world without sound. Through Lisa's adjustment to a hearing aid and a special school, the reader learns that there is more than just one way to communicate. (ages 4–10)

My Sister's Silent World by Catherine Arthur. Chicago: Children's Press, 1979. Heather's sister lovingly tells about eight-year-old Heather and her deafness. Expressive photographs help normal children understand that deaf children are just like *they* are, except for the need to compensate for their hearing loss. (ages 6–9)

Sesame Street Sign Language Fun by Linda Bove. New York: Random House/Children's Television Workshop, 1980. The Muppets and Linda use sign language to communicate opposites, actions, and emotions. In usual *Sesame Street* fashion, this book is not only informative, but charming. (ages 3–6)

Hearing Impaired—
Books for Parents

Deaf Like Me by Thomas and James Spradley. New York: Random House, 1970.

Educating Deaf Children: Psychology, Principles and Practices by Donald Moores. Boston: Houghton Mifflin, 1978.

Hearing-Impaired Children in the Mainstream by Jack W. Birch. Virginia: The Council for Exceptional Children, 1975.

In This Sign by Joanne Greenberg. New York: Holt, Rinehart and Winston, 1970.

Words for a Deaf Daughter by Paul West. New York: Harper & Row, 1970.

Mental Retardation—
Books for Children

Like Me by Alan Brightman. Boston: Little, Brown, 1976. A young retarded boy is aware that he is not able to learn as quickly as others his age, but he demonstrates the same need to be accepted. Color photographs showing children interacting playfully, emphasize the similarities between children, rather than focusing on differences.

Meet Lance, He's a Special Person: Trainable Mentally Retarded by Margaret H. Glazzard. Lawrence, Kansas: H. and H. Enterprises, 1978. Lance, a Down's syndrome child, is pictured in his special class at school. The book and its accompanying phonograph record help normal children better understand the child who is slow to learn. This book is part of an excellent series about children with special needs. (ages 5–9)

My Brother Steven Is Retarded by Harriet L. Sobol. New York: Macmillan, 1977. Eleven-year-old Beth talks movingly of her feelings about her retarded older brother and what it is like to be his sister. She relates her embarrassment, her frustration, and her anger as well as her love for him. The tone is realistic but upbeat. (ages 6–10)

My Friend Jacob by Lucille Clifton. New York: Dutton, 1980. Eight-year-old Sam discusses his best friend and neighbor, Jacob, who is bigger, older, and stronger, but who is mentally retarded. Though Jacob and Sam are of different ages and have different skills, they learn that they have much to offer each other. (ages 6–9)

One Little Girl by Joan Fassler. New York: Human Sciences Press, 1969. Laurie is a young girl who takes longer than most children to learn. But she and her family find out that while she is slow at some things, she learns others quickly. As a result of their awareness, her family begins to reinforce her for her strengths rather than dwell on her weaknesses. (ages 4–8)

Mental Retardation— Books for Parents

Christmas in Purgatory: A Photographic Essay on Mental Retardation by Burton Blatt and Fred Kaplan. Boston: Allyn and Bacon, 1969.

Counseling Parents of the Mentally Retarded: A Sourcebook by Robert L. Noland, ed. New York: Thomas Publishing, 1978.

Retarded Kids Need to Play: A Manual for Parents and Other Teachers by Cynthia C. Hirst and Elaine Michaelis. Champaign, Illinois: Leisure, 1983.

A Step-by-Step Learning Guide for Retarded Infants and Children: Book I by Vicki M. Johnson and Roberta A. Werner. Syracuse, N.Y.: Syracuse University, 1975.

Teaching Your Down's Syndrome Infant: A Guide for Parents by Marci J. Hanson. Baltimore: University Park, 1977.

Other Disabilities— Books for Children

About Handicaps: An Open Family Book for Parents and Children Together by Sara Bonnett Stein. New York: Walker, 1974. This book is a sensitive portrayal of Matt, a young boy who is afraid of handicaps, especially Joe's cerebral palsy. After Matt's father helps him overcome his fear of handicaps, Matt and Joe develop a warm friendship. A separate text for adults, which helps them prepare children for life's realities, accompanies the story. (ages 4–9)

The Balancing Girl by Berniece Louise Rabe. New York: Dutton, 1981. Margaret is a delightful first grader who gets along well in her wheelchair or on leg braces and crutches. This book helps youngsters understand the needs of the handicapped for recognition as competent individuals. The reader will enjoy learning of the increasing respect Margaret gets from her classmates as she balances dominoes at the school carnival. (ages 5–7)

Deenie by Judy Blume. New York: Dell, 1976. This realistic story illustrates Deenie's concerns as she adjusts to life in her Milwaukee Brace. Children who are being watched for scoliosis will identify with Deenie's anxiety and develop confidence from her ability to adapt to her situation. (ages 10–16)

Golden Daffodils by Marilyn Gould. Reading, Mass.: Addison–Wesley, 1982. Fifth grader Janis transfers from a special school to a public school. She faces embarrassment over her handicaps and brace until she learns that her greatest handicap is not her cerebral palsy but her own defensiveness. (ages 8–12)

Howie Helps Himself by Joan Fassler. Chicago: Whitman, 1975. This story shares valuable insight about the day-to-day realities Howie faces in coping with his cerebral palsy. Children, both handicapped and nonhandicapped, will identify with Howie's determination to get around by himself in his wheelchair. (ages 5–8)

Janet at School by Paul White. New York: Harper & Row, 1978. Five-year-old Janet's life in a wheelchair is described with photographs and simple prose, revealing her participation in an active life despite her spinal condition. Youngsters will be inspired by Janet's ability to cope. (ages 5–9)

A Look at Physical Handicaps by Margaret Pursell. Minneapolis: Lerner Publications, 1976. A variety of physical handicaps are explored through words and pictures to demonstrate differences and highlight similarities between normal and physically disabled children and adults. (ages 6–10)

My Friend Leslie: The Story of a Handicapped Child by Maxine B. Rosenberg. New York: Lothrop, 1983. This story, approached from the perspective of Karin, the author's daughter, illustrates how she, her friend Leslie, who suffers multiple handicaps, and their classmates in kindergarten share common experiences and fun. In spite of her many physical problems, Leslie has an outgoing personality and some special talents of her own. (ages 5–9)

Runaway Sugar: All About Diabetes by Alvin and Virginia B. Silverstein. Philadelphia: Lippincott, 1981. Diabetes is described in language that children can easily comprehend. The authors explain its symptoms, causes, and treatment simply and concretely. (ages 8–11)

Sniff, Sniff, Al-er-gee. by Claude A. Frazier. St. Petersburg, Florida: Johnny Reads, 1978. An allergy specialist explains what allergies are, what doctors can do to treat them, and how children can cope with them. (ages 5–9)

Tracy by Nancy Mack. Milwaukee, Wisconsin: Raintree Editions, 1976. Tracy, a young girl born with cerebral palsy, describes firsthand the limitations and challenges she faces from her wheelchair as she relates to family and friends. Actual photographs of her reveal the love her supportive family shares with her. This book offers a positive view of mainstreaming. (ages 5–12)

What If They Knew? by Patricia Hermes. New York: Harcourt, Brace Jovanovich, 1980. Jenny, a ten-year-old, hides her epilepsy from her classmates at her new school until she has a seizure during class. She learns what friendship means through the responses of her classmates. (ages 9–12)

You Can't Catch Diabetes from a Friend by Lynne Kipnis and Susan Adler. Gainesville, Florida: Triad, 1979. Four children are portrayed through interesting text and black-and-white expressive photographs as they are involved in their daily activities. This book explains diabetes and demonstrates how families deal with it. (ages 9–12)

Other Disabilities—
Books for Parents

Autism: Nightmare Without End by Dorothy Johnson Beavers. Port Washington, New York: Ashley, 1982.

Autism: A Practical Guide for Parents and Professionals. Syracuse, N.Y.: Syracuse University, 1979.

Coping with Schizophrenia by Mona Wasow. Palo Alto, California: Science and Behavior Books, 1982.

Creating Community Acceptance for Handicapped People by Roberta Nelson. New York: Thomas Publishing, 1978.

A Difference in the Family: Life with a Disabled Child by Helen Featherstone. New York: Basic Books, 1980.

The Family and the Handicapped Child by Sheila Hewett. Chicago: Aldine-Atherton, 1970.

Handicapped Infants and Children: A Handbook for Parents and Professionals by Carol T. Michaelis. Baltimore, Maryland: University Park, 1983.

Help Me Say It: A Parent's Guide to Speech Problems—How to Spot and Treat Communication Difficulties in Your Child by Carol Barach. New York: Plume Books, 1983.

Helping Troubled Children by Michael Rutter. New York: Plenum, 1976.

Is Your Child's Speech Normal? by Jon Eisenson. Reading, Mass.: Addison-Wesley, 1976.

One Miracle at a Time by Irving Dickman with Dr. Sol Gordon. New York: Simon & Schuster, 1986.

Mainstreaming: What Every Child Needs to Know About Disabilities by Susan Bookbinder. Boston: Exceptional Parent Press, 1978.

Understanding Those Feelings: A Guide for Parents of Handicapped Children and Those Who Counsel Them by Eugene T. McDonald. Boston: Exceptional Parent Press, 1975.

Child Abuse—
Books for Children

A Better Safe Than Sorry Book: A Family Guide for Sexual Assault Prevention by Sol and Judith Gordon. Fayetteville, New York: Ed-U Press, 1985. This excellent book is written for parents and children to read together to help children gain an understanding about sexual abuse and the critical importance of asserting their personal rights. The guide at the back of the book educates parents so they can better respond to their children's questions. It clarifies the difference between loving embraces and sexual abuse. (ages 3–9)

Feeling Safe, Feeling Strong. How to Avoid Sexual Abuse and What to Do If It Happens to You by Susan Neiburg Terkel and Janice E. Rench. Minneapolis: Lerner Publications, 1984. The authors chronicle episodes of sexual abuse, covering obscene phone calls, pornography, exhibitionism, incest, and rape. Each story elicits dialogue through a question-answer format, offering a realistic view of what the child can do to protect himself from sexual assault. (ages 10 and up)

Never Say Yes to a Stranger, What Your Child Must Know to Stay Safe by Susan Newman. New York: Perigee Books, 1985. Each chapter in this impressive resource gives examples of strangers appearing in the everyday lives of youngsters. Children can learn what they need to know to protect themselves in questionable situations. After each chapter a discussion about choices and a clear review of the specific actions a child can take in his behalf is included. (ages 4 and up)

Child Abuse—
Books for Parents

The Child Abuse Help Book by Jim Haskins. Reading, Mass.: Addison–Wesley, 1982.

Cry Softly! The Story of Child Abuse by Margaret O. Hyde. Philadelphia: Westminster, 1980.

Mending Broken Children: A Parent's Manual by George and Barbara Henderson. New York: Thomas Publishing, 1984.

The Silent Children: A Parent's Guide to the Prevention of Child Sexual Abuse by Linda Tschirhart Sanford. New York: Doubleday, 1980.

> TOLL-FREE HOTLINES
> 1-800-422-4453 NATIONAL CHILD ABUSE HOTLINE
> 1-800-421-0353 PARENTS ANONYMOUS HOTLINE

Alcoholism—
Books for Children

An Elephant in the Living Room by Jill M. Hastings and Marion H. Typpo. Minneapolis, Minnesota: Compcare, 1984. This is a charming book about the "family secret" of alcoholism. It describes a child's confusion, strong emotions (love and hate), and the roller-coaster existence children experience as a result of the alcoholic parent's erratic behavior. This workbook for children of alcoholics teaches young people that the alcoholic is not mean: he has a disease. (ages 6–14)

My Daddy Loves Me: My Daddy Has a Disease by Claudia Black. Denver: M.A.C., 1979. This workbook helps children share the reality of living in an alcoholic family. It helps children work through their fears, frustrations, loneliness, and guilt. It is an excellent catalyst for discussion with a child of an alcoholic parent. (ages 6–14)

Alcoholism—
Books for Parents

Another Chance: Hope and Health for the Alcoholic Family by Sharon Wegscheider. Palo Alto, California: Science and Behavior Books, 1981.

Choice Making for Codependents, Adult Children and Spirituality Seekers by Sharon Wegscheider-Cruse. Pompano Beach, California: Health Communications, 1985.

It Will Never Happen to Me! Children of Alcoholics as Youngsters—Adolescents—Adults by Claudia Black. Denver: M.A.C., 1981.

Death and Dying—
Books for Children

How It Feels When a Parent Dies by Jill Krementz. New York: Knopf, 1983. Eighteen children speak candidly about what they experienced and how they felt when a parent died. Children who have suffered grief from the loss of a parent will identify with the guilt, confusion, and anger expressed. And they will gain strength from the sense that, in time, they, too, will be able to go on with their lives.

The Foundling by Carol Carrick. Boston: Clarion, 1977. This is a touching story about death and the need to invest energy back into living. A young boy copes with his grief over the death of a beloved pet and his guilt over wanting to love a new one. (ages 5–8)

Learning to Say Good-Bye: When a Parent Dies by Eda LeShan. New York: Macmillan, 1976. Eda LeShan helps children communicate their feelings about coming to terms with tragic family losses. Her warm, positive approach is strength-building. This is an excellent resource for the child who is trying to cope with the loss of a loved one. The stages of mourning and the fears of death are described realistically. (ages 10–13)

So Long, Grandpa by Elfie Donnelly. New York: Crown, 1981. A young boy adjusts to his grandfather's imminent death, demonstrating his ability to cope with the loss of someone very special. (ages 9–14)

Talking About Death: A Dialogue Between Parent and Child by Earl Grollman. Boston: Beacon Press, 1970. This is a touching, honest book for parents to read aloud with children to help them understand the reality of death. It includes a parents' guide to facilitate positive communication and includes lists of helpful resources. This outstanding book was awarded a UNESCO citation as "one of those books in the world which has changed public opinion." (ages 5 to adult)

There Is a Rainbow Behind Every Dark Cloud by the Center for Attitudinal Healing. Berkeley, California: Celestial Arts, 1978. This book sensitively describes, through pictures and text, the inner feelings of children with terminal illnesses. While it is a book that deals with impending death, it inspires children with an appreciation for the gift of life. (ages 8 and up)

Death and Dying—
Books for Parents

Care of the Child Facing Death by Lindy Burton (ed.). London: Routledge, 1974.

Explaining Death to Children edited by Earl Grollman. Boston: Beacon Press, 1967.

Home Care for the Dying Child: Professional and Family Perspectives by Ida Marie Martinson (ed.). New York: Appleton–Century–Crofts, 1976.

The Long Dying of Baby Andrew by Robert and Peggy Stinson. Boston: Little, Brown, 1983.

Elisabeth Kubler-Ross on Children and Death by Elisabeth Kubler-Ross. New York: Macmillan, 1983.

Should the Children Know? Encounters with Death in the Lives of Children by Marguerita Rudolph. New York: Schocken, 1978.

References

Association for the Care of Children's Health. Washington, D.C., 1984.

Baskin, Barbara Hand, and Harris, Karen. *Notes from a Different Drummer.* New York: Bowker, 1977.

Bernstein, Joanne E. *Books to Help Children Cope with Separation and Loss.* New York: Bowker, 1977.

Cascardi, Andrea E. *Good Books to Grow On.* New York: Warner Books, 1985.

Dreyer, Sharon. *The Bookfinder.* Minnesota: American Guidance Service, 1985.

Fassler, Joan. *Helping Children Cope.* New York: Macmillan, 1978.

Gillespie, John T., and Gilbert, Christine B. *Best Books for Children.* New York: Bowker, 1981.

Griffin, Barbara. *M.L.S. Special Needs Bibliography.* DeWitt, N.Y.: The Griffin, 1984.

Moore, Cory, et al. *A Reader's Guide for Parents of Children with Mental, Physical, or Emotional Disabilities.* Maryland State Planning Council on Developmental Disabilities, 1983.

Smith, Sally. *No Easy Answers: The Learning Disabled Child at Home and at School.* New York: Bantam Books, 1981.

White, Mary Lou. *Adventuring with Books: A Book List for Preschool–Grade 6.* Urbana, Ill.: National Council of Teachers of English, 1981.

CHOOSING A QUALITY PRESCHOOL
OR DAY-CARE CENTER

As an increasing number of mothers join the labor force, quality day care for children becomes a crucial concern for parents today. Besides the center's location and fees, there are a host of other considerations that parents need to be aware of when investigating a preschool or day-care center in order to provide their children with safe, enriching, developmentally sound child care.

The following checklist is compiled in large measure from the position statement of the National Academy of Early Childhood Programs, which has begun accrediting centers with quality programs and services.

Social–Emotional Environment

Caregivers:

—welcome parents to visit the facility at any time and to become involved in the program, so they can become knowledgeable about and comfortable with their child's environment.

—facilitate interaction with parents to better understand the unique needs of each child. There is open communication about potential difficulties, concerns, and positive experiences as staff and parents work together as a team. The focus is on the well-being of the total child: physical, emotional, and intellectual.

—are friendly and accepting, helping each child feel valued; they don't play favorites.

—are positive role models.

—help children resolve conflicts independently.

—use positive guidance techniques that are developmentally suitable. Discipline is fair, kind, and reasonable. Limits and expectations of appropriate behavior are clearly expressed.

—speak with children at their eye level.

—who work with infants and toddlers enjoy cuddling young children.

Children:

—enjoy relaxed mealtimes and snacks. They are welcome to socialize.

—are happy and involved, interacting positively and frequently with each other and with caregivers.

—of both sexes have opportunities to experience a wide variety of social roles through books and creative play—doctor, nurse, banker, teacher, lawyer, astronaut, parent, and so on.

—are provided with opportunities for decision-making and problem-solving.

—are encouraged to express their emotions, both positive and negative.

Learning Environment

—Caregivers stimulate children's interest in their environment.

—Children's hands-on participation is encouraged, with freedom of choice.

—Flexibility is provided for differences in attention span and learning styles.

—Abundant materials are within easy reach of children to enjoy both on a one-to-one and small group basis.

—Children's work is displayed at their eye level.

—Planning with a rich variety of age appropriate materials and activities is apparent (field trips, music, art, creative movement, creative dramatics, science, math, language, etc.).

—Books are plentiful, easily accessible, of fine quality, and developmentally geared.

—Activities provide opportunities with a balance of active/quiet, indoor/outdoor, individual/group, large muscle/small muscle experiences.

—Emphasis is placed on the *process* of the children's involvement rather than on a finished *product* to impress the parents. Creative use of materials is encouraged.

—Caregivers demonstrate respect for cultural differences.

—Children have opportunities for calm and restful naps.

Facility

—Indoor and outdoor play space is safe and uncrowded.

—The environment is cheerful and inviting.

—Space is provided for block building, dramatic play, art, music, and a quiet book corner.

—Crawling space and carpeted areas are provided for nonwalkers.

—Equipment is well-maintained and age-appropriate.

—Electrical outlets are covered.

—Playground has areas for large motor activities (swings, climbing apparatus) as well as creative construction (blocks, boards, boxes, paint, water) with both hard and soft surfaces for play.

—Sized-right bathrooms are clean with functional faucets, paper towels, and soap.

—Space is provided for each child's personal belongings.

—Cleaning supplies and medicines are out of children's reach.

—Suitable space, separate and apart from other children, is provided for children who are ill.

—Cars or buses used for transporting children are safe, well-maintained, and equipped with seat belts. Adequate supervision is provided when transporting children.

Administrative Procedures

—Center is licensed by appropriate agencies.

—Staff–child ratios are maintained at approximately the following ratio:

infants: 4–1

toddlers: 8–1

three-year-olds: 9–1

four-year-olds: 10–1

five-year-olds and older: 12–1

—Children are conscientiously supervised.

—Staff are qualified, having had child-care training and experience.

—Plans for staff development are ongoing, providing regular inservice opportunities.

—Emergency card with health history is on file for each child.

—Emergency procedures are posted.

—Caregivers have first-aid training.

—Well-stocked first-aid kit is available.

—Children and caregivers wash hands before eating and after going to the bathroom. Staff washes hands after changing diapers.

—Meals are balanced and nutritious.

—Food preparation and serving areas are sanitary.

Danger Signals

1. Discipline is harsh and insensitive.
2. Children have an unusual number of bruises.
3. Children are fearful around staff.
4. Caregivers are defensive.
5. Neatness is highest priority. Environment appears sterile.
6. Infants remain in cribs most of the day.
7. Infants are propped for feedings.
8. Children passively watch television.
9. Equipment is poorly designed and maintained.
10. There is a high turnover of staff.
11. Parents are not allowed to visit center unannounced.
12. The center accepts children, whether or not it is full.
13. Sick children intermingle with others.
14. Caregivers stress "right" and "wrong" ways of using materials.
15. Caregivers appear overwhelmed and frustrated. They seem to dislike children.
16. Activities are developmentally inappropriate (i.e., preschoolers are preoccupied with reading, writing, paper-pencil math, and worksheets).

References

Accreditation Criteria and Procedures of the National Academy of Early Childhood Programs. Washington, D.C.: National Association for the Education of Young Children, 1985.

The Book of UPP (Upgrading Preschool Programs). P.O. Box 27043, Phoenix, Arizona 85061. 1985.

Clarke-Stewart, Allison. *Daycare.* Cambridge, Mass.: Harvard University Press, 1982.

Harms, Thelma, and Clifford, Richard M. *The Early Childhood Environment Rating Scale.* New York: Teachers College Press, 1980.

Mitchell, Grace. *The Day Care Book: A Guide for Working Parents—Find the Best Day Care for Your Children.* New York: Fawcett Columbine, 1980.

The Consumer Guide to Choosing Day Care for Children. Office of Public Information. Phoenix, Ariz.: Arizona Department of Health Services, 1985.

Author Photo Credits

Louise Bates Ames photo by Mara Levitt

Dorothy Corkille Briggs photo by Keri Southwick

Myra Cates photo by Rob Raker

Don Dinkmeyer photo by Neil Beracha

Fitzhugh Dodson photo by Don Uuop

Richard Ferber photo by Nick Kaufman

Sol Gordon photo by Gordon Antell

Martin Greenberg photo by Claudia Law-Greenberg

Earl Grollman photo by Michael Romanus

Michael Meyerhoff photo by Center for Parent Education

Eileen Shiff photo by John Hall

Benjamin Spock and Mary Morgan photo by Mark Wallach

Burton White photo by Center for Parent Education

INDEX

curiosity
  development of, 95, 96, 98, 99,
    102, 103, 108
  encouragement of, 103–106
  about sex, 240, 248–249
custodial visits, handling of, 231–
  233

day care, kindergarten as form of,
  129
day-care center, choosing of, 348–
  352
deafness, see hearing impairment
death
  children's understanding of, 200–
    204
  early awareness of, 199, 200
  euphemisms about, 202, 203
  guidelines for explaining of, 212–
    215
  honesty about, 202–204, 210–212,
    213
  self-esteem as factor in dealing
    with, 21–22
  sleep compared to, 203
  theological abstractions about,
    202
death and divorce, explaining of,
  199–215
death and dying, reading lists on,
  345–346
death awareness, stages of, 200–201
decision making
  child's role in family process of,
    229–230, 250
  self-worth and, 278, 296–97
delays, coping with, 287
denial
  negative effect of, 208
  positive use of, 224
depression, as response to crisis, 209
developmental checklist, 305–328
developmentalists, 87
development placement, 132–139
Did the Sun Shine Before You Were

Born? (Gordon and Gordon),
  246
difficult child, needs of, 276
Dinkmeyer, Don, 173–194
Di Pasquale, Glenn, 140
disabilities, reading lists on, 340–
  343
discipline
  baby's introduction to, 110, 113
  defined, 149
  early establishment of, 102
  effective methods of
    communication skills: feedback,
      163–165; I messages, 165
    contracting, 153–155
    environmental control, 157–162
    modeling, 166
    positive reward system, 150–
      155
    rapport building, 151
    reverse time-out, 157
    time-out, 155–156
  importance of, 100, 102, 108,
    110–111, 113
  as learning process, 182–183
  men's and women's views of, 231
  in steprelationship, 230–231, 233–
    235
discouragement *(see also*
    encouragement)
  as basis of misbehavior, 176, 177
  humor as antidote for, 181
disengagement, as response to
    misbehavior, 175
Disney's Busy Poppin Pals, 104n
divorce
  effect on child's feeling of
    lovability, 212
  explaining of, 199–215
    guidelines for, 212–215
  loyalty conflict generated by, 231
  honesty about, 204–205, 212–213
  reading lists on, 333–334
  self-esteem and, 21–22
  statistics on, 199
Dodson, Fitzhugh, 149–169

understanding, age for development of, 103

United Appeal, 235

value judgment, self-esteem and, 8

values, strengthening of, 289–290

virginity, modern status of, 259

visitation rights, disputes about, 222–223

visits, in steprelationship, 231–233

visually impaired, reading lists on, 336–337

vocabulary, development of, 102, 105, 109

walker, for baby, 99–100

walking, age for learning of, 102, 107

walking with a child, pleasures of, 49–50

water, babies' enjoyment of, 46, 104

Watson, John B., 87

wet dreams, 239, 252

White, Burton, 87, 124

on new parents as teachers, 91–118

Williams, Marie, 140

winners and losers, differences between, 267–268

words, baby's understanding of, 102, 105, 109

working-parent families, reading lists on, 332–333

Zigler, Edward, 133, 134